A New Birth
of Freedom

RECENT TITLES IN

CONTRIBUTIONS IN AMERICAN HISTORY

Series Editor: Jon L. Wakelyn

A NEW BIRTH
OF FREEDOM

The Republican Party and Freedmen's Rights, ___ 1861 to 1866 ___

Herman Belz

CONTRIBUTIONS IN AMERICAN HISTORY, NUMBER 52

 GREENWOOD PRESS
WESTPORT, CONNECTICUT • LONDON, ENGLAND

Library of Congress Cataloging in Publication Data

Belz, Herman.
    A new birth of freedom.

    (Contributions in American history; no. 52)
    Bibliography: p.
    Includes index.
    1.   Afro-Americans—Civil rights—History.
2.   Republican Party—History. I. Title.
KF4757.B37   342'.73'085   76-5257
ISBN 0-8371-8902-0

Library of Congress Card Number: 76-5257
ISBN: 0-8371-8902-0

First published in 1976.

Greenwood Press, Inc.
51 Riverside Avenue, Westport, Connecticut 06880

Printed in the United States of America

Contents

Preface

Patterns of race relations and civil rights in the United States assumed essentially modern form during the Civil War and Reconstruction. Within the space of a few years in the 1860s the civil status of nearly four million Negroes—about 13 percent of the American population—underwent profound change as a result of emancipation. The transition from slavery to freedom, especially the social and economic aspects of freedom, has attracted the attention of historians. Far less study has been given to political, constitutional, and legal aspects of emancipation, with which this book deals. Succinctly stated, this book describes how and why the Republican party transformed a series of expedient military steps aimed at denying slave manpower to the enemy into a civil rights policy that rested on settled constitutional principles and was intended to guarantee American citizenship and equality before the law to the freed slave population.

In the days after Appomattox, matters concerning freedmen's rights that Republicans had at first hesitated to assert as war aims, preferring to view them instead as the adventitious by-product of the struggle for Union, came to be regarded as being among the most important of the fruits of victory. To preserve the "new birth of freedom" that emancipation produced, as Lincoln referred to it in his Gettysburg address, Republicans passed the first civil rights laws in U.S. history and, equally unprecedented, amended the Constitution to limit state power over personal liberty and civil rights. These measures, it is all too clear, were to be honored more in the breach than in the observance. They were, alas, but formal laws which, while reflecting a significant change in the attitude of the white majority toward blacks, created public standards for a racially impartial society that would not be fulfilled for generations. Indeed, a century later the work remains uncompleted. Nevertheless, it was of the greatest historical importance that the federal civil rights policy in the aftermath of emancipation was formally established on the principle of equality before the law. Though prejudice against color and black persons' reactions to racial discrimination have from time to time suggested the possibility that Negroes might form a separate national community in the United States, the legal and constitutional framework within which race relations have been dealt with—the very framework set forth in the Republican civil rights settlement of the 1860s—has posited equal citizenship and civil rights in a single national community as the objective of public policy.

For financial assistance in carrying out the research for this study, I wish to thank the American Bar Foundation, the American Philosophical Society, and the University of Maryland. Portions of Chapters 1 and 6 have appeared as articles in the *Journal of Southern History* and in *Civil War History*. William M. Wiecek, Mary F. Berry, and George M. Dennison gave valuable criticism and advice for which I am deeply grateful. Finally I owe thanks to my wife, Mary, for her encouragement throughout the project.

Herman Belz

College Park, Maryland
February 1976

_____ Introduction_____

In 1861, after three decades of antislavery agitation, federal policy toward slave emancipation began as a consequence of the Civil War. Five years later, slavery was abolished by constitutional amendment, and guarantees of personal liberty and civil rights were written into American public law. The Civil Rights Act of 1866 and the Fourteenth Amendment signified the nationalization of individual civil liberty which the Republican party, in control of Congress, regarded as necessary to complete the work of wartime emancipation and to secure reconstruction of the Union. The purpose of this study is to examine how emancipation that was undertaken for military reasons gave rise to federal policies protecting the liberty and rights of freed slaves and how these policies eventually led to the civil rights settlement of 1866.

The settlement of 1866 is usually referred to as a nationalizing process, but it might more accurately be described as the federalization of civil liberty. For in essence it gave the federal government power and responsibility over the liberty and rights of individuals which it had never possessed, without substantially depriving the states of similar power and responsibility. In other words, the settlement provided for sharing of power over civil rights between state and federal governments. In a relative sense, state power was diminished by being made subject to restrictions that were previously unknown. Yet, in an absolute sense, the states lost little power. Significant change occurred, but there was much continuity with the antebellum constitutional system in which states had virtually exclusive authority to define, confer, and regulate personal liberty and rights.

The theory of American federalism was that the national government would act upon matters of concern to all the states, such as diplomacy, national defense, and international and interstate commerce, while the states would govern local affairs. Although in pursuit of its general purposes the federal government could legislate directly upon individuals, levy taxes, and enforce the laws of Congress through a system of national courts, the states could perform these same functions within their own jurisdictions under the power of municipal or local legislation. More importantly, the states alone could determine the condition, status, and rights of persons within their jurisdictions. The noted antislavery legal commentator John C. Hurd acknowledged this fundamental constitutional principle when he stated that the powers granted to Congress for enacting laws of national extent were not such as could confer individual civil rights. "The power therefore of determining by personal laws the *condition* of individuals and their enjoyment of civil liberties," Hurd wrote, "belongs to the States, as the proper object of their own municipal (internal) law."[1]

Furthermore, state legislatures were subject to no effective restraints in exercising the power of local legislation over civil rights, other than those inherent in the electoral process or in judicial review under state constitutions. In the case of Barron *v.* Baltimore in 1833, the Supreme Court confirmed this fact in holding that the Fifth Amendment guarantee against deprivation of life, liberty, or property without due process of law—and indeed all of the first eight amendments to the Constitution—applied only to the federal government, not the states.[2] It was true that two provisions in the federal Constitution, namely, the privileges and immunities and the guarantee of republican government clauses, offered theoretical means by which the federal government might limit state power over personal liberty and civil rights.[3] Nevertheless, despite occasional attempts to interpret these provisions in ways adverse to state power, no effective restraints were forthcoming.[4]

Because states generally acted without interference on questions of individual liberty, state citizenship was the principal locus of ordinary civil rights. It was as state citizens that persons enjoyed the multitude of civil rights that characterized a republican political order. National citizenship existed, or at least could be adduced, from constitutional provisions such as the power of Congress to naturalize aliens. Yet, with the exception of territorial government and the few citizens who were engaged in interstate commerce or overseas interests, the federal government played no effective role with respect to the rights and liberties of American citizens.[5]

Problems concerning the enforcement of the fugitive slave clause of the Constitution led to the only significant departure from this pattern of federal nonintervention in personal liberties. From 1793 until 1842, the return of fugitives was treated as a joint federal-state responsibility. The decision of the Supreme Court in the case of Prigg *v.* Pennsylvania (1842), however, placed this question entirely within federal jurisdiction. As a consequence, the Fugitive Slave Act of 1850 provided for exclusive federal enforcement of the right of recapture. An equal and opposite reaction to the nationalization of the fugitive slave question by Congress was the assertion of state powers in the North to defend the freedom of alleged fugitive blacks and to protect their personal rights.

In contrast to the wartime and postwar interest in freedmen's civil rights, antebellum civil rights efforts, because of the virtually exclusive jurisdiction that states had over the subject, operated at the state rather than the federal level. The personal liberty laws, passed to protect alleged fugitives and free blacks against unlawful detention, were the most conspicuous example of how antislavery reformers employed state power to remove legal burdens and discriminations against Negroes.[6] Abolitionists fashioned arguments based on the federal Constitution in an attempt to restrict the spread of slavery or weaken it fatally where it existed.[7] But the slight success they achieved in removing restrictions on blacks in the antebellum period came about through the application of state legislative power or through interpretation of state constitutions.[8] Of course, the attempt to exclude slavery from the national territories involved the exercise of national power. Nevertheless, the chief emphasis of antislavery constitutional teaching, even in the territorial dispute of the 1850s, was on divorcing the federal government from any connection with or support of slavery. Federal disengagement, it was argued, would free the northern states of the defilement that resulted from contact with slavery and would lead to its eventual destruction without the necessity of federal action.[9] Thus, while the conflict between North and South might in political terms be seen as involving the question of whether slavery or freedom would be nationalized, in a constitutional and legal sense state powers provided the main reliance of antislavery action.

Although wartime emancipation resulted in laws and constitutional amendments that formed the basis for modern civil rights policy, nineteenth-century conceptions of liberty and rights differed greatly from those of our own contemporary times. To understand the historical significance of the changes in the status and rights of Negro slaves that took place between 1861 and 1866, it is necessary briefly to consider these differences.

In our own time, *civil liberties* is a generic term referring to the rights and immunities by which individuals are protected against governmental interference with private, personal freedom and public, or political, liberty. The First, Fifth, and Fourteenth Amendments, for example, prohibit the federal and state governments from infringing on both personal liberty and property, which are private in character, and freedom of speech, press, petition, and assembly, which are public and political in nature. The term *civil rights*, on the other hand, refers to the protection which individuals enjoy against injury and denial of rights by other private individuals. In recent years, too, the term has been used with reference to matters such as employment, income support, housing, and health care, which individuals are said to have a right to demand of government. Civil rights may thus signify not simply negative restraints imposed on government, but also positive obligations to enact social and economic policies for the welfare of individuals. Although negative restraints remain essential, the more distinctive aspect of liberty and rights in the twentieth century has been their positive character, evident especially in the demand for affirmative, active government.[10]

Nineteenth-century liberty was more negative in character. It consisted primarily in restrictions upon government—especially the legislative power—that were intended to permit the individual to have freedom of action insofar as it did not interfere with the liberty of another. In the event of such a conflict, civil suits at common law were available to gain redress for damages or injury. The principal threat to individual freedom, however, was thought to come from government rather than private individuals. Accordingly, civil liberty was seen as consisting in the right of all citizens, equally and without interference from government, to move about freely, work and enjoy the rewards of labor, entertain religious beliefs of whatever character chosen, enjoy the benefits of marriage and the family, make contracts, own or rent property, and bring suit and testify in courts of law. In short, the condition of civil liberty entitled a person to civil rights which protected one's person and property in the sphere of private liberty.

In contrast to the approach favored in the twentieth century, civil rights in the mid-nineteenth century were sharply distinguished from political and social rights. The freedoms of speech, press, assembly, and petition, which today are viewed under the aspect of political freedom, were then considered attributes of personal liberty and hence were counted as civil rights. Since they were believed to be rooted in natural law, these and other civil rights were regarded as inherent natural rights belonging to all free persons. On the other hand, the rights to vote, hold office, and serve on juries were privileges conferred by those who already possessed them—the political community—upon those deemed qualified to assume them. Political rights (or, strictly speaking, privileges) were conferred, moreover, on grounds of expediency and the public good, not as in our own time on the basis of supposed natural right or for the purpose of enabling individuals to fulfill their unique potentialities. [11]

Social rights referred to the sphere of strictly personal relationships, either in the household or outside it, in which personal taste or prejudice could legitimately hold sway and into which the law did not enter. In the late twentieth century, constitutional law retains this distinction between civil and social rights; yet, it is apparent that the private social sphere has been greatly reduced in scope. Schools, voluntary associations, transportation facilities, and places of business and entertainment are perhaps the most conspicuous examples of areas that nowadays are, but were not then, comprehended under the rule of civil rights equality. [12]

Besides considering federalism and the prevailing conception of civil rights, it is also necessary to examine the status and rights of Negroes in the antebellum period in order to understand the significance of wartime emancipation and its civil rights consequences. Starting around 1800, after a hiatus in the revolutionary era which saw slavery abolished in several northern states, discrimination against free and slave blacks became more pronounced. Especially after 1830, efforts to deny blacks their rights and to fix them in more subordinate positions gained momentum. In states where blacks had exercised the suffrage, they were now deprived of it and were subjected to restrictions that occasionally even denied them the right to enter and establish residence in a state. [13] The Supreme Court's decision in the Dred Scott case of 1857, that Negroes were not citizens of the United States in the sense of the Constitution, culminated this decline in the free Negro's status. The Supreme Court, rejecting a line of precedents by which Negro citizenship might have been supported, excluded blacks from the American political community in a way that virtually prohibited amelioration of their status within the existing constitutional system.

On the eve of the Civil War, Negroes were denied not just citizenship, but their very humanity. In the middle of the nineteenth century, an American school of ethnology developed which held that blacks constituted a separate and inferior species of man, not, as had been thought, a variety of the species to which whites belonged. This theory, called polygenesis in contrast to the earlier theory of monogenesis, was used in combination with the ideology of Jacksonian democracy to justify the more pronounced degradation of blacks that took place after 1830. By denying that blacks were men, white persons could maintain belief in the equality of all men—a fundamental premise of democratic ideology—in the face of the evident need or desire to subjugate blacks.[14]

This denial of a common humanity with whites, while embraced by proslavery southerners, also received sympathetic and important consideration by many northerners in the 1850s. It is in light of this denial that the Republican defense of the basic humanity of Negro slaves and their right to personal liberty should be viewed. On this elementary but deeply contested basis, and the corollary notion of the legal personality of blacks under the Constitution, Republicans evolved a civil rights policy out of wartime military emancipation.

NOTES

1. John C. Hurd, *The Law of Freedom and Bondage* (2 vols.; Boston, 1858-1862), I, 483.

2. Barron *v.* Baltimore, 7 Peters 243.

3. Article IV, sect. 2: "the citizens of each state shall be entitled to all privileges and immunities of citizens in the several states." Article IV, sect. 4: "The United States shall guarantee to every state in this union a Republican form of government, and shall protect each of them against invasion. . . ."

4. Cf. Roger Howell, *The Privileges and Immunities of State Citizenship* (Baltimore, 1918), and William M. Wiecek, *The Guarantee Clause of the U.S. Constitution* (Ithaca, 1972).

5. Harold M. Hyman, *A More Perfect Union: The Impact of the Civil War and Reconstruction on the Constitution* (New York, 1973), 8, 426.

In organizing the territories, the federal government could exercise the power of local legislation, defining personal condition and conferring rights of citizens just as states did for citizens within their jurisdiction. Thus, Congress possessed the local police power in the territories. In the early national period, however, this power was not widely employed, because territorial settlers were largely on their own to govern themselves through what was often considered popular sovereignty. In the period of sectional conflict after 1846, federal power over the territories was effectively challenged by the Democrats who argued for popular or territorial sovereignty and by proslavery state sovereignty advocates.

6. Cf. Thomas D. Morris, *Free Men All: The Personal Liberty Laws of the North, 1780-1861* (Baltimore and London, 1974).

7. Howard Jay Graham, *Everyman's Constitution: Historical Essays on the Fourteenth Amendment, the "Conspiracy Theory," and American Constitutionalism* (Madison Wis., 1968), 152-241; Jacobus ten Broek, *Equal Under Law* (New York, 1965; orig. publ. as *The Antislavery Origins of the Fourteenth Amendment* [1951]).

8. Alfred H. Kelly, "The Fourteenth Amendment Reconsidered: The Segregation Question," *Michigan Law Review* 54 (June 1956): 1053, 1055-1056.

9. Eric Foner, *Free Soil, Free Labor, Free Men: The Ideology of the Republican Party Before the Civil War* (New York, 1970), 73-87.

10. Edward S. Newman, *The Law of Civil Rights and Civil Liberties* (New York, 1949), 1, 73; Norman Dorsen, ed., *The Rights of Americans: What They Are—What They Should Be* (New York, 1971), xiii; Edward S. Corwin, *Liberty Against Government: The Rise, Flowering and Decline of a Famous Juridical Concept* (Baton Rouge, 1948), 1-7.

11. Compare Andrew C. McLaughlin and Albert B. Hart, eds., *Cyclopedia of American Government* (3 vols.; New York, 1914), III, 447, in which suffrage is discussed, with James C. Kirby, Jr., "The Right to Vote," in Norman Dorsen, ed., *The Rights of Americans*, 175-193.

12. Cf. W. R. Brock, *An American Crisis: Congress and Reconstruction, 1865-1867* (New York, 1963), 19-20.

13. Leon F. Litwack, *North of Slavery: The Negro in the Free States, 1790-1860* (Chicago, 1961), passim.

14. George M. Fredrickson, *The Black Image in the White Mind: The Debate on Afro-American Character and Destiny, 1817-1914* (New York, 1971), Ch. III, and "A Man But Not a Brother: Abraham Lincoln and Racial Equality," *Journal of Southern History* 41 (February 1975): 39-58.

A New Birth
of Freedom

1

Emancipation legislation and the right of personal liberty, 1862

Although preservation of the Union was the official aim of the federal government in the Civil War, emancipation was a major issue from the start of hostilities. In the months before Sumter, Lincoln initially avoided antislavery measures, despite his uncompromising antislavery attitude, for fear of driving the border states over to the Confederacy. Yet, it was not necessary to reject the official Union theory of war aims to hold that any sound strategy for suppressing the rebellion must rest upon a policy of emancipation. Slavery was a labor system essential to the Confederate war effort which could, it was argued, legitimately be destroyed under the war power of the government as a means of preserving the Union.

In 1862, the Lincoln administration abandoned the border state policy of restraint toward slavery in favor of gradual, compensated, and then immediate military emancipation. It seems clear that, while this change fulfilled distinct ideological tendencies in the Republican party,[1] the principal impetus for it came from military developments. Some historians, believing that emancipation made little substantial difference in the lives of Negroes, have seen in this pragmatic, expedient policy the seeds of failure of Reconstruction efforts and of American race relations in general.[2] It is more accurate, however, to say that although it was not undertaken to promote the liberty and rights of Negro slaves, emancipation produced significant changes and gave rise to a genuine interest in freedmen's rights that were beneficial to blacks. In the confiscation and emancipation legislation of 1862, one can see the beginnings of this development.

The question of personal liberty for blacks arose at the start of the war when escaped slaves began to enter Union lines. To deal with the problem federal authorities, following the example of General Benjamin F. Butler in Virginia, adopted the theory that slaves used for insurrectionary purposes were contraband of war whose services could be appropriated and turned to account for the Union. Although this theory did not recognize the personal liberty and free status of escaped slaves and was not a policy of emancipation, it pointed in that direction. Clearly, it made the drift toward emancipation more acceptable than it would have been if justified on the high ground of antislavery moral principle. Many persons "who would be repelled by formulas of a broader or nobler import" and who were averse to slaves being declared freedmen, observed abolitionist Edward L. Pierce in November 1861, had no objection to their being declared contraband of war.[3]

The contraband theory provided the general framework for federal policy toward escaped slaves in 1861-1862. The policy began to evolve when the War Department approved General Butler's contraband order of May 1861, and several commanders began to employ runaway slaves in military labor. When other commanders refused to receive escaped slaves in their lines or otherwise permitted the recapture of fugitives, Congress intervened by passing an article of war prohibiting military and naval personnel from returning escaped slaves.[4] Republican lawmakers were mainly interested in depriving the enemy of labor which could then be used for the Union cause.[5] But the situation also gave Republicans an opportunity to speak for Negro freedom by arguing that their purpose was to prevent military officers from settling questions of personal liberty outside their jurisdiction.[6]

More directly pertinent to the issue of personal liberty were bills introduced in the Thirty-seventh Congress to free the slaves of rebels. These measures, generally consistent with the contraband theory, aimed at using black manpower for military purposes rather than establishing the free status of former slaves. Nearly all of them failed to provide means of guaranteeing the personal liberty of the freed blacks. For example, the first Confiscation Act, passed in August

1861, provided that if slaves were employed in military labor or service in support of the rebellion, persons claiming their services forfeited their right to slave labor. But the act did not declare that slaves so employed were free. The omission was not inadvertent. A provision stating that slaves used for insurrectionary purposes would be discharged from labor was rejected on Republican initiative, lest the inference be drawn that Congress intended to abolish slavery as a municipal institution.[7] The Confiscation Act of 1861 thus deprived the enemy of slave labor but did not in express terms confer liberty on blacks released from service to rebel masters.[8]

When Congress met in December 1861, the continued failure and inactivity of Union arms made Republican lawmakers more willing to undertake an aggressive antislavery policy. Accordingly, numerous emancipation and confiscation bills were introduced which declared unequivocally that slaves of persons aiding the rebellion were freemen, state laws to the contrary notwithstanding. These proposals did not, however, supply the means of actually securing the right of personal liberty for freed slaves. Only the requirement that persons seeking to enforce claims to slave labor must prove past loyalty served as possible protection for freed blacks, and this was intended as much to guard the interests of loyal masters as the freedom of emancipated slaves.[9]

Although military expediency remained the controlling consideration in emancipation policy, Republican lawmakers in limited ways began to recognize the need to protect personal liberty. Ironically, in its first manifestation this broader outlook was joined with a proposal to colonize emancipated slaves on abandoned plantations. Under legislation submitted by Republicans John Gurley of Ohio and Frank P. Blair of Missouri, special U.S. commissioners would issue certificates of freedom to slaves of persons engaging in rebellion. These certificates would be conclusive of the right of personal liberty against any private individual or state officer seeking to claim the service of a freed slave. Even with their freedom certificates, however, emancipated blacks would remain subject to the regulations of federal commissioners and would be employed in military labor or indentured as apprentices to loyal plantation proprietors.[10]

As antislavery pressures increased in 1862, a more straightforward interest in securing the personal liberty of freed slaves emerged. Bills were introduced which would enable slaves freed under the first Confiscation Act to establish their right to freedom through certificates acquired from U.S. courts, special commissioners, or military officers and which would prohibit kidnapping and enslavement of free persons.11 While these were expedient measures designed to deny manpower to the Confederacy, they also reflected an ideological-humanitarian concern for the freedmen's liberty. As the number of escaped and emancipated slaves increased, a further consideration was the judgment that reenslavement was a practical impossibility because blacks would fight it. In approving the second Confiscation Act in July 1862, Lincoln acknowledged this factor: "[I] believe there would be physical resistance to it [reenslavement], which could neither be turned aside by argument, nor driven away by force." 12 The enlistment of Negro soldiers in 1863 reinforced the view that blacks would not simply be acted upon or be passively disposed of in the aftermath of emancipation. Thus, prudential as well as ideological concerns helped shape Republican attempts to secure the personal liberty of the freed slaves.

The first measure in which Congress actually made provision for the freed slaves' personal liberty was the District of Columbia Abolition Act of April 1862. As originally reported, the bill specified no emancipation procedure but simply released slaves from service. After lengthy discussion of compensation of slaveowners, however, conservative Republican Senator Jacob Collamer of Vermont called attention to the opposite side of the question—the emancipated slaves' personal liberty. If freed blacks went into neighboring Maryland, Collamer pointed out, they would be presumed to be slaves and would need evidence of their freedom to prevent being captured. Persuaded by this advice, the Senate amended the District abolition bill by adding a detailed procedure for carrying out emancipation and securing personal liberty.

The procedure required slaveowners, in order to qualify for compensation, to pay a fee of $.50 and to place a description of their slaves on record in federal court. In turn, emancipated slaves were authorized—upon payment of a $.25 fee—to receive certificates of freedom from the same federal court. In addition, the act prohibited kidnapping or transporting freed persons out of the District with the intent of reenslaving them. In July, Congress passed a supplementary Act which permitted slaves not yet freed, because their owners' absence had prevented the emancipation process from being initiated, to petition the federal court for a certificate of personal freedom. For this certificate the slave had to pay a $.50 fee. Here indeed was emancipation "with all the moral grandeur of a bill of lading" and with actual bureaucratic details to boot.[13]

Regardless of the concern for an emancipation procedure in the District of Columbia, in their principal antislavery undertaking of 1862—the second Confiscation Act—the Republicans were interested mainly in military and political considerations. Confiscation of property and slave emancipation were intended to weaken the enemy, raise money for the Union, and lay the foundation for postwar reform of southern society.[14] Therefore, in a political and strategic sense, in accordance with the contraband theory, slaves were considered along with property as a military and economic asset in war planning.

Nevertheless, an interest in the freedmen's personal liberty was also evinced in the legislative history of the Confiscation Act of 1862. It appeared most clearly in an emancipation bill passed by the House in June 1862. In this measure, the Republicans articulated a definite emancipation procedure and provided a guarantee of the freed slaves' personal liberty, even though their overall purpose was to deprive the enemy of labor and to end the war without abolishing slavery as a municipal institution.

As originally reported by radical Thomas D. Eliot of the Select Committee on Confiscation and Emancipation, the emancipation bill contained no means of actually securing slave liberation. It merely provided that all persons willfully engaging in rebellion forfeited all claims to the labor of slaves. The sole protection for persons released from labor was the provision that, if a master sought to enforce a claim to service, the slave was authorized to plead the claimant's participation in rebellion as a defense, or the claimant must establish his loyalty.[15] The broad sweep of the bill, affecting all who voluntarily supported the rebellion, gave it a radical character and led sixteen Republicans to join with the Democratic opposition in defeating it, 74 to 78. Subsequently, in a compromise move supported by radical Republicans, the House agreed to consider a substitute bill that was less extensive in its emancipation scope but more thorough in its provisions for slave liberty.[16]

Drafted by conservative Republican Albert G. Porter of Indiana, who had opposed Eliot's measure, the new emancipation bill proposed to liberate only the slaves of Confederate and state military and

civil officers rather than all willful participants in the rebellion.[17] As
though to compensate for this more limited scope, the bill also contained an emancipation procedure and safeguards. It directed special
commissioners appointed by the president in each slave state to com-
pile and publish lists of slaves belonging to persons in the designated
classes, and it required the slaveowners to appear in federal court and
prove their loyalty if they wished to avoid forfeiture of the services of
their slaves. Upon the rebel owner's failure to appear, or on proof of
his participation in rebellion if he should appear, the court was to
declare his slaves free and give them certificates of freedom guaranteeing personal liberty in all state and federal courts. As a further protection of personal liberty, Porter's bill took the seemingly obvious
and elementary step—yet one that had not yet been contemplated—of
authorizing federal courts to issue writs of *habeas corpus* to secure the
release of any freed slaves or their descendants who should subsequently be held by any person. Persons illegally detaining freedmen
were in turn to be tried for kidnapping. Finally, slaves not included in
the published lists drawn up by the commissioners to initiate emancipation could apply directly to federal court and receive the benefits of
the act.[18]

Porter defended this emancipation plan on pragmatic and conservative grounds. In the first place, he said, it would affect the leaders of
the rebellion without interfering with the rights of loyal persons in the
South. By liberating an estimated one million slaves, it would assist
the Union and undermine slavery "as a mere political and governing
power," without, however, destroying slavery as a domestic institution. Indeed, Porter said the slavery interest would best be served by
withdrawing the institution from political strife in the manner now
proposed. Nor, he added, would emancipation conducted in this way
produce social upheaval. Pointing to the example of the considerable
free black populations in the border states, Porter argued that large
numbers of slaves could be freed without disrupting southern society
or causing alarm among Unionist planters in the South. Plainly, he
envisioned a peace settlement facilitated and made possible perhaps
by emancipation but based nonetheless on the continued coexistence
of slavery and freedom.[19]

At the same time, Porter emphasized that his bill's approach to
Negro freedom was superior to that of the original emancipation plan.
He regarded Eliot's bill in particular as defective because it took into

account only the possibility that a slaveowner would go into court to claim the service of a freed slave. It provided no safeguard against seizure of emancipated slaves, which Porter thought more likely, or against the prejudice that blacks would encounter in state courts if these were to be the only forum available for defending freedmen's liberty. For this reason and in order to make emancipation secure, Porter said it was essential to give freed slaves the privilege of the writ of *habeas corpus* in federal courts. Observing that under existing law federal *habeas corpus* jurisdiction extended only to cases of detention by U.S. officers,[20] Porter illustrated the centralizing or nationalizing logic of emancipation. His was the first proposal to recognize the necessity, created by wartime emancipation, of permanently altering the federal-state balance by giving the national government power to protect the right of personal liberty against interference from any state officer or private person.[21]

Porter's conservative argument for emancipation did not satisfy the Democratic opposition. John W. Noell of Missouri, a member of the Select Committee on Confiscation and Emancipation, objected that the bill treated slaves as persons and purported to alter their status in disregard of local law. Congress might legislate the seizure of slaves as property as a war measure, Noell contended, but it had no power, even in time of war, to change the relations between persons or the status of individuals under state law.[22] Republicans, however, especially those who found Eliot's emancipation bill too radical, approved Porter's substitute measure, 82 to 54.[23] Thus, the House, which had already passed a property confiscation bill, enacted a companion emancipation plan.

The interest of the House in freedmen's guarantees was not shared by the Senate, which was more exclusively concerned with legitimizing the de facto emancipation that resulted as federal armies moved South and with using the black manpower thus made available. This fact became clear when Republican Senator Lyman Trumbull of Illinois in June 1862 urged passage of the House emancipation bill as a substitute for the confiscation bill being considered by the Senate.

The Senate confiscation bill declared the slaves of rebels free but offered no sanctions or safeguard of personal liberty. In arguing the importance of such guarantees, Trumbull pointed out that the House emancipation bill gave freed slaves the right of personal liberty and the ability to vindicate this right through the writ of *habeas corpus*. In

Trumbull's view, the House measure answered what he perceived as a growing popular demand that something practical be done to promote actual slave liberation. Other Republicans, preferring to leave the status of freed slaves indefinite, objected. Trumbull then withdrew his motion to adopt the House bill, and the Senate went on to approve its own confiscation bill, including an emancipation section, instead of the separate House confiscation and emancipation measures. When the House in turn rejected the Senate bill, a committee of conference on confiscation was formed. [24]

The conference report compromised the differences between the House and Senate as far as the manner of property confiscation was concerned, [25] but followed the Senate bill with respect to emancipation. That is, it did not contain an emancipation procedure or any guarantee of personal liberty. On its face, the antislavery scope of the conference plan was broader than either the House or Senate proposals. The bill did not base emancipation only on judicial process in the form of either conviction for treason or rebellion or *in rem* proceedings leading to forfeiture of the slaves' services. Instead, it declared that slaves of rebels who escaped to Union lines, who were captured from or abandoned by rebels, or who were found in places occupied by Union arms were "captives of war" and forever free. This stipulation would mean a policy of complete emancipation if federal armies were victorious and no compromise peace settlement took place. [26] The bill also prohibited the return of fugitive slaves by the army.

Nevertheless, the conference report contained no means of implementing the broad emancipation decree, nor any guarantee of the freed slaves' personal liberty. Rather, in a clear demonstration of pragmatic military purpose, it authorized the president to employ, organize, and use persons of African descent "in such a manner as he may judge best for the public welfare." The bill also authorized the president to initiate the voluntary colonization of slaves freed by the act. Despite its earlier interest in emancipation safeguards, the House joined the Senate in approving the second Confiscation Act in July 1862. [27]

Many years ago, James G. Randall observed that the antislavery sections of the second Confiscation Act raised puzzling questions of enforcement and implementation. In such an unfamiliar undertaking as slave emancipation, Randall wrote, a definite procedure was to be expected, yet none was provided.[28] As logical as Randall's observation appears in retrospect, it is really somewhat unhistorical and beside the point, for in the final analysis the Republicans in Congress did not conceive of emancipation as a matter of securing personal liberty and civil rights. Rather, emancipation was intended to deprive the Confederacy of slave labor and to range black manpower on the side of the Union. John Sherman of Ohio, for example, objecting to Trumbull's support of the House emancipation bill with its guarantee of personal liberty, explained that he opposed general emancipation of slaves until there existed "some provision for their government, for their education, for their protection, and for their colonization." But as the government could seize and use the property of rebels, so Sherman believed the labor of escaped and freed blacks should be used in ending the rebellion.[29] Furthermore, although Sherman looked forward to a more clearly articulated freedmen's policy, most Republicans evidently thought the Confiscation Act, with its provision for employment of blacks as the president saw fit, adequately supplied the post-emancipation needs of the freed people, for the time being at least.[30]

Although the freedmen's personal liberty and military expediency were not incompatible considerations, few Union men were convinced of the wisdom or necessity of pursuing both ends. Yet, the fact that some were convinced indicates the growth of an interest in the civil rights side of emancipation. A perceptive critic of congressional policy was Henry Winter Davis of Maryland, soon to be an advocate of Negro civil rights in the Thirty-eigth Congress, who at the time Eliot's emancipation bill was being considered in the House advised Republican members that it was defective because it guaranteed no legal protection to freed slaves. It did not give the blacks whom it declared free the right to bring suit to vindicate personal liberty or to enjoy the privilege of the writ of *habeas corpus*, Davis pointed out, and hence it offered no real freedom.[31] Similarly, the radical *Independent* stated that, although the army could enforce emancipation in time of war, after the return of peace there would be need of civil law guarantees of personal liberty for those slaves who were entitled to freedom but ignorant of their rights or were still in the control of their masters. The personal rights conferred by emancipation, the *Independent* reasoned, would need to be made explicit and to be protected by specific remedies at law.[32]

Many abolitionists criticized the Confiscation Act as insufficiently radical. [33] For the most part, however, the abolitionists seemed to object more to the restricted scope of the act rather than to its lack of procedural safeguards of personal liberty. In a typical expression, Maria Weston Chapman called it "an Emancipation bill with clogs on." [34]

Henry Winter Davis offered the most pointed objections to the Confiscation Act from the standpoint of Negro liberty. Like Porter in the House, Davis desired to use emancipation as an instrument of war, without, however, abolishing slavery as a municipal institution. Eager to wage aggressive war, he criticized the Confiscation Act for freeing only the slaves of persons convicted of treason or rebellion, or slaves of rebels who escaped into Union lines. But Davis also attacked its failure to make legal provision for securing the freed slaves' personal liberty. "I suppose no body thought of any *legal* process," he wrote; "*all* was concentrated in the authority to the President to *use* all the negro population at his pleasure against the rebels!" [35]

A radical correspondent evaluating the Confiscation Act confirmed Davis's interpretation of congressional motive as concerned solely with military expediency. "We have a good Confiscation bill from the hands of a Conference Committee," wrote D. W. Bartlett in the *Independent*. "A section authorizes the President to make any use he pleases of black men, bond or free, in this struggle. . . . Congress has solemnly asked the President . . . *to use the black man in this war!* This is something." [36]

The disposition of freed slaves after their use by the government loomed as a great unresolved issue in 1862. In the limited discussion that had developed by this time, the principal question concerned *where* freed slaves would reside, not what status or rights they would enjoy. Some Republicans believed that they would remain on southern soil as a free labor force and that free blacks from the North would join them in reconstructing free states in the South. [37] The only suggestion that emancipated slaves should go North, to be distributed in the free states according to population, came from conservatives trying to provoke and embarrass Republican emancipationists. [38] The readiest answer to the question of the future disposition of freed slaves was colonization.

On several occasions in 1862, including the second Confiscation Act, Congress endorsed the voluntary removal of freed Negroes in a way that cast ironic light on the Republican emancipation policy. Colonization was, of course, an old idea that had never worked and that, even in the altered circumstances of 1862, must have seemed somewhat chimerical. The best explanation of its revival is that it was politically useful as a corollary of emancipation, for it would allay apprehensions about large-scale migration of blacks into the North. [39] What was notable about colonization as it appeared in the second Confiscation Act was the attempt to connect it with the idea of the freed slaves' rights. Thus, the act stated that Negro emigrants, assuming the president chose to initiate colonization, would be settled in a tropical country "with all the rights and privileges of freemen." [40] The fact that this provision was found in none of the earlier colonization measures of 1862 suggests that it was intended to express the emerging interest in the emancipated slaves' personal liberty. [41] Several Republicans, pessimistic about the possibility of securing civil equality for blacks in race-conscious America, said that real freedom for emancipated slaves would come only through colonization with equal rights abroad. [42]

The Confiscation Act of 1862, designed to confirm the de facto emancipation that was taking place with the advance of Union armies, aimed principally at placing black manpower at the service of the Union. Though it declared slaves of rebels free upon entering federal lines, it neglected to guarantee the right of personal liberty. Perhaps most significant, in authorizing colonization, albeit voluntary, it failed by implication to secure the right of remaining within the American republic. Only in a foreign country were Republicans—sensitive to the demands of politics and the strength of race prejudice—willing to make a promise of equal rights for emancipated slaves.

A critic of colonization pointed out the obvious inadequacy of this position. "However it may have failed to be his country," Union publicist William Aikman wrote in 1862 concerning the black man in the United States, "this is his home. . . . After, by a great act of justice, you have raised him from chattelhood into citizenship, and have given him a country, by what rule of right do you propose to banish him from it?" [43]

Congressional Republicans, then, no less than the Lincoln administration, failed to deal with the problem of the freed slaves' personal liberty. Some of them, it is true, were beginning to see that the issue needed attention, even if like Albert G. Porter and Henry Winter Davis they were not prepared to demand the abolition of slavery. Although it is not at all certain that the guarantee of personal liberty was a decisive consideration, in approving Porter's emancipation bill the House at least showed an awareness that effective emancipation required something more than well-intentioned political rhetoric, even if the rhetoric were incorporated in statutory provisions. Yet more compelling was the desire to sustain the war effort politically by declaring for slave emancipation and militarily (so it was hoped) by depriving the enemy of slave labor. The Confiscation Act's authorization of the president to use Negroes as he saw fit, and the 1862 Militia Act's provision for enlistment of blacks in the army, clearly revealed the Republicans' expedient purpose. Motivated by pragmatic considerations rather than by concern for the slaves' personal liberty, they were content to declare the slaves of rebels free and to leave to future developments the determination of their status and rights in the civil order.

NOTES

1. Mark Krug, "The Republican Party and the Emancipation Proclamation," *Journal of Negro History* 48 (April 1963): 98-114.

2. Cf. Aileen Kraditor, *Means and Ends in American Abolitionism: Garrison and His Critics on Strategy and Tactics, 1834-1850* (New York, 1969), 22-23; John S. Rosenberg, "Toward a New Civil War Revisionism," *American Scholar* 38 (Spring 1969): 250-272.

3. Edward L. Pierce, "The Contrabands at Fortress Monroe," *The Atlantic Monthly*, 8 (November 1861): 627.

4. *Congressional Globe*, 37th Cong., 2d sess., 959 (February 25, 1862), 1143 (March 10, 1862); Louis S. Gerteis, *From Contraband to Freedman: Federal Policy Toward Southern Blacks, 1861-1865* (Westport, Conn., 1973), 11-15.

5. *Congressional Globe*, 37th Cong., 2d sess., 1651-1652 (April 14, 1862).

6. Ibid., 358 (January 16, 1862), remarks of Jacob Collamer, 956-957 (February 25, 1862), remarks of John A. Bingham, 1894 (May 1, 1862), remarks of Charles Sumner.

7. Ibid., 409-411 (August 2, 1861), remarks of Orlando Kellogg.

8. *U.S. Statutes at Large*, XII, 319.

9. 37th Cong., H.R. No. 106, December 2, 1861; H.R. No. 107, December 3, 1861; H.R. No. 126, March 20, 1862; H.R. No. 199, January 8, 1862; H.R. No. 421, April 24, 1862; H.R. No. 440, April 30, 1862; H.R. No. 456, May 5, 1862; S. No. 331, May 26, 1862.

10. 37th Cong., H.R. No. 121, December 9, 1861, introduced by John Gurley; H.R. No. 214, January 15, 1862, introduced by Frank P. Blair. Gurley's bill proposed colonization in Florida, Blair's in a foreign country.

11. 37th Cong., S. No. 335, May 1862, introduced by Henry Wilson; H.R. No. 493, June 2, 1862, introduced by James F. Wilson.

12. Roy P. Basler, et al., eds., *The Collected Works of Abraham Lincoln* (9 vols.; New Brunswick, 1953-1955), V, 329.

13. *Congressional Globe*, 37th Cong., 2d sess., 1479 (April 1, 1862), 1522 (April 3, 1862), 3136 (July 7, 1862); *U.S. Statutes at Large*, XII, 376-378, 538-539. The quotation is, of course, from Richard Hofstadter, *The American Political Tradition and the Men Who Made It* (New York, 1948), 132.

14. John Syrett, "The Confiscation Acts: Efforts at Reconstruction During the Civil War," Ph.D dissertation, University of Wisconsin, 1971.

15. *Congressional Globe*, 37th Cong., 2d sess., 2233 (May 20, 1862).

16. Leonard P. Curry, *Blueprint for Modern America: Nonmilitary Legislation of the First Civil War Congress* (Nashville, 1968), 68-69.

17. *Congressional Globe*, 37th Cong., 2d sess., App., 295 (June 4, 1862), remarks of Albert G. Porter.

18. Ibid.; *Journal of the House of Representatives*, 37th Cong., 2d sess., 887-889 (June 18, 1862).

19. *Congressional Globe*, 37th Cong., 2d sess., 2393 (May 27, 1862). App., 294-296 (June 4, 1862).

20. It was actually slightly broader, applying to state officers in cases where they might detail federal revenue collectors or aliens acting under the authority of a foreign nation. Congress made these exceptions after the tariff and nullification crisis of 1832 and the Caroline affair of 1837. See William M. Wiecek, "The Great Writ and Reconstruction: The Habeas Corpus Act of 1867," *Journal of Southern History* 36 (November 1970): 534-535.

21. *Congressional Globe*, 37th Cong., 2d sess., App., 297 (June 4, 1862). Substitute emancipation bills introduced by E. P. Walton of Vermont, Justin Morrill of Maine, and Samuel Casey of Kentucky also contained the *habeas corpus* provision. Ibid., 2362 (May 26, 1862), remarks of Walton and Morrill; 37th Cong., H.R. No. 472, substitute amendment, June 11, 1862.

22. *House Reports*, 37th Cong., 2d sess., Vol. IV, No. 120, Emancipation of Slaves of Rebels, June 17, 1862.

23. *Congressional Globe*, 37th Cong., 2d sess., 2793 (June 18, 1862).

24. Ibid., 2998-3000 (June 28, 1862), remarks of Lyman Trumbull, John Sherman, James R. Doolittle, 3107 (July 3, 1862).

25. James G. Randall, *Constitutional Problems Under Lincoln*, rev. ed. (Urbana, 1951), 278-279; Curry, *Blueprint for Modern America*, 94.

26. Syrett, "The Confiscation Acts," 84.

27. *Congressional Globe*, 37th Cong., 2d sess., 3267, 3275 (July 11, 1862); *U.S. Statutes at Large*, XII, 589-592.

28. Randall, *Constitutional Problems Under Lincoln*, 359-360.

29. *Congressional Globe*, 37th Congress., 2d sess., 2999 (June 28, 1862).

30. Ibid., 3000 (June 28, 1862), remarks of James R. Doolittle.

31. Henry Winter Davis, *Speeches and Addresses* (New York, 1867), 298, 301.

32. *Independent*, January 30, 1862.

33. Moncure D. Conway, *The Golden Hour* (Boston, 1862), 150.

34. James M. McPherson, *The Struggle for Equality: Abolitionists and the Negro in the Civil War and Reconstruction* (Princeton, 1964), 112.

35. Henry Winter Davis to Mrs. S. F. DuPont, July 1862, S. F. DuPont Papers,

Eleutherian Mills Historical Library.

36. *Independent*, July 17, 1862.

37. Robert Dale Owen, *Letter to S. P. Chase: The Cost of Peace, November 10, 1862* (n.p., n.d.), 5; *National Anti-Slavery Standard*, July 13, 1861; *Congressional Globe*, 37th Cong., 2d sess., 2243 (May 20, 1862), remarks of Albert G. Riddle.

38. Ibid., 1356 (March 25, 1862), remarks of Anthony Kennedy and Willard Saulsbury.

39. V. Jacque Voegeli, *Free But Not Equal: The Midwest and the Negro During the Civil War* (Chicago, 1967), 22-24, and passim.

40. *U.S. Statutes at Large*, XII, 592.

41. Ibid., 378, 425, 582, 592.

42. *Congressional Globe*, 37th Cong., 2d sess., 1492 (April 2, 1862), remarks of John Sherman, 1520 (April 3, 1862), remarks of Orville H. Browning, 1604 (April 10, 1862), remarks of Lyman Trumbull, App., 83 (March 19, 1862), remarks of James R. Doolittle.

43. William Aikman, *The Future of the Colored Race in America* (New York, 1862), 13.

2

Military service and national citizenship

The political and military pressures that produced the second Confiscation Act led Congress, in the Militia Act of 1862, to authorize the use of blacks as fighting men. No more than the Confiscation Act was this measure conceived of as a way of promoting Negro liberty and rights. Nevertheless, it contributed to that end by placing blacks in a position as soldiers rightfully to demand equal treatment by the Union government. Furthermore, because military service historically and legally bore a relationship to membership in the national community, blacks enrolled in the federal army were able to claim the rights of American citizenship. Contrary to the Supreme Court's denial of any such possibility in the Dred Scott case, blacks began to act and to be regarded as part of the people of the United States. Although this circumstance did not by itself change the law of citizenship, it began to alter the factual underpinning on which the law rested. If Negroes were to fight for the nation, it would be necessary to recognize them as citizens of the nation.

The question of Negro citizenship first figured in sectional conflict in 1820 when Missouri sought admission to the Union under a constitution that made it illegal for free Negroes and mulattoes to enter the state. Some northerners argued that this exclusion violated the constitutional requirement that citizens of each state shall be entitled to all privileges and immunities of citizens within the several states. Negroes might be discriminated against in local legislation, but, according to this point of view, if they were free born natives of parents belonging to no other nation, they were citizens of the United States

and were protected by the privileges and immunities clause. Southerners, on the other hand, held that the test of citizenship was the
enjoyment of at least all the civil rights of every other person in the
community under like circumstances. And since free Negroes
nowhere—not even in the northern states that claimed to regard them
as citizens—enjoyed the same civil rights as whites, southerners
denied that they were state citizens under the federal Constitution, entitled to the protection of the comity clause. [1]

While Congress admitted Missouri without resolving the question
of citizenship, the controversy stimulated efforts to deny citizenship to
blacks. In state and national forums over the next two decades, the
doctrine developed that free Negroes occupied a status in between
citizenship and alienage. According to a Kentucky Supreme Court
opinion of 1822 that was heavily relied upon in later years, place of
birth made a person a subject, not a citizen. Citizenship in this view
meant something more than the ordinary rights of personal security
and property which applied to everyone. Furthermore, as Negroes
were discriminated against everywhere, the presumption must be that
they were not citizens under the federal Constitution. Living in the
shadow of slavery and under disabilities based on color alone, free
blacks practically speaking were a third thing in American law, neither citizens nor aliens, neither freemen nor slaves. [2]

The argument against Negro citizenship did not go unchallenged.
To begin with, it was well known that when Congress framed the Articles of Confederation it rejected a proposal to restrict the privileges
and immunities of citizens to free white inhabitants. [3] The implication
of this decision was that Negroes could be American citizens. Judicial
opinion also existed to support the claim of Negro citizenship. In a
much cited opinion of 1838, the North Carolina Supreme Court stated
that under American law a person was either a citizen or an alien; no
intermediate status existed. Accordingly, slaves who were manumit-
ted became freemen, and, if born within the state, citizens. [4] The emi-
nent jurist Chancellor Kent reasoned similarly that citizens in American law were free inhabitants, born within the United States or naturalized under federal law. Native-born free blacks and emancipated
slaves were therefore citizens, though under such disabilities as states
might prescribe for free persons of color. [5]

Blacks might be recognized as citizens of a state, but their status
might be more secure if they could be brought under the protection of

the federal Constitution. To this end, abolitionists in the 1830s and 1840s developed a doctrine of national citizenship, based on the privileges and immunities clause, that included the Negro. The citizens of each state, antislavery lawyers argued, were entitled in all the other states to the privileges and immunities that belonged not just to citizens of the particular state in which they happened to be but to citizens of the nation. In other words, a uniform body of privileges and immunities existed under federal guarantee, a national citizenship independent of state authority.[6] Of course, few legal commentators before the Civil War accepted such a sweeping interpretation of the privileges and immunities clause, but even a restrictive reading of it had great significance for free Negroes. For at the very least it meant that a citizen going into another state was entitled to the rights granted to that state's own citizens.[7]

Although the weight of judicial opinion seems to have been against Negro citizenship, the issue had by no means been settled when the Supreme Court addressed it in the Dred Scott case of 1857. In explaining why Scott, a slave, was not a citizen of Missouri in the sense of the Constitution and could not bring suit in federal court, Chief Justice Taney offered an elaborate analysis of the status of the Negro race in American law.

Taney held that when the Constitution went into effect, those who were citizens of states became citizens of the nation. Noting the exclusions and disabilities imposed on blacks in state constitutions and laws in 1787, he stated that nowhere were Negroes citizens of states. As a class, they were not included, and were not intended to be included, he declared, under the word "citizens" in the Constitution, a term synonomous with "people of the United States." Furthermore, although a state could make anyone it pleased a citizen, such a person did not accordingly become a member in the national political community or a citizen in the sense of the Constitution. Taney thus distinguished between state citizenship for exclusively state purposes and state citizenship for national purposes. Having argued that Negroes were not state citizens in 1787, and having shown that only white aliens could be naturalized, he drew the distinction between two kinds of state citizenship in order to close a final avenue by which blacks might receive the constitutional protection of U.S. citizenship.[8]

Denying Negroes membership in the nation was especially important in view of Taney's broad conception of national citizenship based on the privileges and immunities clause. U.S. citizenship, Taney asserted, gave each citizen rights and privileges outside his state and placed him in every other state upon a perfect equality with its own citizens as to the rights of person and property. If free colored persons should be held to be citizens of the United States, they could go into any state they pleased, enjoy full freedom of speech, hold political meetings, and keep and bear arms. They "would be entitled to all these privileges and immunities in every State," the chief justice reasoned, "and the State could not restrict them; for they would hold these privileges and immunities under the paramount authority of the Federal Government." Therefore, said Taney, it could not be supposed that slave states intended to secure rights for Negroes throughout the Union which they denied to blacks in their own borders. The scope and effect of national citizenship made it all the more clear to Taney that blacks were not comprehended by the term *citizen* as used in the Constitution.[9]

If free Negroes were not citizens, however, what status did they possess under the Constitution? Taney in effect held that they formed a third class between citizens and aliens. Unnaturalized foreigners, he explained, owed no allegiance to the country and were under no obligation to defend it. "The African race, however," Taney stated, "born in the country, did owe allegiance to the government, whether they were slave or free."[10] This statement has been interpreted to mean that free Negroes were subject nationals, or, assuming that the Constitution offers only the alternatives of citizenship or alienage, citizens without full rights.[11] Although citizenship of any sort implies at least a degree of government protection (and Taney said nothing of this in relation to Negroes), previous federal policies on land allotment and passports lent support to the idea of intermediate or quasi-citizenship for blacks.[12]

In the aftermath of the Dred Scott decision, the few loopholes open to blacks implying possible citizenship were closed.[13] Ironically, it was wartime Republicans, arguing that slaves owed allegiance and were under an obligation to support the government, who began to illustrate the positive uses to which the doctrine of quasi-citizenship implicit in Taney's Dred Scott opinion could be put.

Given the American tradition of the citizen-soldier and the fact that military service was regarded as an obligation and privilege of citizenship, [14] enlistment in the Union army appeared to be a way for blacks to establish a claim on U.S. citizenship. Negroes had fought in the Revolution and the War of 1812, but in 1861 they were excluded from the nation's military establishment. The Militia Act of 1792, under which the states organized and supplied most of the manpower of Union armies, authorized the enrollment only of white male citizens of the states. Blacks were enrolled in a few of the state militias, but they could not serve if these units were called into federal service. Furthermore, while the regular army statute since 1790 contained no racial exclusion, War Department regulations after 1816 barred Negroes. [15]

Although military service would not by itself be legally conclusive of citizenship, citizenship was seen as involved in the question of army enrollment. Thus, the abolitionist Frederick Douglass appealed to Congress in December 1861 to receive blacks into the army and thereby affirm that Negroes born on American soil were citizens. "Once let the black man get upon his person the brass letters *U.S.*; let him get an eagle on his button, and a musket on his shoulder and bullets in his pocket," wrote Douglass, "and there is no power on earth which can deny that he has earned the right to citizenship in the United States." [16] Henry Winter Davis of Maryland similarly urged Republicans to recognize that if blacks were to become soldiers, "they are to be freemen, ... protected by the laws, recognized by the United States in their position, guaranteed the remedies of the courts of the United States, and armed and drilled to make their rights effectual." [17]

Although radicals advocated the use of Negro troops from the outset, the idea did not gain majority support until military necessity required it. This point came in July 1862, after the failure of the Peninsular Campaign, and was manifested in the passage of the Militia Act, the first statute aimed at enlisting blacks in the army. [18] The principal purpose of the measure was to empower the president to institute a militia draft should the new call for 300,000 troops not be met. [19] It declared that all able-bodied male citizens between the ages of eighteen and forty-five should be enrolled in the militia. This bill omitted the racial qualification of the existing federal law and made Negroes eligible for service in the nationalized militia for the first time. But because almost all the states excluded blacks from their militias by their own authority, the Militia Act provided for direct national enlistment of Negroes. [20]

In abolishing the racial restriction of the federal militia law and providing for national enlistment of blacks, Congress made no determination of the status of Negroes affected by the law. If enrolled in the nationalized state militia, they could conceivably be citizens of a state. [21] Otherwise, if enrolled directly in the federal service, they were, in the words of the law, "persons of African descent," subject to such regulations as the president might prescribe.

Conservatives favored confining Negroes to trench digging and camp labor, contending that slaves so employed might be returned to slavery. [22] Congress imposed no such restriction in the Militia Act, however, and went on to guarantee freedom for slaves who entered military service and their families. The connection between army service and civil liberty which the Militia Act made apparent was underscored in legislative debate. "You arm these slaves, and fight them in the Army," asserted Senator James H. Lane of Kansas, "and when that is done, I say it is out of the power of . . . the General Government to return them to the loyal master in a state of slavery." [23]

Although the Militia Act thus authorized the president to employ black troops, Lincoln remained opposed to the arming of slaves. [24] In the face of continued military defeat, however, and with congressional elections approaching, the pressure to draw on Negro manpower was irresistible. Accordingly, at the end of August 1862, Secretary of War Stanton authorized General Saxton in South Carolina to arm and equip 5,000 Negro troops, and in Kansas and Louisiana Union generals formed Negro regiments. [25] After the Democrats scored impressive victories in the November elections and the Union army was defeated again at Fredericksburg, Lincoln endorsed as general policy the expedient he had allowed in selected areas. In the Emancipation Proclamation of January 1, 1863, he stated that freed slaves would be received into the armed services. Thereafter, the recruitment of Negro regiments was undertaken in full earnest, and a Bureau of Colored Troops was organized in the War Department. [26]

In March 1863, Congress passed the nation's first conscription law. The bill stated that all able-bodied male citizens of the United States between the ages of eighteen and forty-five constituted the national forces and were liable to perform military duty when called upon by the president.[27] In the absence of any racial qualification, this provision might imply that blacks could be enrolled in the army as citizens. But Congress in other legislation continued to treat Negroes as a distinct class, and the War Department did not enlist slaves as citizens.[28] In an amendment to the Draft Act in 1864, however, Congress expressly authorized Negro enlistment.

The 1864 conscription act amendment declared that all qualified male colored persons between the ages of twenty and forty-five, resident in the United States, should be enrolled and "form part of the national forces."[29] This amendment did not state that blacks were citizens of the United States, nor did it require that they be enrolled under the national citizens formula of the 1863 draft law. Congress was content to declare Negroes part of the national forces because the practical need was to get freed slaves into the army and because the citizenship question was too difficult to resolve at this time. Nevertheless, while blacks were not yet regarded as full citizens, they were viewed in congressional military legislation as subjects of the United States, as persons under the Constitution, or as freemen.

Most telling and significant was the assertion of the freed slaves' legal personality under the Constitution. Rejecting the conservative notion that the government could use slaves in the army as a form of property, Senator John Sherman of Ohio declared: "By the Constitution of the United States they are regarded as persons. As such they are represented here. We have the same right to call upon this class of persons for military duty that we have to call upon the white men of the country."[30] Representative James Wilson of Iowa said the enlistment of blacks rested on "the principle of allegiance, the bond which binds the citizen to the Government and the Government to the citizen, insuring protection to the latter and obedience and support to the former."[31] Representative Charles Sedgwick of New York similarly described Negro slaves as "*persons* owing allegiance" and having a right to claim the protection of the Government."[32]

Blacks were enrolled in the army for military reasons, and the arguments used to justify their employment reflected concern for national sovereignty and preservation of the Union more than an interest in Negro rights. Nonetheless, military service was a significant step toward national citizenship for blacks. Although they exaggerated its effects, Democratic opponents of the Negro soldier policy were right in arguing that the logic of admitting blacks to the ranks of fighting men was to admit them eventually to a general civil equality with white persons. [33] This tendency could be seen in a limited way in the matter of Negro soldiers' pay and allowances, in regard to which blacks by the end of the war won a substantial measure of equality, and also the Negro prisoner of war problem. [34]

In a proclamation of July 1863 promising retaliation for mistreatment of captured black soldiers, Lincoln implicitly recognized the new conception of citizen-soldier in which the Negro was coming to be held. The president acknowledged the duty of the government "to give protection to its citizens, of whatever class, color, or condition, and especially to those who are duly organized as soldiers in the public service." [35] Challenged by Democrats seeking to arouse white hostility toward blacks, most Republicans were reluctant to admit the force of the citizenship equality argument. Aside from their own prejudices, equal citizenship for Negroes, needless to say, was politically unpopular. Yet, it seemed indisputable that the black man's entry into military service signified a change in his status in general.

Reviewing the Negro soldier policy, the radical *Independent* observed in 1863: "Military necessity has compelled us to give a vital form to the latent 'American doctrine' of the natural rights of all men." The enlistment of blacks meant that the Negro "is raised and dignified by serving the Government. He is a soldier of the United States! He has a country and a government!" [36] The moment blacks took up arms in the Union cause, said radical Unionist Charles D. Drake of Missouri, "the black race in America felt the power of a new manhood, and stepped firmly into the arena of a higher and better life." Addressing a convention of border state men in Louisville in 1864, Drake admonished: "Let us face the logical result. The black man is henceforth to assume a new *status* among us." Drake denied that Negroes would become in all respects equal to whites, but added that disqualifications, prohibitions, and degradations would be removed, and privileges conferred so that the Negro's freedom would be no empty name but a tangible reality. [37]

Drake in effect described a basic condition of equal citizenship for blacks. Others made the point more explicitly, especially after Attorney General Edward Bates issued an opinion in November 1862 stating that a free Negro was a citizen of the United States. [38] The Texas Unionist Andrew Jackson Hamilton wrote in 1863: "Native-born men—free men—wielding a portion of the political power of

Government, Federal as well as State, and with arms in their hands to defend the flag . . . are citizens in *fact*, in *reason*, and by every right that confers citizenship. And so they will henceforth be considered—the law proceeding from the right." [39] Secretary of the Treasury Salmon P. Chase publicly urged calling blacks into the conflict "not as cattle, not now, even, as contrabands, but as men." In the free states, and as a result of the Emancipation Proclamation in the rebel regions too, said Chase, Negroes were freemen and citizens of the United States. [40]

By its military legislation of 1862-1864, Congress thus effectively denied Chief Justice Taney's assertion in the Dred Scott case that the Negro race formed no part of the people of the United States. Senator Henry Wilson of Massachusetts underscored this point in answering a conservative plea to abide by the Dred Scott ruling that the national government had no power in relation to Negroes, other than to protect the rights of slaveowners. Declared Wilson: "we, acting for the nation, must treat them as persons. . . . We are in time of war, with supreme power to deal with the people of this nation in such a manner as to render our population most effective in the service of the nation." Referring to the South's slave population and indirectly to blacks in general, Wilson announced: "We deal with them as a part of the people of the United States." [41]

In addition to enacting a Negro soldier policy based on the idea that blacks were part of the nation, Republicans also formulated a theory of national citizenship that comprehended the colored race. The central questions that the theory answered were: who are citizens of the United States, and in what does national citizenship consist?

Republican theorists, wishing to bring Negroes under the protection of the Constitution, adopted an inclusive rather than a restrictive approach to citizenship. Defining citizenship in minimal terms, they took as point of departure the proposition, expounded in the Dred Scott case by Justice John McLean, that the most general and appropriate definition of the term *citizen* was a native-born freeman. [42] Thus, John Bingham of Ohio declared: "Those born within the Republic, whether black or white, are citizens by birth—natural-born citizens." Not only free Negroes, but slaves too were American citizens, Bingham reasoned. [43] The New England legalist Timothy Farrar wrote that the people or citizens of the United States included "everybody belonging to the country, without distinction of age, sex, race, or condition." In the sense of the Constitution, citizen meant "all the native or naturalized inhabitants of the land, in contradistinction to aliens only."[44]

Attorney General Edward Bates gave executive department sanction to this view in an 1862 opinion on Negro citizenship. Bates held that any person born in the United States was *prima facie* a citizen. "That nativity furnishes the rule, both of duty and of right as between the individual and the government," he wrote, "is a historical and political truth so old and so universally accepted that it is needless to prove it by authority."[45] The antislavery legalist John C. Hurd held similarly that the word *citizen* as used in the Constitution referred to domiciled inhabitants, native or naturalized under federal law.[46]

Emerging Republican theory on citizenship differed from antebellum theory in making American birth the sole test of national citizenship. Earlier opinion held that national citizenship was derived from and dependent on state citizenship, so that any person born in the United States who was a citizen under a state's constitution and laws was also a U.S. citizen.[47] The trouble with this doctrine, however, was that it allowed each state to exclude any native white or colored person from both state and national citizenship.[48] Accordingly, Republicans came to the conclusion that the qualification for U.S. citizenship must be made exclusively national, and not left to state determination. "Men *born* on our soil are Americans," asserted a Republican pamphleteer, "be they black or white."[49]

As for the content of national citizenship, Republican theorists viewed it in the most fundamental sense as a contract requiring support on the part of the citizen and protection on the part of the government. According to Attorney General Bates, a citizen was a member of the nation and was bound to it by the reciprocal obligation of allegiance on the one side and protection on the other. All citizens were equal in this sense, Bates averred: "the child in the cradle and its father in the Senate are equally citizens of the United States."[50] Congressmen who held that slaves were persons or subjects owing allegiance to the government and liable to be drafted in effect regarded them as citizens in this basic sense. Arguing for equal pay for black soldiers, Edgar Cowan of Pennsylvania insisted: "the negro under the Constitution has a particular legal status, which in my judgment makes him a citizen. . . . He is protected by the law. Being protected, and protection and allegiance being reciprocal, he is therefore a citizen."[51]

Cowan expressed a crucial aspect of Republican citizenship theory when he added that though the Negro was a citizen, he was not fully equal to white persons. [52] All citizens were equal, but the scope of citizenship equality was distinctly limited. Basically, the emerging Republican theory held that national citizenship entitled a person to fundamental natural rights, but not political rights. Failure to make this distinction, observed Attorney General Bates, was the principal reason why so much misunderstanding existed concerning U.S. citizenship. Too often the problem had been approached by assuming that all rights and privileges were incidents of citizenship. Bates denied this assumption, pointing out that political rights were not a constituent element of national citizenship. [53]

In positive terms, national citizenship entitled a person to protection in basic civil rights. The question involved in the citizenship of freed slaves, argued John Bingham in 1862, was whether they should be "permitted to enjoy life and liberty and property under the sanction and shelter of law." Although he did not refer to emancipated slaves expressly as citizens, James Harlan of Iowa saw them enjoying the same rights as persons who were citizens without political rights. Blacks would be equal in their right to personal liberty, to the enjoyment of the fruit of their own labor, and to justice and the protection of the laws. [54]

Citizenship as the reciprocal obligations of allegiance and protection was rooted in the fundamental principles of republican government and natural law. A more specific constitutional foundation for it was the privileges and immunities clause of the Constitution. John Bingham, the principal author of the Fourteenth Amendment which ultimately affirmed Negro citizenship, illustrated the argument in 1862. The Constitution, Bingham pointed out, entitled citizens of each state to all privileges and immunities of citizens in the several states. Thus, when a citizen went into a state, he was entitled not merely to the privileges and immunities of *state* citizenship, but of *U.S.* citizenship as well. There was an ellipsis in the language of the comity clause, said Bingham, which, when supplied, made its nationalistic meaning clear: "'all privileges and immunities of citizens of the United States *in* the several States.' is what is guaranteed by the Constitution." [55]

In demanding the abolition of slavery, Republicans posited a national citizenship based on the privileges and immunities clause. The proposed Thirteenth Amendment, they reasoned in 1864, would enable rights of citizenship originating in national authority and protected by the comity clause to be vindicated for both white and black citizens. According to James Wilson of Iowa, the freedoms of speech, press, religious opinion, and the right to assemble and petition the government were rights of national citizenship guaranteed by the privileges and immunities clause. No state could deny them without breach of the bond which held the Union together, Wilson declared.[56] In similar vein, Andrew Jackson Hamilton wrote that, if slavery were abolished, some meaning and force might be attached to the privileges and immunities clause.[57] Regarding freed slaves as citizens, another Union writer cited the privileges and immunities clause as a guarantee that blacks could not be excluded from residence in any state.[58] A California Republican summed up the argument for equal national citizenship in asserting: "Citizens of one State must be citizens of all; . . . citizens of the nation, everywhere entitled to the same privileges and the same immunities." Local legislation should never be allowed to determine claims to national citizenship and the common rights of the people.[59]

Legal commentators attested to the significance of the privileges and immunities clause as a source and guarantee of national citizenship. Marvin T. Wheat of Kentucky, a proslavery legalist, reasoned that a Negro who was recognized as a citizen in a free state was, by virtue of the comity clause, a citizen of all the other states. Thus, a black man entitled to political and civil rights in a northern state could go before a U.S. court and demand the same rights in a slave state, in spite of the latter's constitution and laws barring blacks from citizenship.[60] The antislavery jurist John C. Hurd saw equally great potential for national protection of civil rights under the privileges and immunities clause. The provision did not merely give a citizen going into a state the rights that the state gave to its own citizens, Hurd wrote in 1862. Rather, the privileges and immunities clause provided an instrument by which fundamental rights could be maintained against state encroachment. The very character of the constitutional provision, Hurd argued, required a national standard of the privileges and immunities of citizens distinct from the law of the state into which a person might go. The comity clause protected state citizens, he believed, but in its operation it gave "something of national citizenship under a quasi-international law."[61]

Republican theorists thus held that persons born in the United

States or naturalized under federal law were citizens of the United States. National citizenship consisted in personal liberty surrounded by fundamental civil rights and was protected against state interference by the privileges and immunities clause. Americans were "a nation of equals," exclaimed James Wilson, and it was the privileges and immunities clause—"of most vital importance to every citizen"—that made them so.[62] Under the pressure of war, Union men were coming to the conclusion, in the words of John Bingham, that "the great privilege and immunity of an American citizen, to be respected everywhere in this land . . . is that they shall not be deprived of life, liberty, or property without due process of law."[63] More and more, Bingham's prewar observation seemed apposite: "This guaranty of the Constitution [the privileges and immunities clause] is senseless and a mockery, if it does not limit State sovereignty and restrain each and every State from closing its territory and its courts of justice against citizens of the United States."[64]

Republican constitutional theory emphasized giving legal force to the idea of national citizenship in order to prevent states from discriminating against blacks in the egregious manner common before the war. The point was not to undermine or diminish state citizenship or deprive states of their accustomed power to regulate it, but rather to give substance to national citizenship alongside it. Republicans sought to give practical expression to a dual citizenship that had existed heretofore only in theory. With respect to citizenship, Republicans proposed a modification, not a revolution, in federalism. State citizenship would still be primary in the sense that a person's principal relationship with government would be at the state level. As had been the case since the founding of the federal union, most of the rights a citizen enjoyed would belong to him as a state citizen. Now, however, he would possess fundamental civil rights in consequence of national citizenship as well, so that, if states were abusive or remiss in protecting individual rights, remedy would lie in national courts, or possibly even national legislation. With the exception of those few Americans who had foreign or interstate interests, national citizenship before the war had been of little practical effect and had not formed a counterweight to the states' power over civil rights.[65] The vitalization of national citizenship would rectify this defect and in that relative sense would diminish the states' powers.

National citizenship would be primary in the sense that it would no longer be derivative of or dependent upon state citizenship. An American citizen was first of all a citizen of the United States and then a citizen of the state in which he resided. The protection which the federal Constitution gave to state citizens could not be denied by a state's denial of citizenship. Hence, in any state in the Union a citizen could demand, as a U.S. citizen, the basic civil rights of personal liberty and security of persons and property, freedom of speech and assembly, and equal protection of the laws. "Where an American lives or travels to (in America) he should have and take with him the rights of American manhood," insisted Union publicist W. W. Broom in 1865. Reflecting the emphasis on basic equality of treatment for all national citizens, Broom concluded: "Those rights should not be lessened nor be abrogated because he leaves one State and emigrates to another. He ought not to be a man in one State and a non-entity in another State."[66]

In 1863, national citizenship theory was in process of formation and many questions remained to be answered. The most perplexing questions concerned the precise scope of citizenship and whether it included voting rights.

The radical *Independent* seemed to take a broad view of national citizenship when it praised Attorney General Bates's opinion on citizenship for giving "to this despised race the full position and the full rights, at home and abroad, on the land and on the sea, of an American citizen."[67] Black abolitionists like Robert Purvis also seemed to see, if somewhat vaguely, broad practical significance in Bates's opinion.[68] And after 1863, the practical import of citizenship, in the view of radicals and abolitionists, was that it provided a means of enfranchising Negroes.[69] Moderate Republicans, however, were much more guarded in their outlook. Criticizing those who saw in Bates's opinion a sweeping advance to Negro equality, the New York *Times* said that the practical advantages of American citizenship to the black man would be small at best. "It simply confers upon his race a few inconsiderable rights," such as commanding vessels, obtaining passports, and suing in national courts, declared the *Times*. The blacks' fundamental rights to life, liberty, and property were no more secure for their being American citizens, reasoned the moderate journal, for in these rights Negroes, like other members of the community, had always been protected by the state governments.[70]

The scope and effect of national citizenship thus remained to be determined. Nevertheless, as a result of the government's recruitment policy, the attorney general's opinion on Negro citizenship, and their own willingness to take up arms, blacks could lay substantial claim to American citizenship. Moreover, Republicans had begun to formulate a theory of national citizenship by which Negroes might be recognized in constitutional terms as part of the people of the United States. Some practical results were also evident, as in the granting of passports to Negroes as U.S. citizens and the acquisition of public lands.[71]

The military necessities which produced emancipation and raised the question of Negro citizenship by the end of 1863 had resulted in the occupation of much Confederate territory. This in turn made reconstruction a prominent issue, and with it the status of the freedmen in the reorganized governments of the seceded states gained in importance as an issue. Indeed, for the next two years this matter overshadowed the question of national citizenship, for however national citizenship might be defined or resolved, Republicans were certain that the freed slaves must remain on the soil of the southern states. The status and rights of blacks as state citizens therefore became part of the reconstruction problem that occupied both the president and Congress in the last two years of the war.

NOTES

1. *Annals of Congress*, 16th Cong., 2d sess., 546, 586, 595-599; Glover Moore, *The Missouri Controversy 1819-1821* (Lexington, 1953), 142-169; Alfred H. Kelly and Winfred A. Harbison, *The American Constitution: Its Origin and Development*, 3d ed. (New York, 1963), 268-269.

2. Amy *v.* Smith, 1 *Littell* 333 (1822); Gordon E. Sherman, "Emancipation and Citizenship," *Yale Law Journal* 15 (April 1906): 263-271; Vincent C. Hopkins, *Dred Scott's Case* (New York, 1951), 96-105; *Citizenship of the U.S., Expatriation, and Protection Abroad*, 64-65; Thomas R. R. Cobb, *An Inquiry into the Law of Negro Slavery in the United States of America* (New York, 1968; orig. pub. 1858), 312-313; Theodore B. Wilson, *The Black Codes of the South* (University, Ala., 1965), 35-41.

3. Article IV of the Articles stated: "the free inhabitants of each of these States, paupers, vagabonds, and fugitives from justice expected, shall be entitled to all privileges and immunities of free citizens in the several states."

4. State *v.* Manual, 4 *Devereux and Battle*, 20-39; Hopkins, *Dred Scott's Case*, 102-103.

5. James Kent, *Commentaries on American Law*, 5th ed. (4 vols.; New York, 1844), II, 258.

6. W. W. Crosskey, "Charles Fairman, 'Legislative History,' and the Constitutional Limitations on State Authority," *University of Chicago Law Review* 22 (Autumn 1954):

12-15; Howard Jay Graham, *Everyman's Constitution: Historical Essays on the Fourteenth Amendment, The 'Conspiracy Theory,' and American Constitutionalism* (Madison, 1968), 175-183.

7. Joseph Story, *Commentaries on the Constitution of the United States* (2 vols.; Boston, 1851), II, 543.

8. Dred Scott *v.* Sandford, 19 *Howard* 404-406.

9. Ibid., 406-407, 416-417, 421-423.

10. 19 *Howard* 420.

11. Dudley O. McGovney, "American Citizenship," *Columbia Law Review* 11 (March 1911): 245-248.

12. In 1841, Congress rejected a proposal to restrict the benefits of a preemption act to whites, and an opinion of Attorney General Hugh Legare upheld the Negroes' right to enjoy the benefits of the act. In regard to travel abroad, the federal government denied regular passports but issued special passports to free Negroes. The State Department held in 1856 that, while Negroes were not citizens, they could receive certificates stating the facts of American birth and free condition and promising protection if wronged by a foreign government. Leon F. Litwack, *North of Slavery: The Negro in the Free States, 1790-1860* (Chicago, 1961), 53-57; Gaillard Hunt, *The American Passport, Its History and a Digest of Laws, Rulings, and Regulations Governing Its Issuance by the Department of State* (Washington, D.C., 1898), 4-16.

13. Litwack, *North of Slavery*, 53, 56.

14. S. T. Ansell, "Legal and Historical Aspects of the Militia," *Yale Law Journal* 26 (April 1917): 472.

15. George Livermore, "An Historical Research Respecting the Opinions of the Founders of the Republic on Negroes as Slaves, as Citizens, and as Soldiers," *Proceedings of the Massachusetts Historical Society* 6 (1862-1863), 86-248; William Whiting, *War Powers Under the Constitution of the United States*, 43d ed. (Boston, 1871), 479-480; Litwack, *North of Slavery*, 31-33; Russell F. Weigley, *History of the United States Army* (New York, 1967), 212.

16. Philip S. Foner, ed., *The Life and Writings of Federick Douglass* (4 vols.; New York, 1952), III, 177; Douglass, *Addresses at a Mass Meeting . . . for the Promotion of Colored Enlistments* (Philadelphia, 1863), 5-7.

17. Henry Winter Davis, *Speeches and Addresses* (New York, 1867), 316.

18. The Confiscation Act of 1862 authorized the president "to employ as many persons of African descent as he may deem necessary and proper for the suppression of this rebellion." *U.S. Statutes at Large*, XII, 590-591. However, blacks were made military laborers under this legislation, not soldiers. Whiting, *War Powers*, 482-483.

19. Jack F. Leach, *Conscription in the United States: Historical Background* (Rutland, Vt., 1952), 139.

20. *U.S. Statutes at Large*, XII, 599; Whiting, *War Powers*, 484.

21. Governor John A. Andrew of Massachusetts apparently regarded blacks in this light. In complying with Lincoln's call for a 300,000-man militia in 1862, he directed that the names of all citizens, white and colored, be enrolled. Washington *National Intelligencer*, August 15, 1862.

22. *Congressional Globe*, 37th Cong., 2d sess., 3204 (July 9, 1862), remarks of Garrett Davis.

23. Ibid., 3338 (July 15, 1862).

24. Roy P. Basler, et al., eds., *The Collected Works of Abraham Lincoln* (9 vols.; New Brunswick, 1953-1955), V, 356-357.

25. Benjamin P. Thomas and Harold M. Hyman, *Stanton: The Life and Times of Lincoln's Secretary of War* (New York, 1862), 241-243; Dudley T. Cornish, *The Sable Arm: Negro Troops in the Union Army, 1861-1865* (New York, 1956), 79-81.

26. Basler, et al., eds., *Collected Works of Lincoln*, VI, 30; Cornish, *Sable Arm*, 129-131.

27. Leach, *Conscription in the United States*, 165.

28. Whiting, *War Powers*, 508-509.

29. *U.S. Statutes at Large*, XIII, 11.

30. *Congressional Globe*, 37th Cong., 2d sess., 3199 (July 9, 1862).

31. Ibid., 37th Cong., 3d sess., 680 (February 2, 1863).

32. Ibid., 629-630 (January 30, 1863).

33. Ibid., 599 (January 29, 1863), remarks of S. S. Cox; 601, remarks of Charles A. Wickliffe; 626-627 (January 30, 1863), remarks of William H. Wadsworth; 653 (January 31, 1863), remarks of George Pendleton; App., 93 (February 2, 1863), remarks of Chilton A. White.

34. Equal treatment for black prisoners of war was largely beyond the control of Union authorities, but the government took the position that no belligerent had a right to treat organized soldiers, regardless of color, other than as public enemies. It threatened retaliation for violations of this rule. Nevertheless, when Confederate officials dealt with captured Negro troops according to southern state laws and reenslaved or shot them, little could be done to stop it. Prisoner exchange, undertaken with difficulty in 1862, was broken off by the Union when blacks were treated in violation of the rules of war. Fred A. Shannon, *The Organization and Administration of the Union Army 1861-1865* (2 vols.; Cleveland, 1928), II, 165-167; Cornish, *Sable Arm*, 157-170, 185-186, 192-195; Thomas and Hyman, *Stanton*, 372.

35. Basler, et al., eds., *Collected Works of Lincoln*, VI, 357.

36. *Independent*, April 16, 1863.

37. Charles D. Drake, *Union and Anti-Slavery Speeches* (Cincinnati, 1864), 414-415.

38. *Official Opinions of the Attorneys General of the United States*, X, 394. Bates's opinion is considered more fully below.

39. Andrew Jackson Hamilton, *Letter of General A. J. Hamilton of Texas, to the President of the United States* (New York, 1863), 5-8.

40. S. P. Chase, *Letter to the Loyal National League* (New York, 1863), 23.

41. *Congressional Globe*, 38th Cong., 2d sess., 1003-1004 (February 22, 1865).

42. *Report of the Decision of the Supreme Court of the United States in the Case of Dred Scott v. Sandford* (Washington, D.C., 1857), 137.

43. *Congressional Globe*, 37th Cong., 2d sess., 1639 (April 11, 1862).

44. Timothy Farrar, "State Rights," *New Englander* 21 (October 1862): 708.

45. *Official Opinions of the Attorneys General*, X, 394. The case which elicited Bates's opinion involved a Negro captain commanding a vessel under federal coasting laws that restricted command to citizens of the United States. Bates held that the Negro, a free black, was a citizen of the United States.

46. John C. Hurd, *The Law of Freedom and Bondage* (2 vols.; Boston, 1858-1862), II, 277.

47. See Justice Curtis's opinion in the Dred Scott case, 19 Howard 406, and Story,

Commentaries on the Constitution, II, 466.

48. Peter Burnett, *The American Theory of Government* (New York, 1861), 49.

49. W. W. Broom, *Great and Grave Questions for American Politicians* (Boston, 1865), 42.

50. *Opinions of the Attorneys General*, X, 388.

51. *Congressional Globe*, 38th Cong., 1st sess., 641-642 (February 13, 1864).

52. Ibid.

53. *Opinions of the Attorneys General*. X, 386.

54. *Congressional Globe*, 37th Cong., 2d sess., 1639 (April 11, 1862); App., 322 (July 11, 1862).

55. Ibid., 1639 (April 11, 1862).

56. Ibid., 38th Cong., 1st sess., 1202 (March 9, 1864).

57. Hamilton, *Letter to the President of the United States*, 5.

58. Adolph E. Kroeger, *The Future of the Country* (n.p., 1864), 21.

59. William N. Slocum, *The War and How to End It*, 3d ed. (San Francisco, 1861), 38.

60. Marvin T. Wheat, *The Progress and Intelligence of Americans; Collateral Proof of Slavery*, 2d ed. (Louisville, 1863), 579-593.

61. Hurd, *The Law of Freedom and Bondage*, II, 334, 351, 353.

62. *Congressional Globe*, 38th Cong., 1st sess., 1202 (March 19, 1864).

63. Ibid., 37th Cong., 2d sess., 1639 (April 11, 1862).

64. Ibid., 35th Cong., 2d sess., 984 (February 11, 1859).

65. Harold M. Hyman, *A More Perfect Union: The Impact of the Civil War and Reconstruction on the Constitution* (New York, 1973), 426.

66. Broom, *Great and Grave Questions*, 42.

67. *Independent*, January 1, 1863.

68. *National Anti-Slavery Standard*, May 16, 1863.

69. Henry Ward Beecher, *Universal Suffrage and Complete Equality in Citizenship* (Boston, 1865), 6; James M. McPherson, *The Struggle for Equality: Abolitionists and the Negro During the Civil War and Reconstruction* (Princeton, 1864), 239-243.

70. New York *Times*, December 17, 1862.

71. In 1861, Secretary of State Seward began issuing passports to Negroes. In 1863, a U.S. land commissioner in California ruled, on the basis of the attorney general's opinion on citizenship, that a free Negro whose right to a quarter section of public land had been challenged on the ground that he was not a citizen was entitled to the benefit of the preemption laws and the Homestead Act. Litwack, *North of Slavery*, 57; *National Anti-Slavery Standard*, May 16, July 18, 1863.

3

Presidential reconstruction and freedmen's policy

After Union armies scored major victories in the summer of 1863, federal policy toward the slave population of the South appeared more distinctly under the aspect of reconstruction requirements rather than simple military expediency. Emancipated slaves were fighting for the Union; their labor was essential to the government's plans for operating abandoned plantations; and as freemen or citizens of the seceded states, they were a potential force in postwar politics. Interwoven with these practical considerations was the growing conviction that elementary justice demanded protection of the freed slaves' personal liberty and rights. The upshot was that by the time Lincoln issued his Proclamation of Amnesty and Reconstruction in December 1863, a large number of Republicans viewed the status and rights of emancipated slaves as part of the general problem of securing the results of the war.

Lincoln first dealt with reconstruction when he appointed military governors in Tennessee, Louisiana, Arkansas, and North Carolina in the spring of 1862. At the same time, responding to radical efforts in Congress to reduce the rebel states to territories and abolish slavery, he inaugurated plans for gradual, compensated emancipation which he hoped the border states would accept. When they did not, and antislavery pressure in Congress produced the second Confiscation Act, Lincoln abandoned the border state policy entirely. After the battle of Antietam in September, he announced a policy of military emancipation in the Preliminary Emancipation Proclamation.[1]

A corollary of the new policy was a more systematic approach to the disposition of escaped and emancipated slaves. One feature of the government's program was the employment of former slaves in military labor. Initiated in the contraband policy of 1861 and endorsed by Congress in the second Confiscation Act, freedmen's labor became general policy through Lincoln's order of August 1862 directing all military commanders to employ blacks as laborers. Recruitment of Negro soldiers was also, as we have seen, promoted by Congress in the Militia Act of 1862 and implemented in 1863 by the formation of black regiments in the occupied South. Like the black labor expedient, it was intended to provide useful roles for freed slaves while strengthening the Union militarily. Voluntary colonization of emancipated slaves, first proposed by Lincoln in December 1861, formed the third element in the government's more systematic method of dealing with emancipation. Like the employment of former slaves, but even more so, colonization was intended to bring political advantage by allaying fears of black migration into the North.[2]

The Emancipation Proclamation completed the radicalization of the administration's slavery policy. Though presented as a strictly military measure, the executive order of January 1, 1863, was understood as enlarging the purpose of the war to include slave liberation.[3] More problematic than its bearing on war aims, however, was the effect of the proclamation on the emerging reconstruction question.

Although the Emancipation Proclamation contained a promise to uphold the freedom of emancipated slaves, it was not clear whether this simply required protection of persons who had become free, or the revision of state constitutions and laws to prohibit slavery as a municipal institution. Historically, the proclamation signifies the decisive turning point in the seemingly irresistible drive to abolish slavery. The liberation of large numbers of slaves notwithstanding, the complete abolition of slavery was no more inevitable than was the success of the Union Army. Therefore, as they contemplated the scope and effect of the emancipation order, Unionists entered into an extensive debate over whether it should form the basis of reconstruction, laying the foundation for new state constitutions that would abolish slavery as a domestic or local institution.

Extreme conservatives, besides denouncing it as utterly impractical, categorically denied any legal validity or effect to the Emancipation Proclamation.[4] Their response was similar to that of Confederates who, although dismissing Lincoln's order as a harmless thunderbolt, betrayed awareness that it altered the nature of the war and thus had profound practical consequences. [5]

Conservative Unionists of less extreme outlook argued that, insofar as the army might give it actual effect, the president's proclamation was a legal exercise of the war power. In this view, the United States enjoyed belligerent rights, martial law superseding municipal or state law in the theatre of war. As a consequence, the relationship between master and slave was destroyed, and slaves who after entering Union lines were able to place themselves subsequently under the laws of a free state might acquire permanent freedom. [6] Conservative Unionists also believed, however, that the Emancipation Proclamation was conceived of as a reconstruction instrument by which to abrogate state constitutions and laws, and in that respect they condemned it.

Former Supreme Court justice Benjamin R. Curtis denounced the Emancipation Proclamation as a measure intended to repeal and annul valid state laws regulating the domestic relations of persons within exclusive state jurisdiction. In effect, said Curtis, the proclamation was to operate as a postwar penalty against loyal as well as disloyal inhabitants of the states for continuing in rebellion. [7] Joel Parker, a prominent conservative constitutional lawyer, also thought the executive order was designed "to operate in a great measure at the close of the war" as a charter of freedom which blacks might plead in the courts to establish their right to personal liberty. [8] Pointing out that Lincoln's proclamation omitted any reference to colonization, Montgomery Throop of New York concluded that it was intended as a permanent guarantee of Negro freedom that would secure blacks the right to reside in southern states in derogation of state constitutions and laws. [9]

Though differing in their outlook toward slavery, Democrats, border state Unionists, and conservative Republicans all agreed that the rebel states should be restored to the Union with their prewar powers intact. To be sure, some wanted to revive slavery or were indifferent to the prospect. [10] Other conservative Unionists condemned slavery but, regarding it for all practical purposes as moribund, opposed setting readmission requirements beyond loyalty to the Union. Emancipation should be recognized as far as it went, but states should be restored with or without slavery as the case might be. [11] Proponents of this view defended state powers and prewar federalism not out of regard for slavery as such, but as a safeguard against the social upheaval that they feared might follow military emancipation. While it was not the only feature of the old order that conservatives wished to retain, the subordination and denial of Negro rights was certainly a prominent consideration.

Postmaster General Montgomery Blair illustrated the dilemma faced by conservatives who supported military emancipation yet feared it might lead to a radical reconstruction policy. In May 1863, Blair defended the Emancipation Proclamation as an irrevocable commitment to protect the liberty of all slaves in rebel areas and denied that the government could ever recognize emancipated persons as slaves.[12] Five months later, after reconstruction had become a subject of intense debate, Blair's concerns had an altogether different focus. In a bitterly antiradical speech, he made only a single brief reference to the emancipation order, and that to recall Lincoln's express intention of compensating loyal slaveowners. Instead, Blair dwelt on the importance of readmitting the seceded states under their prewar constitutions and laws as soon as the rebellion ended. What he feared was a policy that "would make manumission of the slaves the means of infusing their blood into our whole system by blending it with *'amalgamation, equality,* and *fraternity.'"*[13]

Blair's warning against racial mixing expressed the worst fears of the virulent racism that appeared in the miscegenation controversy of 1864,[14] but it was not typical of conservatives in general. Refusing to take the miscegenation issue seriously, most conservatives were content to argue for restoration of state governments on the prewar basis. Conservative Unionists were convinced that the ultimate abolition of slavery was essential to permanent peace, yet they believed that "everything must depend on the mode in which it is done."[15] For some conservatives this meant gradual, compensated emancipation. Others reasoned that slavery was politically dead and before long would be abandoned out of strictly economic considerations, while still others favored a more direct policy which would require persons seeking presidential amnesty to manumit their slaves. In each case, however, the states would dispose of the slavery question and the constitution would be preserved. Reconstruction plans requiring federal interference in state government and local affairs must be resisted and post-emancipation civil rights questions kept within exclusive state control.[16]

In contrast to conservative Unionists, moderate and radical Republicans believed that the Emancipation Proclamation committed the government to a reconstruction policy based on the immediate abolition of slavery. This approach was grounded in an interpretation of Lincoln's emancipation order as a legitimate exercise of the war power which of its own force had permanent consequences. Ironically, a provocative interpretation of military emancipation by the New York *Tribune* helped many Republicans reach this conclusion.

In March 1863, the *Tribune* created a stir in antislavery circles by asserting that any rebel state could preserve slavery by giving up the insurrection. Pointing out that Lincoln had defined military emancipation as a means to the end of restoring the Union, the Republican journal reasoned that even blacks actually freed by Union armies might be returned to slavery upon the restoration of a loyal state government. The constitutions and laws of the nation and states being given their "natural and necessary operation," said the *Tribune*, the Union government could not prevent a citizen of a state from holding another person as a slave. "The President has not assumed to abolish the laws of any State—much less to forbid their reenactment after the perfect restoration of the Union," declared the *Tribune*.[17]

Astonished at this proposition, which seemed designed to appeal to southern Unionism if not to encourage peace negotiations, moderate and radical Republicans and abolitionists insisted on the irrevocable character of executive-ordered liberty. To begin with, they pointed out that the proclamation represented a pledge of public faith that the government could not honorably withdraw.[18] Further, they held that the emancipation order altered the legal status of slaves by conferring the right of personal liberty. It freed slaves "absolutely" in areas to which it applied, stated the *National Anti-Slavery Standard*, and became part of "the fundamental law of the land." Slaves affected by the order became "freemen" in a full legal sense.[19] Abolitionist leader Wendell Phillips reasoned that states could not remand to slavery blacks freed by the proclamation, though, in the absence of an abolition statute, they might enslave free Negroes and white persons. The proclamation, said Phillips, was "essentially a law of the United States" which freed blacks could invoke in federal court against attempts to reenslave them.[20]

Additional arguments for the proclamation declared that it ended slavery in the rebel states and, as a "*law* of freedom," vested personal rights protected by constitutional guarantees.[21] Robert Dale Owen, a prominent antislavery spokesman, held that the emancipation order established the status of slaves as freemen regardless of whether they had physically acquired freedom. They now possessed vested rights which the government could not abrogate.[22] Viewing the proclamation in the light of Attorney General Bates's opinion on Negro citizenship, the abolitionist Edward Gilbert wrote that slaves freed by the order were U.S. citizens whose liberties the government was bound to protect against restored state powers.[23]

These views held that the Emancipation Proclamation had ended slavery in the states where it applied, and to a considerable extent they were advanced more as political-moral than as constitutional-legal arguments. As they considered the matter further in 1863, other antislavery men concluded that, despite its permanent liberating effects, the executive order did not abolish the rebel states' constitutions and laws protecting slavery. Thus, War Department Solicitor William Whiting distinguished between military emancipation operating on slaves personally as individuals, and a change in local law that would abolish the right to hold slaves.[24] In the face of conservative attacks in 1863, several Republican publicists denied that the Emancipation Proclamation was intended to repeal state laws. It was, they explained, a military order, not an arrogation of legislative power.[25] Still other antislavery men, more critical of the administration, stated that the proclamation left the system of slavery untouched.[26] Expressing apprehension lest slavery be left to the outcome of the war, the radical clergyman Joseph P. Thompson declared: "the President's theory of guaranteeing to each loyal State the integrity of its local institutions, might place him in the false position of rebuilding that which his proclamation sought to destroy."[27]

Therefore, most Republicans concluded that, while the proclamation might in some sense be a "law of freedom," by itself it was inadequate as an abolition and reconstruction instrument. Significantly, however, they did not propose to implement and buttress it by the radical expedients of state suicide and territorialization, as reconstruction bills of 1862 had provided. As the mode of reconstruction, they looked instead to action by the states themselves—constitutional conventions that would abolish slavery under executive supervision.

Although the immediate issue was to secure the personal liberty of freed slaves, a few radicals looked to the more general question of the status and rights of blacks after emancipation. The conclusion they began to foresee was that, if restored loyal governments used their powers to restrict Negroes in the prewar manner, it might be necessary to curtail state rights and to revise federal-state relations. Yet, in 1863 even the radicals were reluctant to admit this necessity.

Clergyman Leonard Bacon confessed uncertainty, for example, as to how the legal status of former slaves would be settled "without infringing the reserved rights of the States under the Constitution." Bacon assumed, however, that as loyal men would control the reconstruction process, no drastic change in federalism would be required. In regenerated Virginia, he predicted, "the reserved right of the State to determine the legal condition and relations of its inhabitants will not be employed in the insane attempt to obtain a perpetual entailment of poverty and barbarism by reenslaving an emancipated peasantry." [28] For similar reasons, Secretary of the Treasury Salmon P. Chase, advising Lincoln in November 1863, recommended that the status and rights of blacks after emancipation be left in state hands. In particular, said Chase, no federal laws should be passed by which the freedmen might be regulated, controlled, or virtually reenslaved. [29]

The issue with respect to Negro rights was whether reconstruction would be "safe" in the sense that Unionists who could be trusted with the state police power over civil rights would be controlling it. The answer to this question, however, lay in Lincoln's hands. In the places where state reorganization was underway, the policies being shaped on freedmen's affairs stirred doubts among Republicans and led to serious intraparty conflict. Seeking to sustain loyal governments as a challenge to the Confederacy, the administration proposed to let white southern Unionists resume local self-government—including the disposition of questions concerning the freedmen—in return for abolishing slavery. As an adjunct to this policy, Union officials organized and regulated the labor of emancipated slaves in ways that led many Republicans to reject as inadequate the administration's approach to post-emancipation problems.

Lincoln was reluctant to assume direct control over reconstruction but was committed to upholding the Emancipation Proclamation. Hence, throughout 1863 he urged southern Unionists to form loyal governments and abolish slavery. The focus of reconstruction attention was Louisiana, where Lincoln instructed military authorities to hold a constitutional convention to inaugurate a loyal antislavery government. When these efforts bogged down, the president decided to take reconstruction policy more directly in hand. The result was the Proclamation of Amnesty and Reconstruction of December 1863.[30]

Lincoln's proclamation resolved the debate over reorganization of loyal governments that had taken place in previous months. Its chief significance was to make emancipation the basis of reconstruction. The president offered amnesty to persons who had engaged in rebellion (excluding higher ranking Confederate officials) upon their subscription of an oath to support the Union and the Constitution and all acts of Congress and executive proclamations concerning slavery. Lincoln stipulated that such persons should be encouraged to establish state governments that would be republican in form and that would in no way contravene the oath to support all laws and proclamations on slavery. In other words, reorganized governments were required to recognize and apply the Emancipation Proclamation. Although Lincoln was careful to include points that would appeal to conservatives, his reconstruction policy signified a substantial radical victory.[31]

In a basic political sense, emancipation now ceased to be the fundamental polarizing, radical issue it had been up to this time. As this circumstance was understood, however, new questions of postwar security and guarantees—including the status and rights of the freedmen—assumed political importance. And on this count Lincoln's emerging reconstruction policy aroused strong congressional opposition because it seemed to allow, if not to encourage, apprenticeship for emancipated slaves.

Faced with serious difficulties created by the growing number of freed slaves entering Union lines, the administration had sought to regulate emancipated blacks and employ them in ways beneficial to the Union. While the recruitment of blacks for military labor and army service was the chief mode of accomplishing this dual purpose, Lincoln also proposed apprenticeship for freed slaves. After issuing the Emancipation Proclamation, he told a prominent Democratic general that the states affected by the proclamation need not suffer from it if they would but "adopt systems of apprenticeship for the colored people, conforming substantially to the most approved plans of gradual emancipation."[32] In July, he advised his military commander in Arkansas to press for gradual emancipation with a system of apprenticeship.[33]

For most Republicans, apprenticeship signified a form of servitude that would make emancipation a fraud.[34] They argued instead for free labor governed by contract. Lincoln had not publicly advocated apprenticeship, and after July 1863, he did not refer to it as such in private correspondence. On this as on other matters concerning reconstruction, his thinking remained flexible, if not ambivalent. At times, he seemed willing to allow the states such latitude as would allow them to establish apprenticeship systems; at other times, he seemed to support the contract labor alternative. For example, he wrote to General Nathaniel Banks in Louisiana in August 1863, urging the adoption of "some practical system by which the two races could gradually live themselves out of their own relation to each other, and both come out better prepared for the new." Besides specifically recommending education for black children, Lincoln said "the power, or element, of 'contract' may be sufficient for this probationary period." Its simplicity and flexibility, he added, "may be better." While one cannot be positive that Lincoln was indicating a preference for free labor contracts over apprenticeship, that seems to be a likely inference.[35]

The reconstruction proclamation of December 1863 did not resolve the ambiguity, for Lincoln announced that, as far as he was concerned, the reorganized state governments could deal with post-emancipation problems of the freedmen's status. In a brief reference to the issue, Lincoln stated that he would not object to any provisions adopted by states which recognized and declared the permanent freedom of emancipated slaves, provided for their education, and was "consistent, as a temporary arrangement, with their present condition as a laboring, landless, and homeless class."[36] Elaborating on this point in his message to Congress that accompanied the proclamation on reconstruction, he explained that acquiescence in state policies for former slaves was aimed at alleviating the confusion and destitution that would accompany the revolution in labor systems produced by emancipation. He expressed the hope that white southerners would give up slavery more readily if they could be sure of controlling the "vital matter" of post-emancipation adjustment. The only cautionary note he sounded was a reminder that, in offering to accept state policies for freedmen the president gave up no power to prevent abuses to the ex-slaves.[37]

Whether all of these comments amounted to an endorsement of apprenticeship it is perhaps impossible to say. In private correspondence at the time, Lincoln did not use that term, but rather, in advising Louisiana Unionists, he referred, as he had publicly, to "some temporary provision for the whole of the freed people."[38] Nevertheless, from an antislavery point of view, his reference to "temporary provisions" was ominous, for it suggested something like apprenticeship, if not the institution itself in a formal sense.[39] Nor did Lincoln altogether eliminate the ambiguity. In 1864, he let it be known to interested foreign observers who were seeking to mediate with the Confederacy that, while his plans for reconstruction started with emancipation, states returning to the Union would be permitted to pass laws not inconsistent with the freedom of former slaves in order to relieve the difficulties and strains of immediate emancipation. Like the reference to "temporary provisions," this statement too was perhaps an endorsement of apprenticeship.[40] In reviewing the reconstruction question a year later, Lincoln himself described his position in the amnesty proclamation as recommending apprenticeship for freed slaves, a judgment that was widely shared in subsequent years by Republican contemporaries.[41] Therefore, much as they approved the main outline of Lincoln's reconstruction policy, many antislavery reformers and Republicans began to think that something more was needed to complete the work of emancipation.

Although Lincoln's deference to the states on the question of freedmen's policy could perhaps be seen as resting on the assumption that radical Unionists would control local affairs, events did not bear out this hypothesis. On the contrary, in 1864 the administration began to favor a more conservative approach to post-emancipation problems, as the course of Louisiana's reconstruction politics showed.

Prior to December 1863, Lincoln had supported a coalition of moderate and radical Louisiana Unionists in giving orders for a constitutional convention as the first step in forming a loyal government. After the reconstruction proclamation, Lincoln placed the moderate faction in control of Louisiana affairs by giving General Banks, a moderate allied with local moderate Unionists, a free hand in forming a new state government before holding a constitutional convention. Thus, in January 1864 Banks revived the 1852 Louisiana constitution, without its slavery provisions, and ordered an election for state officers.[42]

After setting up a loyal government, Banks held a constitutional convention. The new Louisiana constitution abolished slavery, opened the courts to all persons, and established free public education for children of both races. Suffrage was restricted to white persons, however, and only under pressure from General Banks and Governor Michael Hahn, reflecting Lincoln's point of view, did the convention give the legislature the power in the future to extend the suffrage to other persons who by military service, taxation, or intelligence might be judged qualified to vote.[43]

Meanwhile, administration policies for dealing with blacks entering Union lines gave a practical meaning to "temporary . . . arrangement for the freed people"—the phrase used in Lincoln's reconstruction message—that further heightened antislavery apprehensions. By the middle of 1862, former slaves needing protection and support created a serious problem for the army. As a general solution to this problem, Lincoln and Secretary of War Edwin M. Stanton favored enlistment of ex-slaves in the army; organization of refugee camps for women, children, old persons, and others unsuited for military service; and establishment of labor systems whereby freedmen would work under contract on abandoned plantations. Adumbrated in separate actions on a small scale in 1862, this policy was implemented more systematically and extensively in 1863 as a corollary of military emancipation. Its main immediate purpose was to relieve the burden placed on the army by the upheaval of emancipation, but it was also seen as a way of easing the transition from slavery to freedom and demonstrating the feasibility and practicability of free black labor. In addition to saving a year's crops, it would show that post-emancipation race relations could in fact be dealt with in an intelligent and competent way. Moreover, by containing the freed slave population in the South, it might have the political advantage of allaying northern fears of an influx of blacks. Thus, it would gain further support for emancipation.[44]

Government labor systems instituted in Louisiana and the Mississippi Valley became the best known and most important of the temporary freedmen's arrangements set up in half a dozen military departments in the occupied South. Initiating the Louisiana system in February 1863, General Banks directed that Negroes be induced, as far as practicable without violence, to return to the plantations where they had previously been slaves. They were to sign one-year labor contracts with planters who would agree to pay wages of $10 per month and provide food, clothing, and medical care. Although freedmen were free to choose among employers, once they did they were bound to a year's labor and were prohibited from leaving the plantation without the employer's permission. Occasionally, after consultation with planters, administrative revisions were made which led to stricter regulation of laborers and the use of army patrols to enforce contracts. For the Mississippi Valley as a whole, General Lorenzo Thomas established essentially the same kind of system.[45]

In the opinion of many antislavery men, the Banks-Thomas labor policy was an exploitive system of apprenticeship operated chiefly in the interest of dishonest, profit-seeking adventurers. Representatives of private freedmen's aid organizations condemned the arrangements as a form of servitude, and even an army officer charged with investigating the system in the Mississippi Valley said it tended toward de facto serfdom. Under these circumstances, abolitionists and radical Republicans argued that the Treasury Department should take control of freedmen's affairs away from the army. Headed by the radical Salmon P. Chase, the Treasury Department was already involved with freedmen's policy through its administration of the Direct Tax Act of 1862 and the Captured and Abandoned Property Act of 1863. Arguing that ex-slaves should logically be dealt with in relation to the land over which the Treasury Department had jurisdiction, radicals pinned their hopes for an enlightened post-emancipation policy on Chase's department.[46]

In late 1863, Chase tried to inaugurate a new freedmen's policy in the Mississippi Valley and enlarge Treasury Department jurisdiction over freedmen's affairs. Criticizing the assignment of freedmen to particular plantations, he proposed a higher wage scale for blacks and a policy of leasing land to freedmen either in groups or as individuals. He also hoped to be able to induce landlords to sell land in small parcels to former slaves. Motivated by a desire to improve conditions for blacks and perhaps also to create an issue on which he might challenge Lincoln for the Republican nomination in 1864, Chase promised the freedmen paternal guidance, humanitarian care, and a limited program of land reform.[47]

Chase attempted to effect these important changes by administrative actions under existing legislation, but Lincoln refused to go along with them. Probably because he regarded the immediate question of post-emancipation policy as inextricably linked to military matters, he ordered General Lorenzo Thomas in February 1864, after a series of conflicts between Treasury agents and military officers had occurred, to take control of "the contraband and leasing business." Lincoln thought the proposed Treasury system was well intentioned, but he believed it would not work because of its "entangling details."[48] Thereafter, Thomas tightened the existing labor regulations in the Mississippi Valley and extended them to plantations which Treasury officials had tried to operate. This development did not end the political and administrative conflict between the Treasury Department and the army over freedmen's policy, but it transferred the struggle to Congress where freedmen's bureau bills were being formulated. For the time being, however, Lincoln had decided the issue in favor of military control.[49]

Through 1863, the question of the former slaves' status and rights was necessarily subordinate to that of whether reconstruction should proceed with or without emancipation. The Negro question was occasionally raised as a specific legal and constitutional problem, but it was seen as bound up with and still subordinate to the politically and militarily more urgent problem of forming loyal governments in the rebel states.[50] Events in Louisiana in early 1864, however, suggested that presidential reconstruction would give control of local affairs to moderate and conservative Unionists who would not go beyond securing personal liberty for freedmen and who might subject blacks to apprenticeship systems. Furthermore, if the freedmen's labor policy established in the Mississippi Valley were any indication of the kind of "temporary arrangement" which Lincoln said he would accept in reorganized loyal states, radicals and abolitionists had all the more reason to oppose administration policy in 1864.

The status and rights of emancipated slaves thus began to emerge as a political issue in the winter of 1863-1864. The conflict that ensued on this issue reflected genuine differences in outlook toward blacks on the part of abolitionists and radical Republicans on the one hand, and the Lincoln administration and its moderate and conservative Republican supporters on the other. More important perhaps were the political gains at stake in the general question of reconstruction. The election of 1864 loomed on the horizon, leading antislavery critics of Lincoln's leadership to seek issues on which to contest his control of the party. State reorganization, slavery abolition, and protection of the freedmen all lent themselves to this purpose. In a more general sense, the problem facing Republican lawmakers and politicians was to gauge popular attitudes toward a postwar settlement. After December 1863, the civil and political rights of the freedmen formed a critical part of this larger concern.

NOTES

1. Roy P. Basler, et al., eds., *The Collected Works of Abraham Lincoln* (9 vols.; New Brunswick, 1953-1955), V, 433-436.

2. V. Jacque Voegeli, *Free But Not Equal: The Midwest and the Negro During the Civil War* (Chicago, 1967), 40-48.

3. Mark Krug, "The Republican Party and the Emancipation Proclamation," *Journal of Negro History* 48 (April 1963): 98-114.

4. Gilbert Dean, *Speech on the Governor's Annual Message, February 12, 1863* (Albany, 1863), 8-9; Thomas H. Baird, *Memorial Praying for the Enactment of Measures to Preserve the Constitution and the Union* (Pittsburgh, 1864), 4-7.

5. Aaron A. Ferris, "The Validity of the Emancipation Edict," *North American Review* 131 (December 1880): 559-560; Robert F. Durden, *The Gray and the Black: The Confederate Debate over Emancipation* (Baton Rouge, 1972), 24-25.

6. Joel Parker, *Letters to Rev. Henry M. Dexter and to Rev. Leonard Bacon* (Cambridge, Mass., 1863), 46-47; Joel Parker, *The War Powers of Congress and of the President* (Cambridge, Mass., 1863), 34; Montgomery H. Throop, *The Future: A Political Essay* (New York, 1864), 90-95; Anon., "Prerogative Rights and Public Law," *Monthly Law Reporter* 25 (January 1863): 143; Henry Weaton, *Elements of International Law*, ed. Richard Henry Dana, Jr., 8th ed. (Boston, 1866), 441; Richard H. Dana, Jr., "Nullity of the Emancipation Edict," *North American Review* 131 (July 1880): 128-134.

7. Benjamin R. Curtis, *Executive Power* (Boston, 1862), 14-15.

8. Parker, *Letters to Dexter and Bacon*, 48-55.

9. Throop, *The Future*, 97-99, 138-139.

10. Truman Smith, *Considerations on the Slavery Question, Addressed to the President of the United States* (New York, 1863), 7.

11. New York *Herald*, November 13, 1863; Henry J. Raymond, *The Administration and the War. Speech at Wilmington, Delaware*, November 6, 1863 (n.p., 1863), 13.

12. William E. Smith, *The Francis Preston Blair Family in Politics* (2 vols.; New York, 1933), II, 237; *National Anti-Slavery Standard*, May 30, 1863.

13. Montgomery Blair, *Speech on the Revolutionary Schemes of the Ultra-Abolitionists, and in Defense of the Policy of the President, at Rockville, Maryland, October 3, 1863* (New York, 1863), 3, 6-11, 20.

14. See Forrest G. Wood, *Black Scare: The Racist Response to Emancipation and Reconstruction* (Berkeley and Los Angeles, 1968), 53-79.

15. Albert Barnes, *The Conditions of Peace. A Thanksgiving Discourse . . . November 27, 1862* (Philadelphia, 1863), 52.

16. Isaac F. Redfield, "On American Secession and State Rights," *Monthly Law Reporter* 26 (December 1863): 84; Raymond, *The Administration and the War*, 14; Barnes, *The Conditions of Peace*, 59-60; J. J. Combs, *Speech at the Union League of*

Washington, September 1, 1863 (Washington, D.C., 1863), 12-14; Charles P. Kirkland, *The Destiny of Our Country* (New York, 1864), 49-59.

17. New York *Tribune*, March 14, 16, 1863.

18. *National Anti-Slavery Standard*, March 28, 1863, letter of Theodore Tilton to the editor of the New York *Tribune*; Joel P. Bishop, *Secession and Slavery: Or the Effect of Secession on the Relation of the United States to the Seceded States and to Slavery* (Boston, 1864), 88.

19. *National Anti-Slavery Standard*, March 28, April 4, 1863.

20. *Independent*, March 26, 1863.

21. Charles D. Drake, *Union and Anti-Slavery Speeches* (Cincinnati, 1864), 339; Andrew Jackson Hamilton, *Letter to the President of the United States* (New York, 1863), 11.

22. Robert Dale Owen, *The Wrong of Slavery, the Right of Emancipation, and the Future of the African Race in America* (Philadelphia, 1864), 177-180.

23. *National Anti-Slavery Standard*, March 28, 1863, letter of Edward Gilbert to the editor of the New York *Tribune*.

24. William Whiting, *War Powers Under the Constitution of the United States*, 43d ed. (Boston, 1871), iii.

25. Grosvenor P. Lowrey, *The Commander-in-Chief: A Defence Upon Legal Grounds of the Proclamation of Emancipation* (New York, 1863), 21-22; Daniel Agnew, *Our National Constitution: Its Adaptation to a State of War or Insurrection*, 2d ed. (Philadelphia, 1863), 29-34; Alexander C. Twining, "President Lincoln's Proclamation of Freedom to the Slaves," *New Englander* 24 (January 1865): 184.

26. Drake, *Union and Anti-Slavery Speeches*, 407-408.

27. Joseph P. Thompson, *Christianity and Emancipation; or, The Teachings and the Influence of the Bible Against Slavery* (New York, 1863), 67, 85-86.

28. Leonard Bacon, "Reply to Professor Parker," *New Englander* 22 (April 1863): 253-254.

29. S. P. Chase to Lincoln, November 25, 1863, No. 28217, Robert Todd Lincoln Collection of the Papers of Abraham Lincoln, Library of Congress.

30. Basler, et al., eds., *Collected Works of Lincoln*, VII, 1; Herman Belz, *Reconstructing the Union: Theory and Policy During the Civil War* (Ithaca, 1969), 154-167.

31. Basler, et al., eds., *Collected Works of Lincoln*, VI, 51-56; Belz, *Reconstructing the Union*, 160-167.

32. Lincoln to John A. McClernand, January 8, 1863, Basler, et al., eds., *Collected Works of Lincoln*, VI, 48-49.

33. Lincoln to General Stephen A. Hurlbut, July 31, 1863, ibid., 358; Tyler Dennett, ed., *Lincoln and the Civil War in the Diaries and Letters of John Hay* (New York, 1939), 73.

34. Apprenticeship was a form of indentured service by which minors, through the instrument of contract, were legally bound to employers or masters for a period of years in order to learn a trade. It was still in existence at this time for both white and black minors. In Maryland, for example, apprenticeship of black minors was common before the war and was resorted to after emancipation in 1864 in an attempt to retain something of slavery. About three thousand black children were apprenticed in Maryland until federal courts stopped the practice in 1867. Apprenticeship could also be

adapted to freed slaves generally. Thus, in New Jersey, which had passed a gradual abolition act in 1804, an immediate emancipation measure in 1846 placed freed slaves in the condition of apprentices with limited personal rights. Robert Dale Owen, "The Claims to Service or Labor," *The Atlantic Monthly* 12 (July 1863): 117; Richard O. Curry, ed., *Radicalism, Racism, and Party Realignment: The Border States During Reconstruction* (Baltimore and London, 1969), 154-156; Arthur Zilversmit, *The First Emancipation: The Abolition of Slavery in the North* (Chicago, 1967), 220.

35. Lincoln to Nathaniel Banks, August 5, 1863, Basler, et al., eds., *Collected Works of Lincoln*, VI, 365. In a subsequent letter to General Hurlbut in Arkansas which was not sent, Lincoln seemed to lean toward free labor rather than apprenticeship in giving instructions to let freed slaves work on abandoned plantations, drawing their own subsistence from the soil, or arrange for loyal men to hire them temporarily on wages. He added that if any blacks made their own arrangements to work, of course they should not be hindered. Ibid., 387.

36. Ibid., VII, 55.

37. Ibid., 51.

38. Lincoln to Thomas Cottman, December 15, 1863, ibid., 66.

39. *Congressional Globe*, 38th Cong., 1st sess., 1206 (March 19, 1864), remarks of A. C. Wilder; Boston *Commonwealth*, December 25, 1863.

40. Glyndon G. Van Deusen, *William Henry Seward* (New York, 1967), 381-382.

41. Basler, et al., eds., *Collected Works of Lincoln*, VIII, 402; John D. Long, *The Republican Party: Its History, Principles, and Policies* (New York, 1888), 92.

42. Fred H. Harrington, *Fighting General: Major-General N. P. Banks* (Philadelphia, 1948), 143-144; Gerald M. Capers, *Occupied City: New Orleans Under the Federals, 1862-1865* (Lexington, 1965), 132-135; Belz, *Reconstructing the Union*, 190-193.

43. Capers, *Occupied City*, 139; Roger W. Shugg, *Origins of the Class Struggle in Louisiana* (Baton Rouge, 1939), 203-207; Francis Newton Thorpe, ed., *The Federal and State Constitutions, Colonial Charters and Other Organic Laws* (7 vols.; Washington, D.C., 1909), III, 1442, 1446.

44. Voegeli, *Free But Not Equal*, 95-112.

45. Gen. Banks Circular, *The War of the Rebellion: A Compilation of the Official Records of the Union and Confederate Armies* (130 vols.; Washington, D.C., 1880-1901), Ser. II, Vol. V, 279; Gen. Thomas Orders No. 9, March 11, 1864, *O.R.*, Ser. III, Vol. IV, 166-169; Capers, *Occupied City*, 224-226; J. Thomas May, "Continuity and Change in the Labor Program of the Union Army and the Freedmen's Bureau," *Civil War History* 17 (September 1971): 247-251.

46. Louis S. Gerteis, "Salmon P. Chase, Radicalism, and the Politics of Emancipation, 1861-1864," *Journal of American History* 60 (June 1973): 55-56.

47. Ibid., 57-59.

48. Lincoln to Gen. Lorenzo Thomas, February 28, 1864; Basler, et al., eds., *Collected Works of Lincoln*, VII, 212.

49. *O.R.*, Ser. III, Vol. IV, 166-170; Gerteis, "Salmon P. Chase," 60.

50. Adolph E. Kroeger, *The Future of the Country* (n.p., 1864), 21.

4

Congressional reconstruction and freedmen's rights

Lincoln's amnesty proclamation satisfied the radical demand that reconstruction be based on the Emancipation Proclamation, and it was widely endorsed by conservative Unionists as well.[1] Soon, however, new sources of division became apparent. While insisting on emancipation, Lincoln seemed ready to give control of freedmen's affairs to the states. Moreover, within the occupied South he supported Unionists who took a severely minimal view of Negro rights as consisting almost exclusively in personal liberty, and that perhaps hedged about by restrictive regulations, if not outright apprenticeship systems. In contrast, a growing number of antislavery reformers and Republicans held that to be successful reconstruction required national recognition and guarantee of the liberty and rights of emancipated slaves. The evolution of a congressional plan of reconstruction in 1864 was, among other things, a reflection of this outlook.

The conservative Republican Montgomery Blair later described the congressional reconstruction plan of 1864 as a turning point which foreshadowed the centralization of Republican policy that occurred after Lincoln's death.[2] There was truth in the observation, for the Wade-Davis bill, as the congressional plan was known, aimed at restricting state power over personal liberty and civil rights in an unprecedented way—and for the unprecedented purpose of protecting freed blacks in the South. Intended as a means of organizing loyal state governments, the plan reflected the Republicans' concern for congres-

sional authority over reconstruction, for the future security of the
Union, and for the development of the Republican party in the South.
But it also contained guarantees of personal liberty and civil rights for
former slaves which showed the increased importance of the freed-
men's question in reconstruction politics and in the ideology of the
Republican party.

The evolution of administration policy in Louisiana and the Mississippi Valley produced objections to executive reconstruction that
eventually formed the basis for an alternative congressional plan. For
all the emancipationist satisfaction it gave, Lincoln's reconstruction
message was suspect in some radical quarters because it held out the
possibility of judicial modification of the Emancipation Proclamation.[3] Furthermore, by offering amnesty without a time limit and
promising to restore real property, the presidential plan threatened to
restore to power the very elements that had provoked secession. Except for chattel slavery, declared the *National Anti-Slavery Standard*,
the administration seemed bent on leaving southern society as much
as possible what it was before the war.[4]

Failure to guarantee the freedmen's rights was an important issue
in the adverse judgments of executive reconstruction that appeared in
1864. Many abolitionists were quick to fault the administration for
proposing to let presidentially restored states regulate freedmen's
affairs. In the view of the *National anti-Slavery Standard*, that would
be "too much like giving the lambs to the nurture and admonition of
wolves." According to the abolitionist Wendell Phillips Garrison, the
administration policy would free the slave but abandon him in an
anomalous position between bondage and citizenship. Reaching the
same conclusion, the antislavery leader Wendell Phillips said the
president's proclamation "frees the slave, but ignores the negro."[5]

As the Lincoln-Banks policy unfolded in Louisiana, antislavery
critics charged that it amounted to a system of apprenticeship or serfdom. Phillips conceded that the president was committed to the liberty of the Negro but thought Lincoln's concern "to let the white race
of the South *down easily*" meant a mere technical liberty for the freedmen that was no better than apprenticeship. Banks's "whole system
of orders," he asserted, had "not one element of the recognition of the
manhood of the black in it—not one element of contract." Expected
to serve, subject to the provost marshal if insubordinate, his wages
fixed, "The negro is a serf," Phillips concluded.[6]

The Boston *Commonwealth* reiterated the charge, stating that maintenance of existing slavery was as nothing compared to the formation of a state government based on an exploitive system such as Banks's in Louisiana. According to the abolitionist Charles K. Whipple, Banks's actions showed that he wished to avoid all recognition of the freed slave as a man, a citizen, a landholder, or a voter. In May 1864, the Worcester *Spy* summarized a large segment of anti-slavery opinion in declaring: "There has been something worse than failure in the treatment of questions growing out of the slave question." Banks's policy seemed to preserve the spirit of the old labor system without the name.[7]

Like more moderate Republicans, radical critics assumed that restored states would eventually resume their customary role in regulating personal civil rights and liberties. While wartime circumstances permitted, therefore, it seemed necessary to establish national guarantees of freedmen's rights. Criticizing the Lincoln administration's willingness to defer to state rights, the Boston *Commonwealth* impatiently asked: "Are you going to slink any more behind the sham, the miserable evasion, that the protection of personal rights and liberty for every citizen of the United States within the limits of any state belongs entirely to the state and in no case to the United States?" As a long-range solution, the *Independent* urged Congress not only to abolish slavery on the ground that it denied the equality of all men, but also to prohibit distinctions in state law that were not based on moral considerations applicable to every class and group. Pointing out that once rebel states were readmitted the federal government could not interfere in local legislation, Wendell Phillips advocated a constitutional amendment that would prohibit states from making any distinction among their citizens on account of race or color.[8]

Critics of executive reconstruction also began to demand Negro suffrage as a safeguard of freedmen's rights. The Louisiana policy, complained the *National Anti-Slavery Standard*, "lifts the ballot out of the reach of every freedman at the South." The Boston *Commonwealth* insisted that disfranchisement of colored native citizens in Louisiana was indefensible, while Wendell Phillips warned that unless blacks were included as voters it would be necessary to hold the rebel states as territories for years until northern immigrants formed a loyal majority. Nonetheless, the suffrage question was only beginning to be raised. Most critics of the administration were content to insist, with the *National Anti-Slavery Standard*, that the basic principle in post-emancipation policy should be absolute liberty to the freedmen to go where they pleased, choose their employers, and protect themselves by contract under national guarantees against local legislation.[9]

Corroborating the radical estimate of the situation was the approving judgment of conservative Unionists that, although Lincoln supported emancipation, he would block demands to revolutionize southern society and institutions. Noting that the crucial issue would be the content of the state constitutions in the South, the conservative jurist Montgomery Throop pointedly observed that emancipation would be no obstacle to reunion if other conditions were favorable. [10]

That these "other conditions" included freedmen's policy was evident in Montgomery Blair's assessment of presidential reconstruction. Speaking before the Maryland legislature in January 1864, Blair underscored the administration's intention to remit freed blacks to the states. Lincoln's reconstruction announcement, he said, signified a "willingness to refer the changes in state constitutions relating to slavery . . . to the people and States most affected." Blair also predicted that the government would recognize the seceded states' constitutions as existing and obligatory in everything but slavery. [11] Conservatives were thus pleased with administration tendencies on the Negro question but were disturbed at the growing radical criticism. "I hate terribly to seem to share the apprehension of the Copperheads about radical theories & practices" concerning "negro suffrage and negro rights," wrote Henry J. Raymond to conservative Senator James Doolittle of Wisconsin in April 1864, "but I really believe our chief danger *just now* lies in that direction.[12]

Because of political and military exigencies and, to a limited extent, because of ideological reasons, Republican lawmakers in 1864 began to recognize the need for post-emancipation guarantees of freedmen's rights. The appearance of constitutional theories and proposals for protecting civil rights both reflected and helped shape this emerging outlook.

Although emancipation provided the stimulus and the occasion, constitutional theorizing about civil rights involved more than simply the situation of the freed slaves. Just as before the war slavery had been regarded as a threat to civil and political liberty in general,[13] so its abolition was undertaken with the idea of enlarging the freedom of all Americans, not just the emancipated slaves. This helps explain the apparent contradiction, so often noted, between northern prejudice against blacks and the desire to abolish slavery. The movement to abolish slavery, especially as it found expression in wartime policies, hardly placed the welfare of Negro slaves uppermost. Nevertheless, legal instruments for safeguarding civil rights, whether conceived specifically with reference to or motivated by concern for emancipated slaves, were to have great importance for the freedmen.

Illustrating the "declaratory" tendency in constitutional thought— that is, the disposition to propose what are in fact radical changes while holding that the existing constitution already authorizes them—jurists Edward F. Bullard and Marvin Warren contended that the Constitution prohibited slavery and protected personal civil rights and liberties. Because of slavery, Bullard argued, fundamental rights—the privilege of the writ of *habeas corpus*, freedom from unreasonable search and seizure, the deprivation of life, liberty, or property without due process of law, freedom of speech as an attribute of general citizenship under the comity clause—all had been denied. As the blacks had suffered most egregiously, Bullard held that after emancipation they must be protected by a federal law allowing them the benefit of the writ of *habeas corpus* "and all other measures to insure [their] future freedom." Bullard was concerned with more than the liberty of former slaves, however; thus, he advocated federal legislation making the writ of *habeas corpus* available to all persons "without regard to color." Reasoning that Congress could apply Fifth Amendment guarantees against the states by the same sovereign power with which it collected duties in southern ports, Bullard concluded that basic civil rights would be enforceable in national courts and thus protected against contradictory state laws.[14]

The Ohio legal writer Marvin Warren held that the guarantees of the bill of rights absolutely protected the rights of American citizens— at all times, in all places—against violations by state or federal authorities or at the hands of private individuals or mobs. No constitutional amendment was necessary for Congress to enact penal laws against deprivation of civil rights, regardless of its source. In Warren's view, however, this fact did not mean that the national government would supersede the states in regulating and protecting civil rights and liberties. Yet, when rights were violated or states were unwilling or unable to protect their citizens, Warren contended, the federal government had a duty to stand between a state and its citizens. More than Bullard, Warren was concerned with civil rights protection beyond the problems created by emancipation. Aware that his nationalist doctrine would be of great benefit if applied to blacks, he carefully confined citizenship to white persons and denied any intent to determine the question of Negro citizenship.[15]

Other Republican legalists turned to the contract clause of the Constitution for national protection of civil rights against state violation. Timothy Farrar, pointing out that land grants and other forms of property holding had received immunity from state interference through the contract clause, advised that civil rights could be given a similar guarantee. As state constitutions were solemn agreements by the people among themselves and with their government, Farrar reasoned, they were contracts within the meaning of the federal Constitution. Arguing that no class of rights needed protection more urgently, he saw particular advantage in the fact that, under the contract clause, disputes over civil rights could be settled in national rather than state courts.[16] Joel P. Bishop, a prominent legal writer, showed how to adapt the contract clause more directly and specifically to post-emancipation problems. In an analysis of reconstruction, Bishop proposed that the national government require the constitutions of reorganized states to contain a contract with the United States not to infringe on the rights of freedmen or persons serving the Union.[17]

The guarantee of a republican form of government to each state in the Union provided another theoretical basis for federal civil rights protection.[18] The Founding Fathers had conceived of the guarantee clause as a way of maintaining existing state governments against domestic upheaval; during the Civil War, the clause became an instrument by which Republicans tried to change state constitutions and laws.[19] Thus, Ohio Republican John Hutchins argued in December 1862 that Congress could secure the liberty of emancipated slaves by giving each state a republican form of government under which no person could be deprived of liberty or property without due process of law. In the same session of Congress, Senator Ira Harris of New York introduced legislation to give the seceded states provisional republican governments prohibiting slavery and guaranteeing freedmen's rights. Henry Winter Davis of Maryland developed the idea further, positing the guarantee clause as solid constitutional foundation for organizing loyal governments and protecting the freedmen's liberty.

Like other law-minded Unionists, Davis placed great importance on national legislation that would give freed blacks "the courts of the United States to protect them against the local tyranny." [20]

Against the background of these theoretical explorations of civil rights protection, Congress turned in December 1863 to the problem of implementing the president's reconstruction ideas. Several Republicans introduced legislation which would either enact the Emancipation Proclamation as a law of the United States or abolish slavery outright in all the states or alone in the seceded states. [21] Some of the bills in question, like the emancipation legislation of 1862, merely declared slavery abolished and showed no concern with implementation. Other bills, however, reflected awareness of the need to protect post-emancipation liberties. For example, Illinois radical Owen Lovejoy proposed that all freed persons should be protected "as all other free citizens" against unreasonable searches and seizures and should be permitted to sue and be sued and to testify in U.S. courts in the same manner as white persons. Further, Lovejoy made kidnapping of freed slaves a federal crime cognizable in national courts. Observing that "the rights of the blacks, now more and more seem to be inextricable from those of the whites," the *National Anti-Slavery Standard* praised Lovejoy for providing all that antislavery men desired as protection for the freedmen. [22]

While these measures remained in committee, more far-reaching proposals were introduced that made the protection of freedmen an explicit part of reconstruction policy. The first to do so was presented in December 1863 by radical Republican James M. Ashley of Ohio. Ashley's bill accepted the 10-percent population basis of the executive plan and authorized the president to appoint provisional military governors, charging them with administering civil affairs in accordance with preexisting state laws, the laws of slavery excepted. Beyond the abolition of slavery, Ashley sought to abolish state black codes and safeguard freedmen's rights. Thus, his bill prohibited enforcement of state laws excluding Negro testimony, denying blacks the right to a jury trial, punishing persons for teaching blacks to read or write, and interfering with U.S. mails or abridging freedom of speech or of the press. It also authorized federal courts to issue writs of *habeas corpus* releasing freedmen illegally deprived of their liberty, and it made kidnapping and peonage or debt slavery federal crimes. Meanwhile, conventions elected on the basis of 10 percent of the 1860 voting population were to form new state constitutions prohibiting slavery and guaranteeing the liberty of the emancipated blacks. Finally, Ashley omitted any racial qualification for voting in the convention election—a Negro suffrage provision that curiously attracted no notice at the time, probably because it seemed so premature and politically unrealistic. [23]

When introduced in December, Ashley's reconstruction bill seemed essentially an extension or confirmation of the executive plan. By February 1864, however, when it was revised and reported out of committee by Chairman Henry Winter Davis in the form of a new bill, it had taken on a distinctly anti-administration character.

The most important circumstance producing this new situation was the course of events in Louisiana. The Lincoln-Banks reconstruction policy, as we have seen, aroused opposition among abolitionists for what was regarded as inadequate recognition of freedmen's rights. In February 1864, radical Republicans in Congress attacked the administration on this score. Representative A. C. Wilder of Kansas expressed apprehension that the president's approval of temporary arrangements for ex-slaves suggested a system of apprenticeship, while James M. Ashley said the fact that former slaveowners had made no complaint about the Banks regime was itself sufficient condemnation of the government's policy. Radical Senator B. Gratz Brown of Missouri warned against binding the freed people under provost marshalships, as in Louisiana, that he said amounted to "slavery under new conditions and names." What was needed, declared Brown, was "true, substantial liberty" and "a democratic equality before the law . . . for all men." [24]

The freedmen's question was by no means the only issue in the emerging congressional opposition to executive reconstruction. Efforts to create a movement by which Secretary of the Treasury Salmon P. Chase might replace Lincoln as the Union party nominee had been underway for several weeks and came to a head at this time. Chase and his supporters sought to change government policy toward emancipated slaves, but they were also concerned to use the freedmen's rights issue for political purposes. [25] Criticism of excessive military influence in civil affairs also lay behind opposition to presidential reconstruction. Even the "most trembling conservative in Congress," reported one Washington correspondent, "is compelled to admit that *some* legislation is necessary to revive the old State organizations." [26]

Too, a feeling existed that restoration in Louisiana was proceeding too fast for the country's and for the party's own good. Policies of reconstruction were blended inseparably with those of warfare, admonished B. Gratz Brown, and carelessness in the former—as in inviting southerners prematurely to resume "franchises and ownerships and social control"—would lead to failure in the latter.[27] Hence, pressure appeared on several points for a change in the government's reconstruction policy.

The measure which Henry Winter Davis reported in February 1864 from the Select Committee on the Rebellious States proposed to create provisional civil governments in the seceded states until new state governments could be organized. It directed a provisional governor appointed by the president to administer civil affairs in accordance with existing state laws, except those recognizing slavery. After all white male citizens were enrolled and 10 percent of the enrolled had taken an oath to support the federal Constitution, the governor was to hold an election for delegates to a constitutional convention.[28] Only citizens able to swear an oath of past loyalty could vote for or be delegates to the constitutional convention, and rebel civil and military officers and those bearing arms voluntarily against the Union were excluded.[29]

Besides proscribing former rebels and repudiating the Confederate debt, the most important provisions of the Davis bill sought to secure the Emancipation Proclamation and guarantee freedmen's liberty and rights. First of all, state constitutional conventions were required to prohibit slavery and to guarantee the freedom of all persons. By its own force, the bill also proposed to emancipate all slaves by prohibiting the recognition or enforcement of the laws of slavery. Furthermore, it provided that freedmen deprived of their liberty under a claim to labor should be discharged by U.S. courts on a writ of *habeas corpus*, and it made kidnapping of former slaves a federal crime punishable by a fine of at least $1,500 and five to twenty years imprisonment. Finally, the bill required that state laws for the trial and punishment of white persons should extend to all persons.[30]

These substantive provisions were intended to eliminate discriminatory black codes and to establish intrastate equality before the law for emancipated slaves.[31] If state powers were restored in their "original plenitude," Henry Winter Davis speculated, how would freed blacks secure their rights? "What provision is there to protect them?

Where is the writ of *habeas corpus*? How are the courts of the United States to be open to them? Who shall close the courts of the States against the master?" All of these rights the reconstruction bill would secure. Its purpose, Davis said, was to preclude or predetermine the judicial question of the validity of the Emancipation Proclamation by making new state constitutions the rule of decision in cases involving freed blacks, instead of existing judicial rules which might otherwise prevail in state courts. When recognized by Congress, he declared, state constitutions were irrefutable authority in any state or federal court. [32]

Missouri Senator B. Gratz Brown further illuminated the approach to civil rights which characterized the reconstruction bill. Proposing to amend a related measure with civil rights provisions similar to those of the reconstruction committee's plan, Brown argued for "the double affirmance of the new attitude of freedom by local and Federal authority." [33] Codes to secure the liberties of all persons under the law must be ratified and brought up from below, as well as enacted from above. Like Davis, Brown wished to bypass or guard against state judicial interpretation of Negro freedom on the basis of the Emancipation Proclamation. He therefore held that, in reorganizing the seceded states, the first step must be to form new constitutions, "the only sufficient assurance that the law of the locality is in accord with the law of the nation." Summarizing the emerging consensus among Republican lawmakers, Brown said reconstruction must proceed "under the guardianship of congenial national authority through authentic law and its safeguards, and not pell-mell under the auspices of amnesty proclamations." [34]

Concern for the civil rights of white citizens as well as freed slaves was also evident in Republican support of the reconstruction bill. Thus, Representative Ignatius Donnelly of Minnesota, in addition to demanding security for emancipated blacks, urged going beyond the restoration of state authority that Lincoln's policy seemed to promise. To regenerate the South Donnelly would establish a free press, guarantee freedom of speech, and build systems of education for both black and white. Several other Republicans believed that in guaranteeing republican government to the rebel states Congress must improve and expand the sphere of liberty generally in the seceded area. [35]

On May 4, 1864, the House passed the reconstruction bill by a 73 to

59 vote. Dissatisfaction with presidential policy in Louisiana and a desire to slow down the course of state reorganization and to systematize it under national law led all but a few conservative Republicans to vote for the congressional plan. [36] In the Senate, however, where it was placed in the charge of the radical Ben Wade, the bill lay in committee for two months while developments that had a direct bearing on reconstruction occupied congressional attention.

The first development was the attempt, begun in December 1863, to prohibit slavery by constitutional amendment. Although Republican leaders doubted that such a measure could be passed, the proposed Thirteenth Amendment was approved by the Senate in April. In mid-June, it came before the House but failed to receive the necessary two-thirds approval. This meant that the reconstruction bill was the only practical antislavery step that Congress could take before the end of the session. The second event that affected strategy toward the Wade-Davis plan was the nomination of Lincoln and Andrew Johnson of Tennessee as Union party candidates at the Baltimore convention in June 1864. On the reconstruction question that was expected to be an issue in the presidential election, this action identified the party with the Lincoln-Banks policy in Louisiana. The Wade-Davis bill, however, might provide a way of distinguishing the party from the administration on this issue. [37]

In July, Wade brought the reconstruction bill before the Senate. With the session almost over, sentiment to postpone the matter was strong, and a half dozen Republicans, including both radicals and nonradicals, joined the Democrats in voting 17 to 16 for a substitute amendment that put reorganization aside and simply excluded electoral votes from seceded states. In arguing for this course, B. Gratz Brown, sponsor of the substitute, said conditions in the South were too unsettled to warrant definitive reconstruction legislation. The House refused to concur in the substitute, however, and the next day the Senate receded from its amendment, thereby enabling the Wade-Davis bill to pass. [38]

In all this maneuvering, the question of the freedmen's status and civil rights was not directly at issue. An amendment to the House bill extending suffrage to blacks, added by the Committee on Territories in May, was dropped when Wade brought the measure before the Senate. Brown's substitute proposal was not chiefly motivated or supported by a belief that greater guarantees could be secured for the freedmen by postponing the issue.[39] Nevertheless, the Wade-Davis bill was in essence an antislavery measure containing legal safeguards of the freedmen's personal liberty which answered what was expected to be a key issue in the election, namely, the disposition of slavery in relation to reconstruction.[40]

Presidential and congressional plans of reconstruction had much in common, including antislavery resolve.[41] The outstanding difference was that the congressional plan insisted in a far more definitive way on the immediate abolition of slavery, whereas the executive policy allowed the method and conditions of abolition to remain more or less a contingency of reconstruction politics.[42] Lincoln continued to affirm the Emancipation Proclamation and oppose any return of slaves actually freed.[43] In July 1864, he went so far as to say that a necessary condition of any peace settlement would be the "abandonment of slavery." In subsequent months, however, his commitment to total abolition seemed to waver. In September, Secretary of State Seward, presumably speaking on behalf of the administration, stated that when the rebellion ended all outstanding questions, including slavery, would be settled by the courts and legislative councils. This statement seemed to indicate that some alternative to unconditional abolition still was possible.[44]

In the view of most Republican congressmen, the government had to go beyond Lincoln's insistence, asserted in December 1863 but not elaborated or enlarged upon since then, that returning states must not contradict the Emancipation Proclamation. The trouble with this position was that the scope and effect of the proclamation were an open question. Indeed, the Republicans generally regarded the proclamation as not having abolished slavery. Furthermore, it seemed necessary to demand far more than Lincoln's amnesty proclamation promise to accept any temporary arrangements for the freed people that the states might devise. What was required was the immediate and complete abolition of slavery in state law, the restriction of state powers over personal liberty, and the establishment of national guarantees of personal liberty and rights for the emancipated slaves. These were what the Wade-Davis bill attempted to provide.

Lincoln pocket-vetoed the Wade-Davis plan, primarily because it would have forced him to start the reorganization of loyal government in Louisiana all over again. In an attempt to prevent a split in the party, he then issued a proclamation stating that the congressional reconstruction proposal was a satisfactory alternative to the administration's policy, and that he would implement it if the people of any state wished to follow it. [45] The issue did not end here, however, for, amid war weariness and disappointment at the failure of Grant's Virginia campaign, radical critics seized on Lincoln's handling of the reconstruction bill in a final attempt to force his retirement as the Republican nominee. The Wade-Davis manifesto of August 1864, an attack on executive reconstruction, was the evidence of this purpose. [46]

Although concern for freed blacks was not the immediate source of the manifesto, differences between executive and congressional policy toward slavery, the freedmen, and reconstruction figured prominently in it. Actual emancipation notwithstanding, argued Davis, the administration's policy left slavery in the same legal status it occupied at the start of the war and added no guarantees for slaves who had become free. Despite the antislavery constitution in Louisiana, the administration did not systematically require new state constitutions and laws going beyond the Emancipation Proclamation. In Davis's view, this policy seemed to leave the freedmen's liberty open to state court interpretation of the proclamation in the light of prewar precedents and gave the freed blacks no legal remedy against illegal detainment. The Wade-Davis bill, however, Davis contended, added "a congressional title and judicial remedies by law" to the disputed liberty bestowed by the executive proclamation of freedom. Moreover, it gave protection to the freed slaves by adhering to the principle that slavery could be abolished only through state constitutions and laws or by amendment of the federal constitution. [47]

Because the congressional plan excluded blacks from political rights, a few abolitionists professed indifference to its defeat. In their view, judicial guarantees of liberty did not redeem the measure. [48] Most antislavery men, however, considered the safeguards of the bill—its majority rather than 10-percent requirement for starting reorganization as well as its provisions against slavery—to be important improvements over presidential reconstruction. The intemperate nature of the Wade-Davis attack redounded to Lincoln's benefit by drawing attention away from the real differences that existed between president and Congress on reconstruction. Following Sherman's victory in Georgia which made a united party effort easier, Republicans dissociated themselves from the radical criticism and supported

Lincoln. Contrary to expectation, reconstruction was not directly or explicitly an issue in the 1864 election.[49]

The congressional plan of reconstruction reflected concern for the freedmen's civil rights in its formative stages, and already the matter was quite as much one of political tactics and expediency as ideology and principle. Indeed, the political consideration seemed more compelling than principle, as demonstrated by the fact that essentially the same reunion plan was defeated in 1865, in the altered political situation following Lincoln's reelection.[50] Yet, the political motivation of the reconstruction bill in 1864 and of the Wade-Davis critique was inseparable from the realization that if the Democrats should capture the presidency, emancipation would very likely be halted, if not reversed.[51] Aware of this possibility, congressional planners sought to provide a measure of national protection for the freedmen's liberty and rights.

Principally, the Wade-Davis bill sought to make emancipation effective, but the remedies it provided—extension of *habeas corpus* jurisdiction to federal courts and the requirement that blacks be dealt with according to the same law as whites—had utility beyond the minimum personal liberty of emancipation. To be sure, the legal guarantees of the bill were of limited scope. The privilege of the writ of *habeas corpus*, for example, was given only to emancipated persons who might be illegally detained under state authority. Even so, the contrast with the Confiscation Act of 1862, which contained no legal means for making good its declaration of freedom, was significant. However tenative the civil rights ideology underlying the Wade-Davis bill, it had potentially great civil rights consequences.

The congressional reconstruction plan of 1864 also provides evidence of Republican attitudes toward protecting civil rights in the context of federalism. As lawmakers tried to secure emancipation, they concluded that state powers over civil rights, virtually unlimited in prewar days, needed to be restrained. To effect such restraint meant not so much taking power from the states absolutely as diminishing it in a relative sense by establishing supervisory federal safeguards. Although the Wade-Davis prohibition of slavery and legal inequality under state law deprived states of power previously used, the larger point was that the states would continue to bear the primary or main responsibility for regulating and protecting civil rights. Yet, the *habeas corpus* provision of the bill and the requirement of intrastate legal equality for blacks signified an unprecedented national oversight of state performance in this regard, which presumably included corrective national action when that was necessary.

In the reconstructed Union envisioned by congressional planners, states would remain the centers of republicanism. The federal system would be modified, as indeed the abolition of slavery by any means seemed to require. But the rupture in federal-state relationships signified in the Wade-Davis bill was far less than that augured in earlier territorial reconstruction bills.[52] This more moderate outlook was not simply the outgrowth of an innate constitutionalism that rejected extreme solutions, but was also the result of compromise between the goal of securing the results of the war, including freedmen's liberty, and preserving the benefits of a decentralized federal system. The chief difference would be that now the national government would have a new and distinct, if limited, role to play in protecting individual rights. While this development has often been seen as a revolutionary one that produced a centralized, sovereign national government, Republicans then saw it as a repudiation at long last of state sovereignty and a restoration of the balanced governmental arrangements which the founding fathers had designed. The great test for the nation, abolitionist William M. Grosvenor wrote in illustrating this view, lay "in the task of constructing out of such materials as the war would leave us, governments for the rebellious States which should prove a source of strength and not a burden to the nation."[53]

By 1864, then, the problem of guaranteeing the status and rights of emancipated slaves had become a definite part of the reconstruction question. The congressional plan promising at least minimum national safeguards had been set aside, but the possibility existed that it would be revived at the next session of Congress. Meanwhile, actual emancipation continued to take place, creating for Union armies into whose lines the freed people came a welfare and relief problem of considerable magnitude. The congressional response to this problem was the Freedmen's Bureau Act of 1865.

NOTES

1. Herman Belz, *Reconstructing the Union: Theory and Policy During the Civil War* (Ithaca, 1969), 169-172.

2. Montgomery Blair, "The Republican Party As It Was and Is," *North American Review* 131 (November 1880): 426.

3. *National Anti-Slavery Standard*, January 2, 1864; *Independent*, December 17, 1863; Benjamin F. Butler to Wendell Phillips, December 11, 1863, quoted in Jessie Ames Marshall, ed., *Private and Official Correspondence of General Benjamin F. Butler* (5 vols.; Norwood, Mass., 1917), III, 204.

4. *National Anti-Slavery Standard*, April 30, 1864; New York *Tribune*, December 11, 1863, letter from "Freedom"; Boston *Commonwealth*, December 25, 1863, speech of Wendell Phillips; New York *Tribune*, February 13, 1864, speech of William Lloyd Garrison.

5. *National Anti-Salvery Standard*, December 19, 1863; *Liberator*, December 18, 1863, letter of "M. du Pays"; *National Anti-Slavery Standard*, January 9, 1864.

6. Ibid., February 13, May 14, 1864; Phillips to George W. Julian, March 27, 1864, quoted in I. H. Bartlett, *Wendell Phillips: Brahmin Radical* (Boston, 1961), 268; *National Anti-Slavery Standard*, May 14, 1864.

7. Boston *Commonwealth*, April 8, 1864; Worcester *Daily Spy*, May 3, 1864.

8. Boston *Commonwealth*, December 25, 1863; *Independent*, April 14, 1864; *National Anti-Slavery Standard*, January 9, 1864; New York *Tribune*, February 17, 1864.

9. *National Anti-Slavery Standard*, February 27, 1864; Boston *Commonwealth*, April 8, 1864; *National Anti-Slavery Standard*, April 23, May 14, 1864.

10. Springfield *Weekly Republican*, December 19, 26, 1863; Washington *Evening Star*, December 10, 1863; Washington *National Intelligencer*, December 10, 1863; Montgomery Throop, *The Future: A Political Essay* (New York, 1864), 186, 332-333.

11. Montgomery Blair, *Speech on the Causes of the Rebellion and in Support of the President's Plan of Pacification* (Baltimore, 1864), 3-4.

12. Henry J. Raymond to James Doolittle, April 30, 1864, Doolittle Papers, Library of Congress.

13. Phillip S. Paludan, "The American Civil War Considered as a Crisis in Law and Order," *American Historical Review* 77 (October 1972): 1032-1033.

14. Edward F. Bullard, *The Nation's Trial: The Proclamation: Dormant Powers of the Government* (New York and Albany, 1863), 47-48, 53-55, 60.

15. Marvin Warren, *A Solution of Our National Difficulties, and the Science of Republican Government* (Cincinnati, 1863), 10, 49-50.

16. Timothy Farrar, "State Rights," *New Englander* 21 (October 1862), 719-720.

17. Joel P. Bishop, *Secession and Slavery* (Boston, 1863), 112.

18. "The United States shall guarantee to every state in this union a Republican form of government, and shall protect each of them against invasion." U.S. Constitution, Art. IV, sec. 4.

19. Belz, *Reconstructing the Union*, 124-125, 203-205; William M. Wiecek, *The Guarantee Clause of the U.S. Constitution* (Ithaca, 1972), 166-243.

20. *Congressional Globe*, 37th Cong., 3d sess., 78 (December 11, 1862); 37th Cong., S. No. 538, February 17, 1863; Henry Winter Davis, *Speeches and Addresses* (New York, 1867), 325-326. See also Harold M. Hyman, *A More Perfect Union: The Impact of the Civil War and Reconstruction on the Constitution* (New York, 1973), 272.

21. 38th Cong., H.R. No. 21, 22, 24, December 14, 1863; H.R. No. 118, January 11, 1864; H.R. No. 330, March 14, 1864; S. No. 3, December 14, 1863; S. No. 111, February 10, 1864; S. No. 159, March 10, 1864. MS, National Archives, file of printed bills, RG 233.

22. 38th Cong., H.R. No. 21, H.R. No. 22, December 14, 1863; *National Anti-Slavery Standard*, December 26, 1863.

23. 38th Cong., H.R. No. 48, December 21, 1863, MS, National Archives, 38A-B1, RG 233; Belz, *Reconstructing the Union*, 185.

24. *Congressional Globe*, 38th Cong., 1st sess., 1206 (March 19, 1864), 1358 (March 30, 1864), 987-988 (March 8, 1864).

25. William F. Zornow, *Lincoln and the Party Divided* (Norman, Okla., 1954) 23-54; Gerteis, "Salmon P. Chase, Radicalism, and the Politics of Emancipation, 1861-1864," *Journal of American History* 60 (June 1973): 57-58.

26. *Congressional Globe*, 37th Cong., 3d sess., 1507 (March 3, 1863); *National Anti-Slavery Standard*, January 30, 1864.

27. *Congressional Globe*, 38th Cong., 1st sess., 987 (March 8, 1864).

28. The bill was later amended to require a majority, rather than 10 percent, of the enrolled population to swear the oath before an election could be held. It should be noted that this bill also rejected the proposal for Negro suffrage contained in Ashley's plan.

29. 38th Cong., H.R. No. 244, February 15, 1864, sec. 1-4.

30. Ibid., sec. 7, 12, 13, 10.

31. *Congressional Globe*, 38th Cong., 1st sess., 1740 (April 19, 1864), remarks of Nathaniel Smithers, 38th Cong., 2d sess., 969 (February 21, 1865), remarks of H. W. Davis.

32. Ibid., 38th Cong., 1st sess., App., 45 (February 25, 1864), App. 84-85 (March 22, 1864).

33. The related measure was a Negro enlistment bill. Brown proposed that it confirm the Emancipation Proclamation as a law of the United States, to be recognized as such by all state and federal courts, and authorize all freed persons to sue and be sued and give evidence in all courts in the same manner as other citizens. Ibid., 553 (February 10, 1864).

34. Ibid., 986-987 (March 8, 1864).

35. Ibid., 2038 (May 2, 1864), remarks of Ignatius Donnelly; 1354 (March 30, 1864), remarks of James M. Ashley; 1770 (April 20, 1864), remarks of John M. Broomall; 2014 (April 30, 1864), remarks of John W. Longyear; 2104 (May 4, 1864), remarks of George S. Boutwell.

36. Belz, *Reconstructing the Union*, 213.

37. Worcester *Daily Spy*, June 9, 1864; New York *World*, June 10, 1864; St. Louis *Missouri Democrat*, June 23, 1864; *The Principia*, July 7, 1864; Belz, *Reconstructing the Union*, 213-216.

38. *Congressional Globe*, 38th Cong., 1st sess., 3449 (July 1, 1864); Belz, *Reconstructing the Union*, 217-223.

39. Brown himself, however, may have aimed at securing more substantial rights for the freedmen. He said he was unwilling to support a reconstruction bill that disfranchised the vast amount of loyal men in the rebel states, a reference probably to the exclusion of Negro voting from the Wade-Davis bill. At a later date he hoped it would be possible to assert the rights needing to be secured in the rebel states. *Congressional Globe*, 38th Cong., 1st sess., 3460 (July 1, 1864).

40. St. Louis *Missouri Democrat*, March 28, 1864; *Congressional Globe*, 38th

Cong., 1st sess., 3449-3450 (July 1, 1864); Hyman, *A More Perfect Union*, 266.

    41. Belz, *Reconstructing the Union*, 237-239.

    42. St. Louis *Missouri Democrat*, May 11, 1864.

    43. Lincoln to Charles D. Robinson, August 17, 1864, in Roy P. Basler, et al., eds., *The Collected Works of Abraham Lincoln* (9 vols.; New Brunswick, 1953-1955), VII, 499-500.

    44. William H. Seward, *The Great Issues: Speech at Auburn, N.Y., September 3, 1864* (n.p., 1864), 7; V. Jacque Voegeli, *Free But Not Equal: The Midwest and the Negro During the Civil War* (Chicago, 1967), 145-151; Ludwell H. Johnson, "Lincoln's Solution to the Problem of Peace Terms, 1864-1865," *Journal of Southern History* 34 (November 1968), 576-586.

    45. Basler, et al., eds., *Collected Works of Lincoln*, VII, 433-434.

    46. After the Chase presidential drive collapsed, radicals met in Cleveland at the end of May to nominate General John C. Fremont. Their purpose was to undercut the Union Republican convention to be held in early June. When this effort failed to gain popular support, radicals talked of yet another convention which might be held before the Democrats met at the end of August. Its purpose would be to force Lincoln from the nomination by choosing a radical who would somehow be acceptable to War Democrats as well as radical Republicans. General Benjamin F. Butler was most often mentioned as a possible candidate, with Fremont being persuaded to withdraw. Nothing came of these machinations. Zornow, *Lincoln and the Party Divided*, 110-112.

    47. New York *Tribune*, August 5, 1864.

    48. Boston *Commonwealth*, July 15, 1864; *Liberator*, August 19, 1864, letter of "M. DuPays"; *The Principia*, August 11, 1864.

    49. Detroit *Advertiser and Tribune*, July 6, 1864; Cincinnati *Gazette*, July 7, 1864; *Independent*, July 21, August 4, 11, 1864, letters of George B. Cheever; Belz, *Reconstructing the Union*, 230-231.

    50. Belz, *Reconstructing the Union*, 244-276.

    51. Hyman, *A More Perfect Union*, 266-267, 270-271.

    52. Belz, *Reconstructing the Union*, 66-99.

    53. William M. Grosvenor to Charles Sumner, December 29, 1864, Sumner Papers, Harvard University Library.

5

Freedmen's bureau legislation and civil rights

The purpose of creating a federal freedmen's bureau was to provide humanitarian assistance to former slaves and relieve Union armies of the emergency welfare responsibility that emancipation had placed upon them. In a limited and oblique way, the recruitment of blacks into the federal army and the organization of freedmen's labor in military camps and on abandoned plantations were attempts to meet this responsibility. These policies, however, were intended mainly to promote military and political interests, with the result that antislavery reformers criticized them for failing to protect the freed slaves' liberty, rights, and welfare in general. While the congressional reconstruction plan of 1864 was in part directed to this end, the principal attempt to assist southern blacks and recognize their new status came in freedmen's bureau legislation.

Though dealing with temporary welfare relief, freedmen's bureau bills raised questions concerning the status and rights of former slaves and the nature and extent of federal power in relation thereto. On the assumption that the benefits of full civil liberty now belonged to the ex-slaves, the framers and supporters of freedmen's bureau legislation regarded it as a means of protecting the blacks' newly acquired rights. Others, however, including many Republicans, contended that if emancipation made slaves free men, then the kind of regulatory devices that supporters of a freedmen's bureau proposed were wrongly conceived. To supervise the freedmen, critics reasoned, was to deny their free status.

Criticism of freedmen's bureau proposals, though couched in terms of civil liberty, was to some extent based on anti-Negro sentiment. Such criticism was disingenuous and rhetorical, inspired by the political motive of embarrassing the radical supporters of freedmen's legislation rather than regard for the emancipated slaves' rights. Opposition to freedmen's bureau legislation in 1864-1865 was also based on a widely shared and genuinely held laissez-faire point of view which questioned the wisdom of governmental supervision of the former slaves. According to this outlook, the freedmen should be left on their own as much as possible, unencumbered by governmental restraints and able like white persons to go to the law for redress of injury or discrimination.

Opposition on laissez-faire grounds was reinforced by constitutional apprehensions. Supervision of freed slaves by the proposed bureau, even if confined to the period of the war and its immediate aftermath, would intrude deeply into the traditional power of the states to regulate personal liberty and civil rights. It therefore augured a potential revolution in federalism which blended with race-sensitive politics in freedmen's bureau deliberations.

As early as 1862, the future of the former slaves began to be debated. Freedmen's bureau legislation took shape in light of this debate and provided a focus for discussions of the matter. The basic reference points were (1) that the freed blacks should be left alone, on the assumption that they were freemen, if not citizens, with ordinary civil rights, and (2) temporary guardianship should be established over them, with the purpose of enabling them to exercise their rights.

Voegeli has shown that among northerners emancipation aroused fears of black migration out of the South.[1] Hence, the first and most fundamental antislavery answer to the question of post-emancipation policy was to insist that the freedmen be left alone to remain where they were—on the soil of the southern states. Antislavery men pointed out that as a laboring class blacks would be indispensable to the economic recovery of the region. What was more, owing to environmental conditions, racial characteristics, and the laws of political economy, emancipation would induce northern free Negroes to go South. Leave them alone, advised radical Republican Owen Lovejoy, and the freedmen would take care of themselves.[2]

This argument did not, of course, mean that emancipated slaves literally would be left alone by civil authority. The assumption was that ordinary civil rights—personal liberty and locomotion, the right to make contracts, to buy, sell, and lease property, to sue and be sued and to testify in court—would be upheld through ordinary litigation at common law. Blacks would be able to enforce their rights through civil suits for injury to person or property. This was the meaning of Iowa Republican Senator James Harlan's assertion in July 1862 that emancipated slaves "will be equal with white men in their right to justice and the protection of the laws."[3]

Since the laissez-faire position prevailed, it was necessary to guard against restrictive regulations that would leave emancipation incomplete. The *American Baptist* insisted that nothing should be done with the freedmen and warned against intervention that would lead to apprenticeship systems.[4] In December 1861, the abolitionist Gerrit Smith criticized a Republican proposal to colonize emancipated slaves under military rule in Florida on the basis that the plan would amount to apprenticeship imposed against their will. Apprehension about undue restraints on freed slaves was also evident in Republican criticism of a plan to apprentice black children in the District of Columbia who were without parents or guardians and to provide support for elderly ex-slaves. Opposing the measure, Senator Lot M. Morrill of Maine declared: "give them their rights; they ask no favors of you; . . . they do not ask you to assign guardians."[5]

As actual emancipation proceeded in 1863, however, radicals and abolitionists emphasized the government's responsibility to help the freed people adapt to their new condition of liberty. Without abandoning the goal of laissez-faire legal equality, they took the position that emancipated slaves needed temporary guardianship. The Emancipation League of Boston, for example, canvassed the opinions of army superintendents of contrabands as to whether southern blacks needed preparatory training and guardianship. Responses were mixed, but the league's call for a bureau of emancipation suggested that many antislavery men believed supervision necessary. The *National Anti-Slavery Standard* confirmed this view in arguing that the government should depart from the let-alone policy and direct the movement and employment of freed slaves. The reformer Robert Dale Owen agreed that little use could be made of freed blacks if the government did not govern them when they reached Union lines.[6]

Apart from wartime exigencies, some reformers had second thoughts about the wisdom of a strict laissez-faire approach to emancipation. The *Independent* reasoned that blacks needed guardianship because of their lack of training. They "are children, in a great measure, and must be treated accordingly," the radical weekly declared. Drawing an analogy to the Indian question, the Boston *Commonwealth* recommended creation of a freedmen's bureau on the ground that blacks formed a separate interest or class. The natural rights of the freed people should be secured, observed the *Commonwealth*, but more than "a cold and forced justice" was needed to guarantee their rights. [7]

That emancipated slaves would form an agricultural labor force in the South was taken as axiomatic, by men of all political persuasions. Therefore, the ex-slaves' relationship to the land and to their former masters were important issues in discussions of freedmen's affairs in 1863. Recognizing that old patterns of subordination might continue in new forms, the Boston *Commonwealth* urged "a minute and careful code of laws to regulate the labor of the freedmen." Freedmen's aid societies proposed leasing rebel lands under a system of government regulation that would protect both the loyal lessee and the former slaves. After surveying army contraband camps, James E. Yeatman, a leader in the freedmen's aid movement, stated: "It is the duty of the Government to exercise a wholesome guardianship over these new-born children of freedom; to guide, direct and protect them at least in their infancy." [8]

In their preliminary report, the American Freedmen's Inquiry Commission (AFIC), a group appointed by the War Department in 1863 to study post-emancipation problems, reflected the antislavery emphasis on supervision of former slaves. [9] While the AFIC noted the importance of legally recognizing the freedmen's liberty and rights, it argued chiefly for their temporary guardianship. As a model, it suggested the system of apprenticeship employed in the British West Indies in the 1830s, a plan that had been condemned by the abolitionists. The AFIC argued that the West Indian plan was defective in details only, not in principle. It was an open question, the commissioners stated, whether and how soon ex-slaves would be able peacefully to maintain their rights in the face of the prejudice and dependency created by slavery. The AFIC accordingly recommended that the government organize freed blacks' labor on abandoned and confiscated plantations and ultimately allow them, if qualified, to lease or purchase land outright. Though it would be but temporary, guardianship was the dominant theme of the 1863 report. [10]

In the eyes of most antislavery reformers, such an approach was consistent with the idea of legal equality for emancipated slaves. [11] "Protection—education—these are what we need to give him, as well as that equality before the law which is the right of all men," declared the *Commonwealth*. [12] Others, however, including many antislavery supporters, held that special governmental supervision of the freedmen contradicted the principle of legal equality. From this standpoint, there was no essential difference between the War Department labor system which the abolitionists criticized in 1863 and the legislative plans for a freedmen's bureau which they advocated in 1864. And in truth, though abolitionists and radicals might believe that ordinary civil liberty was not incompatible with government supervision, the issue was not that simple.

In the context of nonradical emancipationist thought, regulation of emancipated slaves might have little in common with ordinary civil and legal equality. There was little of republican liberty, for example, in Unionist F. P. Stanton's view that the freedmen should become the wards of the government under a system of apprenticeship with humane rules for their education, employment, and governance. Another emancipationist described former slaves as "in a state of infantile weakness and inexperience . . . subjects of the Government, but not a part of the Government." The work of organizing their labor, he reasoned, "must assume paternal form." Missouri emancipationist Charles D. Drake frankly endorsed apprenticeship to teach blacks to utilize their freedom, while Louisiana Unionist Michael Hahn, soon to become the reconstruction governor of the state, said strict vagrancy laws would assure the availability of freedmen's labor. Hahn explained that labor contracts could be arranged to protect employers, and he reassured planters that they would not suffer from the change to free labor. [13] While this argument was perhaps calculated to gain support for emancipation, it converged with the advice of conservative critics who were hostile to the idea of legal equality for blacks and believed the nation must assume guardianship over them. [14]

As the government's labor policies in the occupied South came under attack and the potential dangers of freedmen's supervision appeared in 1864, some abolition reformers shifted their emphasis again to the laissez-faire theme. After extensive investigation of the freed slaves' circumstances. Samuel Gridley Howe of the American Freedmen's Inquiry Commission advised Senator Charles Sumner of

Massachusetts that, while blacks were "a poor race physically," he favored "the *let alone* system, unless our protection is demanded by the sufferers themselves." In the border states, said Howe, freed blacks needed no special provision other than protection of their legal rights. Though military protection would be necessary in the rebel states, Howe warned against adopting any system that, under the pretext of protection, would impose a disguised slavery. [15]

The AFIC's final report in May 1864 reflected heightened concern for the ex-slaves' equality and rights. Declaring that the freedmen's legal status was the primary issue, the commissioners recommended guarantees of civil and political rights in reorganized loyal governments. They also advised a federal constitutional amendment prohibiting slavery that would forbid discrimination in civil and political rights on account of color. Meanwhile, the commission cautioned, "The risk is serious that under the guise of guardianship, slavery, in a modified form, may be practically restored." A freedmen's bureau was needed, but former slaves should not be compelled to make labor contracts, nor should they be interfered with in their relationship to their employers or regulated as to local movement. Blacks must find remedy for ill treatment not in special laws or a special organization, concluded the AFIC, but in "the safeguard of general laws, applicable to all, against fraud and oppression." [16]

It was against this background of public discussion that the Thirty-seventh Congress first introduced measures to deal with freed slaves. In contrast to the general laissez-faire view that prevailed among reformers outside Congress, initial congressional efforts in 1862 proposed government supervision of freedmen's labor. [17] In February 1862, for example, the Senate passed a bill for the care of Negroes which created a board of receivers and guardians to manage abandoned property and employ "indigent persons" on the Sea Islands of South Carolina. Under regulations aimed at protecting the freed people, the guardians were charged with providing food, lodging, clothing, and medical care, as well as keeping accounts of wages. While the bill was rendered superfluous when the Treasury Department introduced regulations that were similar to its provisions, it nevertheless provoked arguments that anticipated later freedmen's bureau debate. Thus, on the one hand radical Republican Ben Wade of Ohio insisted that emancipated slaves must be supervised, put to work, and protected against rapacious whites bent upon controlling the land, while on the other hand conservative John Carlile of loyal Virginia said that the bill converted the government "into one great lordly slaveholder." The Republicans, perhaps sensitive to Carlile's charge, voted to delete the word "guardians" before passing the bill.[18]

In June 1862, Congress enacted a bill for the collection of direct taxes in rebel states which provided a limited statutory basis for government supervision of freedmen. The chief purpose of the measure was to provide for the public sale of land on which taxes had not been paid. Although this measure was seen to threaten the abolition aim of installing ex-slaves on the land, Republicans did not object.[19] Regarding the freedmen as an agricultural labor force under government control, lawmakers directed the tax commissioners to lease abandoned lands and make contracts and temporary rules and regulations securing "proper and reasonable employment" for "persons and families"—i.e., freedmen—residing on the soil.[20] Two years later, Thomas D. Eliot of Massachusetts said this act marked the first expression of congressional concern for the freed slaves. He added, however, that it was dictated by a desire for revenue, not by humanity.[21]

As antislavery reformers in 1863 came to recognize the necessity for direct governmental supervision of the freedmen, they sought in particular to establish a central agency that could coordinate the diverse public and private efforts that were being undertaken to aid former slaves. The first such proposal to be introduced in Congress was offered by Representative Thomas D. Eliot in January 1863. In December 1863, Eliot reintroduced the measure, and two weeks later he reported a second freedmen's bureau bill from the Select Committee on Emancipation.[22] Both of these measures provided for government supervision and support of emancipated slaves. Eliot and his colleagues apparently regarded legislative guarantees of freedmen's liberty and rights as unnecessary, premature, or unimportant; accordingly, they were primarily concerned with giving protection and immediate welfare assistance. Nevertheless, some slight evolution of ideas about the status and rights of former slaves can be seen in these proposals.

Eliot's first bill called for the creation of a bureau to adjust and determine "all questions touching the general superintendence, disposition, and direction" of freed slaves. The commissioner of the bureau was further directed to make suitable regulations "for the needful, economical, and judicious treatment" of persons covered by the act. Eliot's second bill, reported from the Select Committee on Emancipation, retained these provisions but in addition authorized freedmen and persons of African descent, who were also included in the bill, to occupy, cultivate, and improve abandoned and other lands to which the United States had acquired title. [23]

Even if the original bill assumed land occupation by freed slaves, which seems doubtful, explicit recognition of this point in the second bill was significant. Without it, the first plan referred to freedmen's rights only in conjunction with those of society, stating that bureau regulations were to be shaped "to the end that said freedmen and the government of the United States shall be mutually protected, and their respective rights and interests duly determined and maintained." [24] Abandoning this balancing formulation, the emancipation committee by adding the land occupation provision at least pointed in the direction of a free labor right. The terms on which freedmen might occupy the land were not defined, and bureau agents were given a wide charge to advise, organize, and direct the former slaves' labor as well as adjust their wages and receive all returns arising from the use of the land. [25] Nevertheless, the contrast with Eliot's original proposal, which said nothing about a possible right of occupation for freedmen, was significant.

The emancipation committee bill contained other indications of evolution beyond Eliot's original conception of the freedmen's status. One was a provision authorizing bureau agents to arbitrate disputes among freedmen, "except when resort to a provost judge or other legal tribunal becomes necessary." [26] While this provision gave bureau officials quasi-judicial power to settle minor conflicts, it also implied that in more important matters freedmen had the right to bring suit in courts of law. Noteworthy too was the abandonment of a provision for enforcing colonization laws. By March 1864, when this section was deleted, the administration's gradual emancipation and colonization plan had long since failed, and reference to colonization was an embarrassment to the bill. The right to remain in the United States was a fundamental civil right now receiving recognition. [27]

As chairman of the Select Committee on Emancipation, Eliot opened the debate on the freedmen's bureau bill in February 1864. Presenting it as a humanitarian relief measure, he argued that the government was under an obligation to guarantee protection and guidance to those whom it set free. In Eliot's view, this purpose was related to the larger objective of securing liberty and rights. Referring to Lincoln's exhortation, contained in the Emancipation Proclamation, that freed slaves labor faithfully for reasonable wages in all cases where allowed, Eliot observed: "So they will, if allowed. But who is to allow them?" In other words, Eliot's theory was that the proclamation conferred certain rights on the former slaves, one of which—the right to labor for wages—the bill would protect and uphold. In similar vein, Eliot said the purpose of the act was to give legislative assurance that freed blacks who were not recruited into the army, but remained at home, would not be forced into serfdom.[28]

While Eliot was certain as to what must be avoided, he was unclear about the status of the freedmen in a positive sense. On the one hand, he referred to them as subjects of the government who owed allegiance and were entitled to protection. Together with the fact of native birth, this reference was the usual description of a citizen, although Eliot did not call freed blacks citizens. On the other hand, he spoke of "a nation of freedmen" which emancipation had created—a rhetorical reference perhaps but one that implied that blacks formed a legally distinct class. Of like import were Eliot's allusion to blacks as "children of the Government" and the fact, despite his denial that the purpose was to separate the freedmen from the rest of the population, that the bill applied to all blacks. That is, free Negroes as well as freed slaves might be brought within the scope of the act. Despite these possible contradictions, Eliot saw the bill as giving the freedmen "the rights of man."[29]

Republicans who defended the freedmen's bureau bill gave far more attention to the practical importance of organizing emancipated labor than to civil rights recognition. William D. Kelley of Pennsylvania approached it as a way of cultivating abandoned lands and employing idle labor. He warned that freed blacks "must not be permitted to contract habits of idleness, indolence, and vagrancy." Representative Hiram Price of Iowa said the issue was not whether the former slaves' labor should be made available to the government, but how it should be done. According to Price, the bill proposed "simply an organization to direct in a proper channel the physical, and bone-and-sinew energy of the black race . . . —only this and nothing more."[30]

Democratic objections to the bill centered on federalism and race.

"If there is any power clearly and exclusively within the province of the several States," reasoned Anthony Knapp of Illinois, a member of the emancipation committee, "it is that to control and direct the social relations of their inhabitants." Yet, the bill proposed to give this power to the federal government. Knapp pointedly recalled President Lincoln's reconstruction promise to accept "State action alone" in resolving freedmen's affairs, while George Pendleton of Ohio said the government's existing labor systems for freed blacks were satisfactory. Led by S. S. Cox of Ohio, Democratic critics also accused freedmen's bureau planners of promoting miscegenation and Negro equality. [31]

At the same time, Democrats called attention to the civil rights aspect of the problem by charging Republicans with hypocrisy in regard to freedmen's liberty. If the Emancipation Proclamation made the blacks freedmen in anything but name, asserted Knapp and Martin Kalbfleisch of New York, then they came under state jurisdiction. Only if they were still slaves and the U.S. government their new master could the blacks be separated out and controlled as the bill proposed, contended the Democratic critics. William Wadsworth of Kentucky protested that the measure claimed a power of exclusive jurisdiction over persons who were "freemen by the assumption of the friends of the bill." Without any constitutional warrant, said Wadsworth, the bill would impose on "the *free people* of the States" federal officials to fix wages, direct labor, and adjudicate rights without judge or jury. [32]

These criticisms reflected jealousy for state powers. For the purpose of maintaining traditional state control over personal liberty and rights, the Democrats were willing to consider the former slaves freemen with civil rights. The political and rhetorical nature of the argument aside, the debate revealed the possible contradiction between the supervisory aspect of the freedmen's bureau bill and the Republicans' assumption that emancipated slaves were entitled to laissez-faire legal equality.

On March 1, 1864, the House passed the freedmen's bureau bill by a 69 to 67 vote. The division followed party lines for the most part, with only three northern Republicans and seven border state Unionists joining Democrats in opposition. [33] In the Senate, the bill was referred to the Select Committee on Slavery and the Freedmen, under the chairmanship of Charles Sumner. No action was taken on it for

several weeks, apparently because of the struggle between the War
and Treasury Departments for control of freedmen's affairs.

In late 1863, as we have seen, Secretary Chase inaugurated efforts
to bring former slaves under what reformers saw as the more humane
regulations of the Treasury Department. Conflicts between army officers and Treasury agents ensued, which ended in Lincoln's February
1864 order to General Lorenzo Thomas to take charge of the land
leasing and freedmen's question. Thomas proceeded to vindicate the
army's authority, and, when the Senate freedmen's committee at
length reported the House bill, it reflected dissatisfaction with this
outcome by proposing to place the bureau in the Treasury Department.

In Senate deliberations on the freedmen's question, the status and
rights of emancipated slaves was a more prominent issue. The substitute bill reported by Sumner's committee differed most conspicuously
from the House measure in placing the emancipation bureau in the
Treasury rather than the War Department. Too, it applied only to
persons emancipated since the beginning of the war.[34] Though it provided for "general superintendence of all freedmen" in a manner similar to the House bill, the Senate substitute directed the bureau "in the
spirit of the Constitution, to protect these persons in the enjoyment of
their rights."[35] While the practical force of this injunction was uncertain at best, it seemed to signify growing awareness of the civil rights
side of the freedmen's question.

As in the House bill, bureau agents were given power to arbitrate
disputes among freedmen, and in the event disputes were taken into a
civil or military court, they were to act as next friends of the former
slaves. The Senate bill also provided that, in judicial or quasi-judicial
proceedings, there should be no disability or exclusion on account of
color.[36] No such provision for legal equality was present in the House
bill.

The land provisions of the Senate bill also differed from those of the
House proposal. The bureau was authorized to take possession of all
abandoned or confiscable real estate and to rent or lease it. If no proper lessees could be found, the land was "to be cultivated or occupied
by the freedmen on such terms . . . and under such regulations as the
commissioner may determine." No freedmen was to be "held to service" other than by voluntary contract, reduced to writing and for a
period no longer than twelve months. The Senate bill also directed

agents to act as "advisory guardians" to see that freedmen neither suffered from ill treatment or failure of contract nor were themselves negligent in fulfilling contractual obligations. Where freed slaves rented plantations or small holdings, bureau officials were to assist in adjusting wages and organizing their labor. [37]

These provisions meant that, while the Senate bill took into account the possibility that freedmen might be lessees, primarily it viewed them as contract laborers on government-leased plantations. Indeed, according to a careful student of the subject, the Senate bill seemed to point in a direction opposite that of landownership for emancipated slaves. [38] In contrast, the House bill, though it did not define the terms on which blacks could occupy abandoned lands, did not prescribe labor contracts for the freedmen. While the House proposal more clearly implied a right of landholding, the Senate measure recognized the civil rights side of the question in ways that the House bill did not. Although the reasons for offering a substitute bill remain somewhat obscure, there is evidence that the House bill was rejected in the Senate in part because it did not seem to provide adequate protection for freedmen's rights.

When forced to explain how the House bill, which he supported, was defeated in his own committee, Charles Sumner attributed the outcome to objections B. Gratz Brown raised to the measure's failure to guarantee the freedmen's liberty. According to Sumner, Brown believed the bill "handed over the freedmen to a 2nd slavery." Sumner complained about embarrassing differences of opinion on the question and added that, in Brown's view, the House proposal "furnishes no protection to the freedmen, so as to keep them from being made serfs or apprentices." What was more, Brown felt so strongly about the bill that "he would speak & vote against it in the Senate." [39] Whether the rest of the committee on slavery and the freedmen shared Brown's apprehensions is not known, but since there was no apparent reason for nonradicals to place the bureau under the radical Secretary of the Treasury Salmon P. Chase, the possibility cannot be disregarded. [40] In any case, Brown's objections were consistent with his concern for establishing legal guarantees of the freedmen's liberty and rights.

Whether Sumner was persuaded by Brown's views or was merely trying to disarm critics, in debate he argued the superiority of the substitute Senate bill partly on the ground that it safeguarded freedmen's rights more effectively than the House proposal. Sumner noted that positive government assistance was needed to give emancipated slaves opportunities on the land, and he warned that care must be taken to prevent a system of serfdom or apprenticeship from being established. Sumner believed the Senate bill was superior in this respect because it authorized bureau agents to aid in adjusting wages and to guard against violations of contracts by employers. Indeed, in his view voluntary labor contracts were an essential element of security. The House plan did not specify such labor contracts and lacked positive guarantees against a system by which blacks "may be annexed to the soil . . . in direct conflict with their newly acquired rights," Sumner judged.[41]

Indicating how complex the issue of freedmen's rights could be when dealt with under the pressure of race, politics, and ideology, several senators objected that the substitute bill itself failed adequately to recognize the free status of the ex-slaves. As in the House, some of this criticism came from Democrats trying to defeat any freedmen's bureau bill and repudiate what they regarded as revolutionary programs of social equality.[42] The principal opposition, however, came from antislavery Republicans who took a laissez-faire view of the freedmen's question.

James Grimes of Iowa led the intraparty protest against the "general superintendence" of freedmen that the Senate bill prescribed. According to Grimes, the proposal gave the bureau power to control the freed blacks on the assumption that, like Indians, their condition required them to be governed apart. Moreover, the commissioner's power to set the terms on which freed blacks would occupy abandoned lands was tantamount to "peon slavery." Grimes said the former slaves' abject circumstances negated the voluntary character of labor contracts they might enter. "Are they free men or are they not?" he asked. "If they are free men, why not let them stand as free men?"[43]

Senator Timothy Howe of Wisconsin also questioned the provision for general superintendence of freedmen. Howe contended that many freed blacks were earning a good living, and he said the bill gave the commissioner "the right to control the action and the efforts of all these freedmen." Without fully endorsing this criticism, radical Senator Henry Wilson of Massachusetts lent it support by suggesting that the substitute bill was more concerned with plantations than freedmen. Noting the emancipated blacks around Washington, Wilson said those who lived under government organization were the worst off and were "held ... under a rule which is irksome to them." Wilson, who as chairman of the Military Affairs Committee preferred to place the bureau in the War Department, believed the House bill would allow the freedmen independently to take possession of the land.[44]

This intraparty attack astonished Sumner and led him to suggest improvements in the bill.[45] In an attempt to reassure laissez-faire critics, he added a provision stating that "every such freedman shall be treated in every respect as a freeman, with all proper remedies in courts of justice; and no power or control shall be exercised with regard to him except in conformity with law."[46]

Not satisfied, laissez-faire Republican critics demanded further changes to protect the freedmen's rights. Thus, Grimes successfully proposed that both the commissioner and the freedmen, and not just the commissioner alone, should agree to the terms for occupying unleased land. On the theory that restrictions on bureau agents would protect the former slaves, Grimes also won approval for Senate confirmation of top level bureau appointments. Similar, though more controversial, was Wisconsin Senator James Doolittle's suggestion that bureau agents be regarded as in the military service and be made liable to trial by military commission for various offenses, including any willful act of oppression of freedmen or loyal inhabitants. In the absence of courts in southern states, Doolittle reasoned, such a provision was needed to make officers accountable in their treatment of the freed people. Again, a majority of senators agreed.[47]

Although sectional and racial antagonisms within the party seem to have been behind this laissez-faire criticism of the bill, with the session drawing to a close Sumner accepted the Republican amendments as friendly and supported them.[48] A proposal that was accorded very different treatment, though it also was ostensibly aimed at protecting freedmen's rights, was one for Negro migration introduced by Waitman T. Willey of West Virginia. Protesting the irresponsible power of bureau officials, Willey recommended that the freedmen be protected by relocating them in northern states. To this end, he offered an amendment to the bill authorizing the commissioner of the bureau, when it was not possible to employ freedmen, to provide homes and employment for them with humane and suitable persons at fair and just compensation for their services. To commence the relocation work, the Willey amendment authorized the commissioner to initiate correspondence requesting the cooperation of governors and municipal officials in the states. This would protect the freed blacks, Willey said, by assuring residence in free states where they would have equality before the law and the same rights as other citizens. [49]

Willey's amendment divided Republicans and produced an unusual alignment across party lines. The arch conservative Willard Saulsbury of Delaware joined with antislavery men such as B. Gratz Brown of Missouri in supporting the Negro removal plan, while Democrat Charles Buckalew of Pennsylvania denounced it as "monstrous" and Republican Samuel C. Pomeroy of Kansas objected that the freedmen could not be controlled or disposed of in the manner that Willey proposed. Radical Republican Charles Sumner insisted that the idea of transporting freed blacks into the northern states was "entirely untenable." [50]

What made it untenable, of course, was widespread anti-Negro sentiment in the North. Since the start of serious emancipation efforts in 1862, black migration had been a controversial issue, and though many freedmen had made their way North, there was strong popular opposition to government actions to assist their relocation. In the fall of 1862, the War Department, meeting immediate resistance, abandoned efforts to arrange for the employment and support of black refugees in Illinois. Nor was eastern opinion more favorable to blacks on this issue than western, as Governor John A. Andrew of Massachusetts showed in declining a Union commander's offer to send two thousand blacks to the New England states. [51]

Indeed, northern prejudice made congressmen acutely sensitive to the issue of Negro migration from the start of freedmen's bureau planning. In the first meeting of the House Select Committee on Emancipation in December 1863, Republican Godlove Orth of Indiana proposed that no action should be taken to encourage emigration by freedmen. Sharing this viewpoint, Democrat Anthony Knapp of Illinois moved an amendment to the bureau bill, stating that nothing in it should authorize the introduction of any persons of color into any state whose laws prohibited them. Eliot's committee rejected this motion by a vote of six Republicans (including Orth) to one Democrat, but the result signified a desire to steer clear of the issue rather than support the migration of blacks. [52]

In June 1864, Republican opponents of the Willey amendment acknowledged political reasons for avoiding any reference to black migration in national legislation. To open public correspondence on the subject, Samuel C. Pomeroy of Kansas declared, would enable "a political party to make a fuss about it, and it will become an unpopular thing." Henry Wilson of Massachusetts held that the provision for official correspondence with state governors was liable to misrepresentation and would excite opposition. Wilson said he supported black relocation, but only if it were carried on by private voluntary means. [53]

The Senate agreed to Willey's amendment, 19 to 15. Analysis of the vote suggests that its proponents were mainly trying to embarrass Sumner and his fellow radicals and defeat the bill rather than protect Negro rights. The principal division was between western and eastern Republicans. B. Gratz Brown, James R. Doolittle, James W. Grimes, James Harlan, John B. Henderson, Timothy Howe, Alexander Ramsey, and Henry S. Lane—all westerners—voted for the migration proposal, along with easterners Ira Harris, Solomon Foot, William Sprague, Henry B. Anthony, and Daniel Clark. Six border state Democrats and conservative Unionists also voted for it. The fifteen opponents of Willey's amendment included four Democrats and eleven Republicans, seven of whom were easterners: Edgar Cowan, Lafayette S. Foster, Lot M. Morrill, Edwin D. Morgan, John C. Ten Eyck, Charles Sumner, and Henry Wilson. Only Lyman Trumbull, Benjamin F. Wade, Morton Wilkinson and James H. Lane from western states supported it. [54] On each side of the question radicals uncharacteristically joined with conservatives.

Since anti-Negro sentiment was particularly strong in the West, it is doubtful that western Republicans supported black migration in order to promote freedmen's rights or thought that the bill could pass the House with such a provision. Their purpose was to embarrass the bill and put its radical supporters in the position of opposing a measure that could be construed as aiding blacks. Another source of the division that now manifested itself within the party concerned the recruitment of freedmen in the South.

Concurrently with the freedmen's bureau bill, Henry Wilson advocated legislation to permit states to fill their draft quotas by recruiting southern blacks. Wilson's rationale was that this policy would prevent the loss of industrial labor through conscription, a subject on which Massachusetts businessmen had lobbied for over a year. Western Republicans strongly objected to such a policy because it would give an unfair advantage to wealthier eastern states which could purchase black substitutes to fill their quotas.[55] B. Gratz Brown, a supporter of the black migration amendment and an opponent of state recruitment of blacks, called attention to the connection between these issues in the freedmen's bill debate. If it was desirable to have an official system to put blacks into military service for the state of Massachusetts, Brown asked, why should not a similar system, as in the Negro relocation proposal, be used to fill the ranks of industry throughout the North?[56]

After Willey's proposal was adopted, the Massachusetts senators fought back and managed to remove the most politically explosive part of the amendment. At first Sumner tried to have the entire amendment struck out but was defeated by a tie vote. Wilson then moved to delete only the language authorizing correspondence with state governors for the purpose of placing freedmen in northern states. By voice vote, the Senate accepted this compromise.[57]

The Senate bill thus authorized the commissioner of the freedmen's bureau, if he was unable to locate abandoned lands on which to employ emancipated slaves, to find homes and employment for them "with humane and suitable masters." Although Wilson said the bureau could open a correspondence with anyone in any part of the country for the settlement of freedmen and the Democrat Buckalew believed that the substance of the objectionable proposal remained in the bill, in a practical political sense the Negro migration idea had been defeated.[58]

The Senate then passed the substitute freedmen's bill by a 21 to 9 vote. On the recommendation of Thomas D. Eliot, however, the House refused to concur and voted to postpone consideration of the matter until the December session.[59]

To a considerable extent, attitudes toward the freedmen's question were politically motivated. Even so, recognition of the status and rights of emancipated slaves was a legitimate issue on which genuine disagreement was emerging. Samuel Gridley Howe gave evidence of this fact when he described the difference in opinion among members of the American Freedmen's Inquiry Commission. Howe and Robert Dale Owen agreed on the importance of a laissez-faire course toward the freedmen, Howe wrote, but fellow commission-member James McKaye did not. "The Col. goes for some system which will amount to apprenticeship—& which will be *enforced*," Howe declared.[60] Fur-

thermore, while Eliot conceived of the House bill as recognizing the
rights of the freedmen, others such as B. Gratz Brown on the Senate
emancipation committee thought it inadequate. Some House members may also have had reservations about the House freedmen's bureau bill. Henry Winter Davis implied as much when he observed that
the powers given the new bureau made passage of the measure in the
House remarkable and not likely to be repeated.[61] Yet, the alternative Senate plan, drawn up by Sumner along lines advised by the
American Freedmen's Inquiry Commission, was in turn criticized by
antislavery men for imposing guardianship on freed blacks. Finally, if
support for Willey's Negro migration idea was largely political, other
attempts to amend the Senate bill reflected a genuine concern with
the problem of recognizing the blacks' free status under a system of
laissez-faire legal equality.

Conflicting opinions on freedmen's rights were also heard outside
Congress. In describing the vulnerable position of the freedmen, with
Treasury agents and army officers vying for control and pardoned
rebel owners waiting to recover their lands, businessman-reformer
John Murray Forbes urged Sumner to give the black man a guardian.
"The purpose would not be to control him," Forbes added, "but to
stand between him & the white man, & protect him in the new right he
has acquired to work for himself & his family." Forbes and others
believed that the House bill offered the kind of friendly government
interposition that was needed, and so they advised Sumner not to risk
defeat by proposing an alternative bill.[62] In the view of abolitionist
editor William Goodell, however, the House bill unwisely gave "irresponsible, indefinite, unlimited authority" to the superintendent of
the bureau. "*Protection*, with very little if any extra Supervision, is, I
think, what the freedmen most need," Goodell declared.[63]

Antislavery opinion also criticized the Senate bill for doing either
too little or too much for the freed slaves. Could it not be changed "so
as to secure more complete & available *protection* . . . & also open
some door for the better care of the helpless among them?" an antislavery correspondent asked Sumner. On the other hand, abolitionist
Josephine S. Griffing commented that, in providing relief and protection for the emancipated blacks, the fact of their new status had to be
considered. "Even the Bureau bill, in the hands of our wisest legisla-
tors," she wrote, "did not steer clear of apprenticeship in fact, though
they did in form." There would be no safety for the freedmen until it

was understood that they "are now free by the laws of the country, and are to be treated as men, having their rights guarantied," she admonished. Horace Greeley warned against "any specious project for 'taking care' of the freedmen by . . . salaried superintendents."[64]

Despite disagreement over the most proper way to recognize the freedmen's status, consensus was reached on the temporary nature of the proposed bureau. This understanding was consistent with and reinforced both the laissez-faire position and traditional federalism. Assuming that the bureau would last only during the war, Thomas D. Eliot evidently believed no explicit time restriction was needed and hence put none in the House bill. But since the bureau would govern persons who otherwise were under state jurisdiction, Democrats, rejecting the Republicans' war powers justification, objected to it as unconstitutional. At the very least, they insisted on a time limitation in the bill, as assurance that no permanent policy of protection for blacks was intended. To clarify this point, Charles R. Buckalew of Pennsylvania proposed an amendment stating that the bureau would continue only during the rebellion.[65]

Republicans agreed without demur. "It is obvious to everyone that we cannot carry on this system within States in the Union represented here in Congress," declared Samuel C. Pomeroy, a member of the Senate emancipation committee. "These freedmen are to be citizens of the States, and when States come back into the Union we cannot undertake to exercise control over them." While some Republicans believed the bureau would be needed for a year or two after the war, the Senate accepted the wartime restriction.[66] This acceptance implied that the results of emancipation could be dealt with in the state-centered federal system, with such safeguards as the congressional plan of reconstruction, which was then under consideration, would provide.

With the Freedmen's bureau question deadlocked, before adjourning Congress tried to deal with freedmen's policy in a limited way as an aspect of the management of abandoned plantations. When passage of either the House or Senate bureau bill began to seem unlikely, Senator Lot M. Morrill of Maine proposed a supplementary abandoned property bill that authorized Treasury agents to lease lands and provide for the employment and general welfare of freedmen within Union lines. Accepting Morrill's argument that this provision would not change government policies but would merely give them a statutory basis, both houses approved the bill.[67] Treasury officials evidently regarded it as an indication of political support, for shortly thereafter the department issued a new set of regulations for the employment of former slaves on abandoned lands. The jurisdictional conflict between the War and Treasury Departments for control of freedmen's affairs thus continued, providing the context in which the Freedmen's Bureau bill of 1865 finally took shape.

NOTES

1. V. Jacque Voegeli, *Free But Not Equal: The Midwest and the Negro During the Civil War* (Chicago, 1967), *passim.*

2. Daniel S. Dickinson, *Speech at the Great Union War Ratification Meeting, October 8, 1862* (New York, 1862), 10; *Congressional Globe*, 37th Cong., 2d sess., 441 (January 22, 1862), remarks of Thaddeus Stevens, 2243 (May 20, 1862), remarks of Albert G. Riddle, App., 212 (May 25, 1862), remarks of Luther Hanchett, 1817 (April 24, 1862), remarks of Owen Lovejoy; *National Anti-Slavery Standard*, April 26, May 17, June 24, 1862.

3. *Congressional Globe*, 37th Cong., 2d sess., App., 322 (July 11, 1862), remarks of James Harlan.

4. Quoted in *Liberator*, December 5, 1862.

5. *National Anti-Slavery Standard*, January 4, 1862, letter of Gerrit Smith to John Gurley, December 16, 1861; *Congressional Globe*, 37th Cong., 2d sess., 1474-1477 (April 1, 1862), remarks of Daniel Clark and Lot M. Morrill. The proposal was defeated.

6. *Facts Concerning the Freedmen* (Boston, 1863), 3; James M. McPherson, *The Struggle for Equality: Abolitionists and the Negro in the Civil War and Reconstruction* (Princeton, 1964), 180-181; Boston *Commonwealth*, February 21, 1863, Memorial of the Emancipation League; *National Anti-Slavery Standard*, January 24, 1863, editorial; Robert Dale Owen, *The Policy of Emancipation* (Philadelphia, 1863), 36.

7. *Independent*, August 20, 1863, editorial; Boston *Commonwealth*, January 17, 31, 1863, editorials.

8. Ibid; *Report by the Committee of the Contrabands' Relief Commission of Cincinnati, Ohio, Proposing a Plan for the Occupation and Government of Vacated Territory in the Seceded States* (Cincinnati, 1863), 10-13; James E. Yeatman, *A Report on the Conditions of the Freedmen of the Mississippi, presented to the Western Sanitary Commission, December 17th, 1863* (St. Louis, 1864), 16.

9. Robert Dale Owen, Samuel Gridley Howe, and James McKaye formed the AFIC, which represented the antislavery establishment. Charles Sumner was influential in its creation. John G. Sproat, "Blueprint for Radical Reconstruction," *Journal of Southern History* 23 (February 1957): 33-34.

10. 38th Cong., 1st sess., *Senate Executive Documents*, No. 53, "Preliminary Report Touching the Condition and Management of Emancipated Refugees, Made to the Secretary of War by the American Freedmen's Inquiry Commission," June 30, 1863, 13-14; Samuel Gridley Howe to Charles Sumner, June 11, 1863, Howe Papers, Harvard University Library.

11. *Liberator*, February 13, 1863, letter of Parker Pillsbury to William Lloyd Garrison.

12. Boston *Commonwealth*, January 31, 1863, editorial.

13. F. P. Stanton, "The Freed Men of the South," *Continental Monthly* 2 (December 1862): 733; William H. Kimball, "Our Government and the Blacks," ibid., 5 (April 1864): 431-435; Charles D. Drake, *Union and Anti-slavery Speeches* (Cincinnati, 1864), 289; Michael Hahn, *What Is Unconditional Unionism? Speech at the Union Association of New Orleans* (New Orleans, 1863), 10.

14. Emma Willard, *Via Media: A Peaceful and Permanent Settlement of the Slavery Question* (Washington, D.C., 1862), 2-11; Samuel T. Glover, *Slavery in the United States—Emancipation in Missouri* (St. Louis, 1863), 7-13; Thomas Baird, *Memorial* (Pittsburgh, 1864), 13-14; Charles Ward, *Contrabands: Suggesting an Apprenticeship Under the Auspices of the Government, to Build the Pacific Railroad, January 8, 1863* (Salem, Mass., 1866), 3-5.

15. S. G. Howe to Charles Sumner, December 19, 1863, Howe Papers, Harvard University Library; Harold Schwartz, *Samuel Gridley Howe: Social Reformer 1801-1876* (Cambridge, Mass., 1956), 264-265.

16. 38th Cong., 1st sess., *Senate Executive Documents*, No. 53, "Final Report of the American Freedmen's Inquiry Commission to the Secretary of War," May 15, 1864, 73, 99, 109-110. See also Robert D. Owen, *The Wrong of Slavery, the Right of Emancipation, and the Future of the African Race in the United States* (New York, 1864); James McKaye, *The Mastership and Its Fruits: The Emancipated Slave Face to Face with His Old Master* (New York, 1864).

17. The first bill on the subject called for colonizing freed slaves in Florida, where they would be employed on confiscated lands and protected by government agents under military supervision. 37th Cong., H.R. No. 121, December 9, 1861, introduced by John Gurley; *Congressional Globe*, 37th Cong., 2d sess., App., 234 (May 26, 1862).

18. 37th Cong., S. No. 201, February 14, 1862, introduced by LaFayette Foster; Willie Lee Rose, *Rehearsal for Reconstruction: The Port Royal Experiment* (Indianapolis, 1964), 32-103; McPherson, *The Struggle for Equality*, 158-167; *Congressional Globe*, 37th Cong., 2d sess., 960 (February 26, 1862), remarks of Benjamin F. Wade, 1114 (March 7, 1862), remarks of John S. Carlile.

19. Rose, *Rehearsal for Reconstruction*, 200-201.

20. 37th Cong., S. No. 292, April 29, 1862, sec. 10. The measure was introduced by James Doolittle, conservative Republican from Wisconsin. Similar direct tax collection and freedmen's labor regulation bills were proposed by Francis P. Blair, Jr., Republican of Missouri in the House (H.R. No. 214, January 15, 1862), and Doolittle in the Senate (S. No. 121, December 18, 1861).

21. *Congressional Globe*, 38th Cong., 1st sess., 569 (February 10, 1864).

22. 37th Cong., H.R. No. 683, January 19, 1863; 38th Cong., H.R. No. 1, December 7, 1863, H.R. No. 51, December 22, 1863, January 13, 1864.

23. H.R. No. 683, sec. 1, 4; H.H. No. 1, sec. 1, 4; H.R. No. 51, December 22, 1863, sec. 5 (sec. 6 in amended bill).

24. H.R. No. 683, sec. 4; H.R. No. 1, sec. 4.

25. H.R. No. 51, sec. 5 (sec. 6 in amended bill, January 13, 1864).

26. H.R. No. 51, January 13, 1864, sec. 6.

27. H.R. No. 683, sec. 3; H.R. No. 1, sec. 3; *Congressional Globe*, 38th Cong., 1st

sess., 890 (March 1, 1864), remarks of Thomas D. Eliot, App., 45 (February 25, 1864), remarks of Henry Winter Davis; New Orleans *Tribune*, October 25, 1864, resolutions of the Convention of Colored Men, Syracuse, October 4, 1864.

28. *Congressional Globe*, 38th Cong., 1st sess., 568-570 (February 10, 1864).

29. Ibid., 572-573 (February 10, 1864).

30. Ibid., 773 (February 23, 1864), 888 (March 1, 1864).

31. Ibid., App., 54 (March 1, 1864), remarks of Anthony Knapp, 894 (March 1, 1864), remarks of William H. Wadsworth, 760 (February 19, 1864), remarks of Martin Kalbfleisch; 38th Congress, *House Reports*, Vol. I, No. 2, "Report of the Minority of the Select Committee on Emancipation on the bill to establish a Bureau of Freedmen's Affairs, Jan. 20, 1864," 3; *Congressional Globe*, 38th Cong., 1st sess., App., 54 (March 1, 1864), 891 (March 1, 1864), remarks of George Pendleton, 709-711 (February 17, 1864), remarks of S. S. Cox, 761 (February 19, 1864), remarks of Martin Kalbfleisch, App., 52 (March 1, 1864), remarks of Anthony Knapp.

32. "Report of the Minority of the Select Committee on Emancipation," 3; *Congressional Globe*, 38th Cong., 1st sess., 894 (March 1, 1864).

33. Ibid., 891 (March 1, 1864).

34. 38th Cong., S. No. 227, sec. 1, H.R. No. 51, May 25, 1864, sec. 1. Charles Sumner introduced S. No. 227 on April 12, 1864. It was then reported in the form of a substitute amendment to H.R. No. 51 on May 25.

35. H.R. No. 51, May 25, 1864, sec. 4.

36. Ibid., sec. 6.

37. Ibid., sec. 5-6.

38. LaWanda Cox, "The Promise of Land for the Freedmen," *Mississippi Valley Historical Review* 45 (December 1958): 415.

39. Charles Sumner to Charles Eliot Norton, May 2, 1864, Norton Papers, Harvard University Library.

40. Democrats Buckalew, Conness, and Carlile, and Republicans Brown and Pomeroy opposed the House bill. Only Sumner and Jacob Howard, a radical Republican, supported it. Pomeroy may have thought Eliot's bill unduly restrictive, for in subsequent debate he criticized excessive supervision of the freedmen. The Democrats may have been trying to create a deadlock between the two houses in an attempt to prevent any bill from passing. David H. Donald, *Charles Sumner and the Rights of Man* (New York, 1970), 175, notes that the reasons for rejecting the House bill are not entirely clear but suggests that the main reason was agreement with the AFIC view that freedmen and lands belonged under the same authority.

41. *Congressional Globe*, 38th Cong., 1st sess., 2799-2800 (June 8, 1864).

42. Ibid., 2801 (June 8, 1864), remarks of William A. Richardson, 3336 (June 28, 1864), remarks of Thomas H. Hicks, 3346 (June 28, 1864), remarks of Thomas A. Hendricks.

43. Ibid., 2972 (June 15, 1864).

44. *Congressional Globe*, 38th Cong., 1st sess., 3331 (June 28, 1864).

45. Donald, *Sumner and the Rights of Man*, 176.

46. *Congressional Globe*, 38th Cong., 1st sess., 3299 (June 27, 1864).

47. Ibid., 3299-3300, 3327 (June 28, 1864).

48. After discussion with Sumner, the critics withdrew other amendments, indicating that their purpose was to improve rather than obstruct the bill. Grimes withdrew a

proposal to remove the freedmen from the scope of the bureau commissioner's "general superintendence" (ibid., 3300), and Howe, a proposal to give "general superintendence" to all who applied for it, so that bureau rules would not be forced upon freedmen who could take care of themselves (ibid., 3330).

49. Ibid., 3329 (June 28, 1864).

50. Ibid., 3330, 3334-3335 (June 28, 1864).

51. Voegeli, *Free But Not Equal*, 58-61.

52. 38th Cong., House of Representatives, Select Committee on Emancipation, minutes of meetings, National Archives, R.G. 233, HR 38A-E 23.2.

53. *Congressional Globe*, 38th Cong., 1st sess., 3334-3335, 3337 (June 28, 1864).

54. Ibid., 3330 (June 28, 1864).

55. Richard H. Abbott, "Massachusetts and the Recruitment of Southern Negroes, 1863-1865," *Civil War History* 14 (September 1968): 198-199, 202-203.

56. *Congressional Globe*, 38th Cong., 1st sess., 3334 (June 28, 1864). Harlan, Howe, and Lane voted against Wilson's recruitment bill and for the Negro dispersal plan. Grimes and Brown criticized Wilson's bill but abstained on the vote approving it. Abbott, "Massachusetts and the Recruitment of Southern Negroes," 206.

57. *Congressional Globe*, 38th Cong., 1st sess., 3337 (June 28, 1864).

58. Ibid., 3341 (June 28, 1864).

59. Ibid., 3350 (June 28, 1864), 3527 (July 2, 1864).

60. Samuel Gridley Howe to Charles Sumner, December 19, 1863, January 8, 1864, Howe Papers, Harvard University Library.

61. Davis is quoted in Theodore Tilton to Charles Sumner (April 1864), Sumner Papers, Harvard University Library.

62. John Murray Forbes to Charles Sumner, April 11, 1864, Edward L. Pierce to Sumner, April 7, 1864, George W. Curtis to Sumner, April 15, 1864, Charles Eliot Norton to Sumner, May 7, 1864, C. B. Fesseden to Sumner, April 24, 1864, Sumner Papers, Harvard University Library; New York *Tribune*, April 12, 1864, editorial.

63. William Goodell to Sumner, April 13, 1864, Sumner Papers, Harvard University Library.

64. J. A. Hawley to Sumner, June 23, 1864, Horace Greeley to Sumner, February 7, 1865, Sumner Papers, Harvard University Library; *Liberator*, August 26, 1864, letter of J.S.G. on "Legislation for the Freedmen."

65. *Congressional Globe*, 38th Cong., 1st sess., 3300, 3346-3347 (June 28, 1864), remarks of Thomas S. Hendricks.

66. Ibid., 3301 (June 28, 1864).

67. Ibid., App., 256, 3325 (June 28, 1864), 3514 (July 2, 1864).

6

The freedmen's bureau
act of 1865

The ideas of laissez-faire legal equality that were evident in the debate on the freedmen's bureau bills of 1864 played a conspicuous part in formulating the act of March 1865. The single most important of these ideas was the principle of no discrimination according to color. Ironically, it was not the radicals with the reputation of being the special friends of the freedmen who insisted on this principle, but rather Republicans who sought to uphold the interest of loyal white refugees in the South. The Republicans regarded the proposal for a permanent department of freedmen's affairs, which the radicals now advocated, as an unwholesome and unsound form of guardianship. These same Republicans believed that emancipated slaves should be recognized as freemen or citizens and, in the contemporary idiom, should be left severely alone to make their own labor arrangements and provide for themselves. How the famous civil rights principle of no distinction according to color formed the basis for the Freedmen's Bureau Act of 1865 is the subject of this chapter.

Two main features marked the legislative situation with respect to freedmen's affairs in December 1864. The first was continued conflict between the War and Treasury Departments for control of freedmen's policy in the occupied South. As we have seen, the Treasury Department issued a new set of rules concerning the employment of freedmen on abandoned plantations. The Treasury rules were approved by antislavery radicals but opposed by army freedmen's officials, who persuaded Lincoln to suspend them. In certain locations, however, Treasury agents tried to implement the new instructions, and conflict between the War and Treasury Departments persisted.[1]

The second feature of the legislative situation was a recently inaugurated movement to aid loyal white refugees in the South. Early in the war, southern refugees had been assisted by the Sanitary Commission and by 1864 were attracting more widespread attention.[2] The American Freedmen's Inquiry Commission, for example, stated that the aid required by blacks was no different from that which southern whites fleeing from the Confederacy would need. Similarly, the commission compared the protection given the families of Negro soldiers with that required by the families of white men under the same conditions. Assessing the outlook for southern reconstruction, the Boston businessman and reformer Edward Atkinson suggested that a freedmen's bureau might be needed more to organize and civilize poor whites than emancipated blacks. The white refugee problem also contained obvious political significance, for southerners choosing not to remain within the contracting Confederacy formed a potential constituency for the Republican party.[3]

The American Union Commission (AUC), some of whose officers played an important part in shaping the final freedmen's bureau bill, was the principal organization for aiding loyal white refugees. Founded in 1864 by moderate antislavery reformers, the AUC from its inception aimed at rebuilding southern society along northern lines.[4] Refugees were not only to be given emergency relief, but their civil and social condition was also to be restored "upon the basis of industry, education, freedom, and Christian morality."[5] To promote this end, the AUC helped southern whites obtain seed and equipment for farming; transported refugees to their homes or relocated them in new ones; operated schools and industrial training homes; advocated temporary occupation of abandoned lands for immediate sustenance and recommended changes in land tenure; and urged emigration, new industry, and a free press in the South.[6] Adopting an argument usually applied only to blacks, the AUC also tried to keep poor whites in the South on the theory that they were unsuited to the climate, business, and customs of the North.[7]

The AUC had special significance for the evolution of the freedmen's bureau bill because of its assertion of the principle of no discrimination according to color as the basis for extending aid to south-

ern white refugees. According to Lyman Abbott, an officer of the
organization, AUC representatives were often asked in 1864-1865
whether care of the freedmen was part of its purpose and operations.
The answer to this question, Abbott explained, was emphatically to
affirm that "the American Union Commission recognizes no distinction of caste or color. It is organized to aid the people of the South—
not the black men because they are black, nor the white men because
they are white, but all men because they are *men*, upon the ground of a
common humanity alone." But Abbott went on to say that the association was careful to avoid duplication of charities and conflict of
organizations by maintaining cordial understanding and cooperation
with freedmen's aid societies.[8] In other words, the AUC acted as a
white refugee organization, but it did so under the idea—usually associated with the protection of Negro civil rights—that distinctions
should not be made according to race. As in its argument against poor
white immigration into the North, the AUC exhibited an unconven-
tional and ironic attitude of racial impartiality. Partly owing to the
efforts of the commission's leaders, this same attitude was to find expression in the drafting of the freedmen's bureau bill.

Alongside the work of assisting white refugees, freedmen's aid societies continued their endeavors and pressed their views on Congress
with the hope of securing a federal agency to supervise freedmen's
affairs.[9] At length, in February 1865, a committee of conference formulated a measure to resolve the differences between the House and
Senate freedmen's bills of 1864.[10] To solve the problem of choosing
between the War and Treasury Departments as a home for the bureau, the committee proposed to create a new department of freedmen's affairs. Furthermore, showing concern for the laissez-faire
criticism of the 1864 bills, it sought more clearly to recognize the freed
slaves' new status of civil liberty without, however, altering the basic
structure of supervision provided by the earlier measures.

The conference committee bill, which was chiefly the work of radicals Thomas D. Eliot and Charles Sumner, committed to the new department the "general superintendence of all freedmen" in the rebel
states and charged the commissioner, or head, with establishing regulations protecting former slaves in the enjoyment of their rights, promoting their welfare, and securing to them and their posterity the
blessings of liberty. Agents of the department, described as "advisory
guardians," were instructed to aid freedmen in adjusting their wages,

protect them against failure of contract, arbitrate their disputes, and assure fair trial for them if they became involved in litigation. The provision in the Senate bill of 1864 which authorized the bureau head to find homes and employment for freedmen whom he was unable to employ was retained in modified form in a section which allowed the commissioner, in such a situation, "to make provision" for former slaves with humane and suitable persons at a just compensation for their services. The conference report also stipulated that department agents should be deemed in the military and should be liable to trial by military commission for, among other crimes, willful oppression of any freedman. [11]

The conference committee made certain minor changes in the 1864 legislation, apparently for the purpose of allaying apprehension about excessive controls being placed on the freedmen. Department agents were no longer instructed to see that freedmen upheld their part of labor contracts into which they entered or to "organize" their labor. As though to assure laissez-faire critics that power would not be abused, the bill stated that the object of the department was "the good of the freedmen." The bill retained the declaration of the Senate measure that every freedman "shall be treated in all respects as a freeman, with all proper remedies in courts of justice, and no power or control shall be exercised with regard to him except in conformity with law." [12]

Land occupation arrangements in freedmen's bills provided an opportunity to recognize the civil liberty of emancipated Negroes. In this respect, the conference committee measure differed appreciably, though not fundamentally, from the 1864 legislation. The 1864 measure, in both Senate and House versions, primarily envisioned a system of plantation leases under which freed slaves would be employed as contract laborers. Only subordinately did it hold out the possibility of independent tenure. The conference bill reversed this order of priority by stating that abandoned lands should be rented or leased to freedmen, or should be permitted to be cultivated, used, or occupied by them for a one-year period, on terms to be agreed upon by the department and the former slaves. Lands not required for freedmen could be leased to others, in which case ex-slaves could be employed under voluntary contracts approved by the department. This provision was described by Thomas D. Eliot as a "material modification" of the 1864 legislation. Although it did not offer a clear expectation of permanent landownership because of the one-year limitation on freedmen's leases or occupation, in theory it pointed more directly to independent landholding than either of the previous bills.[13]

While the conference report tried to obviate the conflict between civilian and military authority evident in the passage of the 1864 bills, it failed to do so because the proposed new department, a civilian agency, was in a practical sense the equivalent of the Treasury. Therefore, at one level the issue remained the same as in 1864. But this formal jurisdictional dispute was now bound up with the controversy over how best to recognize the freedmen's liberty and rights.

Discussion of these issues outside Congress throws light on the legislative debate of February 1865 that produced the final freedmen's bureau bill. As in 1864, the argument for civilian control was in part based on the contention that the free labor policy of the military regime of General Banks in Louisiana imposed virtual and effective serfdom on emancipated blacks.[14] Proponents of a civilian agency also charged that army officers regarded the freed people as inferior and were indifferent to their interests and advancement.[15] Still another view was that the conference bill should be supported as an experimental measure, on the theory that any freedmen's measure was better than none at all.[16] Supporters of the conference bill believed, too, that it substantially recognized the rights of the freedmen. "Details are of less moment than principles," declared the radical *Independent*. "The point to be gained is that the rights of the freedmen and the obligations of the Government to them should be recognized and authoritatively affirmed.... The present bill seems to do that."[17]

Opponents of a civilian agency, who included army freedmen's officials actively lobbying against the conference bill, warned that without military protection the civil liberty of freed blacks was threatened by commercial and speculative interests seeking to control postemancipation affairs.[18] One critic argued that placing the freed people under the same authority as abandoned plantations gave "an unpleasant twinge, as if, after all, we still clung to the idea of slavery."[19] Not only had the Treasury leasing system seemed to fail, but experience also showed that blacks did better when they rented or occupied lands assigned them than when they entered labor contracts.[20] Many Negroes themselves emphatically declared that working for a share of the crop and the profit was preferable to working for mere wages. [21] Yet, the conference bill, critics pointed out, proposed a scheme of controlled labor as though the former slaves were incapable of supporting themselves. [22]

Political and bureaucratic rivalries formed a large part of the conflict between civilian and military control. [23] Ideas about freedmen's rights were also involved. Opponents of a civilian agency believed that military regulation was more consistent with a laissez-faire, equal rights approach to post-emancipation policy. Only the army, they reasoned, had the power to uproot the prejudicial codes and customs of slavery and protect freedmen's rights in the aftermath of abolition. [24] Once the war power had established freedmen's liberty on an equal rights basis, blacks should be left alone under the peacetime powers of the states. [25] A corollary of this laissez-faire outlook was an insistence on treating the races equally. "We do not want a civil control of the black man, while there is no civil control of the white man," an opponent of the conference bill wrote. [26] The military power which protected and aided whites should do the same for blacks. [27] Thus, although many antislavery men and women supported the conference bill, others saw the War Department as the proper place for the freedmen's bureau, in part because they wanted to avoid the danger of overlegislating for the former slaves. [28]

In the context of this public discussion, congressional debate on the conference bill reflected concern with the status of the freedmen and the degree of government regulation to which they should be subjected in contrast to other persons. The basic argument for the proposal, as in 1864, was that temporary care of the former slaves was a necessary corollary of the government's emancipation policy. The freed people were "unused to self-reliance and dependent for a season somewhat upon our sympathy and aid," declared Thomas D. Eliot, manager of the conference report in the House. Charles Sumner, reasoning that if the measure failed blacks would remain under a policy that made them "the mere accident of the Treasury," said the new department was needed to recognize and protect the freedmen's basic rights. [29]

Elaborating on this theme, Lot M. Morrill argued that because blacks possessed no security of personal right in the South, the government must mediate between them and their former masters by providing employment, support, and protection. William D. Kelley of Pennsylvania reasoned that the former slaves had no relationship to the country and its institutions other than life and nativity. In the rebel states, he pointed out, they could not be witnesses nor could they bring suit in court to protect themselves. Implying that the bill would rectify this situation, Kelley asserted: "We are to guide them, as the guardian guides his ward, for a brief period, until they can acquire habits and become confident and capable of self-control." In short, the government must organize the emancipated people into society. More sanguine than most others, Eliot and Sumner, the principal framers of the conference bill, confidently announced that it gave the freedmen every legal and civil right.[30]

As in the Senate debate of 1864, the leading critics of the bill were Republicans who attacked it from a laissez-faire point of view. The power of general superintendence which the bill extended over the freed people, together with the authority given the new department to "make provision" for them when unable to find employment, seemed in particular to subject blacks to undue restriction. Arguing that the fewer restraints imposed by government, "the sooner we shall make men of them," Representative James Wilson of Iowa urged that the freedmen be given entire responsibility for disposing of their own labor. In the Senate, fellow Iowan James Grimes objected that the proposal for Negro migration which he had supported in attenuated form in 1864 had been transformed in the present measure into a potential means of hiring out blacks for indefinite periods without their consent.[31]

Several Republicans protested that the bill rested on the assumption that the Negro race needed guardianship. According to John P. Hale of New Hampshire, it gave the lie to twenty years of abolitionist teaching that freed slaves could take care of themselves. Supporters of the bill had insisted that the regulations of the new department would affect the freed people only with their voluntary consent rather than coercively. Why then, asked John B. Henderson of Missouri, should government agents make bargains and contracts for them? William Sprague of Rhode Island contended that the bill would destroy the blacks in the same manner that government policies had destroyed the Indians. He therefore recommended giving the freedmen the power to protect themselves through the suffrage; then no special government agency would be needed.[32]

Similar criticism outside Congress suggests that to a greater extent than in 1864 these objections reflected more than mere intraparty political tensions. One Washington correspondent of antislavery out-look wrote sharply that the conference bill "contemplated a sort of serfdom as a substitute for slavery." "A majority of the antislavery men of the North," he added, "believe that if the negro must have a master, as the friends of Sumner's bill admitted by supporting it, it makes very little difference whether that master comes from South Carolina or from Massachusetts." [33]

While this kind of criticism from whites might be discounted ac-cording to whether its motivation was political, racial, or ideological-humanitarian, the laissez-faire point of view expressed by blacks possessed an undoubted cogency. The New Orleans *Tribune*, repre-senting the substantial free black community in Louisiana, approach-ed the freedmen's question from this perspective. Condemning the Treasury labor plan of 1864 as "mitigated bondage," the *Tribune* re-jected the notion that blacks needed superintendence. "Give the men of color an equal chance," advised the black journal, "and this is all they ask. Give them up at once to all the dangers of the horrid com-petitive system of modern commerce and civilization; and . . . they will, more quickly than their fellow white man, find a happy issue out of all their sufferings." The *Tribune* opposed "protection and tutor-ship" and recommended the creation of a board of elected freedmen to represent the emancipated population. But what blacks were given instead, complained the *Tribune*, was the conference committee freedmen's bureau bill: "the eternal question of tutorage, presented in its most complete and comprehensive form." Urging suffrage as self-protection, the black newspaper thus assailed "this final effort to domination." [34]

The most prominent black advocate of a laissez-faire post-emanci-pation policy was Frederick Douglass. In January 1862, when reform-ers and political men first began to ask what should be done with the freed slaves, Douglass expounded the view that he maintained throughout the war. "Do nothing with them," he wrote: "Your *doing* with them is their greatest misfortune." Three years later, adverting to the evident sympathy for Negroes among antislavery people, he of-fered the same advice. "I look over this country at the present time," he told the Massachusetts Anti-Slavery Society, "and I see Educa-tional Societies, Sanitary Commissions, Freedmen's Associations, and the like, —all very good: but . . . there is always more that is be-nevolent, I perceive, than just, manifested toward us." Attempts to "prop up the Negro" or prepare him for freedom were misconceived. The freedmen, Douglass concluded, should be given equal civil and political rights and be left to stand alone, and if they could not, then they must fall. Although he offered no specific comment on the freedmen's bureau bill, Douglass's laissez-faire arguments were implicitly critical of the articulated supervisory scheme of the conference committee. [35]

If the laissez-faire critique offered by the congressional Republicans reflected concern for the rights of blacks, their second major argument against the conference bill focused on the needs of white refugees in the South. Invoking the principle of no discrimination according to race, Republican critics insisted on equal rights for white southern war victims and objected to the conference report because of its exclusive attention to blacks. In part, this line of attack originated in the fear—conditioned generally by northern anti-Negro prejudice—that the freedmen might receive privileges and benefits not available to whites. The argument also reflected commitment to the idea that race was not a reasonable basis on which to classify or distinguish among people.

As on the guardianship issue, representatives from the racially sensitive midwestern states led the way in demanding aid for loyal white refugees. Republican Henry S. Lane of Indiana, noting the absence of any provision for white refugees in the conference report, commented sarcastically: "I have an old-fashioned way of thinking which induces me to believe that a white man is as good as a negro if he behaves himself." Pointing to the land provisions of the conference measure, John B. Henderson of Missouri asked why a distinction was made in favor of blacks over white men. James Grimes of Iowa asserted that destitute Unionist whites deserved the same advantages as emancipated slaves, while John P. Hale of New Hampshire objected to giving all the abandoned lands to the freedmen and declared: "in cases of this kind, I let the white and the black stand together." With evident pleasure, the Washington correspondent of the conservative New York *Herald* reported that Republicans—to the consternation and despair of Charles Sumner—were coming to the conclusion "that the poor white refugees of the South had some rights as well as the negroes." [36]

Although intraparty criticism was more pronounced than in the previous session, the conference report passed the House on February

9, 1865, with only four Republican votes cast in opposition.[37] One of these votes—that of Robert C. Schenck of Ohio—was particularly significant, for it appeared alongside an attempt to formulate an alternative freedmen's bill that would satisfy both the laissez-faire critics and those who desired to assist loyal white refugees.

As an indication of the considerable bipartisan support it would receive, Schenck's alternative plan originated in a Democratic resolution of January 1865 urging legislation to aid loyal southern refugees.[38] As chairman of the Committee on Military Affairs, to which the resolution was referred, Schenck on January 24 introduced a bill combining this purpose with aid to the freedmen. On February 9, he reported this freedmen and refugees bill back from committee with amendments.

Schenck's plan was to create in the War Department a bureau of refugees and freedmen which would continue during the rebellion and have effect in rebel states and in loyal districts within the operation of the army. Notably brief in comparison to previous freedmen's proposals, the bill contained only two substantive provisions. The first gave the bureau authority to supervise, manage, and control all subjects relating to refugees and freedmen, while the second authorized the president to provide relief assistance to freedmen and refugees and assign to the bureau for their benefit the temporary use of abandoned lands.[39]

On the same day that the House voted on the conference report, Schenck, who was regarded as an influential radical, presented his freedmen and refugees bill as a laissez-faire, equal rights alternative.[40] Assuming that a military framework was necessary for any freedmen's legislation, Schenck in presenting his plan stressed the temporary nature of the problem facing Congress. The condition of the freedmen was merely an incident of the war, he reasoned, and would end about the time the war concluded. Accordingly, he believed there was no need to create a permanent department of government to deal with post-emancipation affairs.[41]

Schenck's most telling argument invoked the principle of no distinction according to color within the framework of laissez-faire legal equality. In contrast to the bill of the conference committee, he pointed out, the proposal of the military affairs committee "makes no discrimination on account of color." This feature, he said, was a "peculiarity" of the plan. Faithful to the laissez-faire point of view, Schenck added that the principal danger for both freedmen and white refugees was that too much government assistance would encourage them to remain paupers. Thus, the purpose of the bill was to put the former slaves and white refugees "in a condition to shift for themselves and become independent of this help from the authorities of the country at the earliest time." [42]

Schenck's attempt to formulate and win support for an alternative freedmen's bureau bill was abetted by the American Union Commission. In early January, upon learning of the House resolution directing an inquiry into the condition of loyal refugees, the president of the AUC, Joseph P. Thompson, wrote to Schenck describing the work of his organization and requesting a conference. [43] Representatives of the AUC then went to Washington and circulated among members of Congress a memorial outlining the white refugee problem and recommending a course of action. [44] At the invitation of a bipartisan group which included a few members of Congress, the AUC held a public meeting at the Capitol on February 12, 1865, to publicize the loyal white refugee issue and to win backing for Schenck's bill. Among several speakers in the hall of the House of Representatives, Joseph P. Thompson and the black abolitionist Henry Highland Garnet underscored the laissez-faire theme in rejecting the idea of class legislation and in cautioning against a long state of dependence for both blacks and whites. [45] Meanwhile, army freedmen's officials John Eaton and Asa Fiske tried to influence opinion against the bill of the conference committee. [46]

On February 18, Schenck brought the freedmen and refugees bill to the floor of the House. Although the conference bill had already been approved and was awaiting action in the Senate, the chances of passing the new measure appeared good. On its introduction, both Republicans and Democrats had expressed support. Democrat John Chanler of New York called it a "pertinent, wise, and proper" means of caring for the emancipated blacks. The New York *Times*, reflecting moderate Republican opinion, praised Schenck's bill as much more satisfactory than the "cumbersome, . . . impracticable, and ineffective" bill of the conference committee. Given this favorable response and the subsequent AUC lobbying effort, a solid base of support quickly emerged which enabled the measure to pass without debate. As he brought the bill to a vote, Schenck reminded members that it was "broad and general in character and makes no distinction on account of color." By voice vote that was almost unanimous, the House agreed to follow Schenck's recommendation of approving the freedmen and refugees plan and letting the Senate choose between it and the conference bill. [47]

In the upper chamber, meanwhile, Charles Sumner on February 13 brought forward the conference committee bill, arguing that the choice was between this measure and none at all. [48] Other issues took precedence, however, and by the time Sumner got the matter to the floor again on February 21, the Schenck bill stood as an alternative. Significantly, it received immediate and bipartisan backing.

As they attacked the conference report for its paternalistic restrictions on blacks and neglect of white refugees, laissez-faire critics referred approvingly to the new House bill. James Grimes stated that it accomplished all that was necessary, in language that had a definite and well-understood meaning in contrast to the merely rhetorical guarantees of liberty contained in the conference proposal. Democrat Reverdy Johnson of Maryland believed the House bill met the needs of both former slaves and loyal white refugees. After two days of debate, the Senate rejected the conference report, 14 to 24, with twelve Republicans joining Democrats and border state conservatives in opposition. A second committee of conference was then requested. [49]

The second conference committee, consisting entirely of members who had sat on neither the House nor Senate emancipation or freedmen's committees, reported a measure substantially in accord with the Schenck bill. [50] It proposed to establish a bureau of refugees, freedmen, and abandoned lands within the War Department, to continue during the rebellion and for one year thereafter. Within rebel states and in districts embraced by the operations of the army, the bureau was to exercise supervision and management of abandoned lands and to control all subjects relating to refugees and freedmen. As in Schenck's bill, provision was made for immediate relief of destitute refugees and freedmen. The section of the bill dealing with land was more elaborate and extensive than the corresponding section in the Schenck measure. The commissioner of the bureau was authorized to set aside abandoned and confiscated lands and to assign forty acres to each male citizen, whether freedman or refugee. After three years' use of the land at rent equal to 6 percent of its value, the freedman and refugee occupants could purchase it and receive "such title as the United States can convey." [51]

The most significant feature of this bill was its abandonment of the idea that the freedmen should be contract laborers under the indefinite supervisory power of a new government department. The first conference report, it is true, theoretically gave first call on the land to the freed blacks, with secondary provision for leases to other persons. Nevertheless, defenders of the bill seemed to envision the former slaves continuing as plantation laborers under a contract labor system essentially the same as existing Treasury Department arrangements.[52] In contrast, the second conference bill envisioned the freedmen as independent farmers, perhaps even as property owners, under their own supervision. Absent were provisions instructing bureau agents to help freed slaves adjust or apply their labor, as well as the stipulation authorizing the commissioner to "make provision" for them. Also omitted were all references to bureau agents acting as advisory guardians, arbitrators, or next friends of the freedmen in court proceedings.

A degree of federal intervention was necessary, as laissez-faire critics conceded. However, placing the bureau in the War Department, limiting its existence to a definite period, and charging it with emergency aid and support would minimize the government's role. The conference committee headed by Schenck further expressed its antipaternalistic attitude in giving the bureau control over "subjects relating to freedmen and refugees" rather than giving the commissioner an express general power to superintend and regulate the freedmen themselves as in earlier bills. In the view of its supporters, the language of the latter proposals was indeed designed to prevent the power of the bureau from being restricted to that of mere arbitration of legal questions involving emancipated slaves.[53] The Schenck formulation, while it did not refer to the adjustment and determination of questions concerning the freedmen—which would have been tantamount to arbitration—seemed to point in that direction. Though it would not necessarily lead to significant differences in practice, the Schenck conference proposal was intended to limit the power of the bureau and to express more clearly the commitment of the bill's framers to the idea that emancipated slaves were freemen with ordinary civil rights.

Although laissez-faire civil equality purposes characterized the second conference bill, the forty-acre provision has usually been cited as the most important feature of the legislation. In particular, it has been taken as evidence of a more radical commitment to give land to the freedmen. [54] The intention of Congress in the second conference plan, however, was to allow temporary use of rebel estates, with the rather remote possibility of subsequent ownership, rather than to extend a firm promise of a title in fee simple.

The closest Congress ever came to promising land to the freedmen was the approval by the House in 1864 of a southern homestead bill which proposed to give outright forty or eighty acres of public land to Union soldiers and army laborers regardless of color. But only in a very limited and indirect sense can this piece of legislation be viewed as a freedmen's bill. [55] The freedmen's bureau legislation of 1864 contained no promise of land to former slaves, and though the first conference report theoretically proposed to place them on the soil, this arrangement was to be only temporary. "The time has come," said Charles Sumner in February 1865, "when they should enjoy the results of their labor at least for a few months." [56]

While friends of the freedmen urged temporary use of rebel estates, proponents of aid to white refugees broached the same idea. Joseph P. Thompson of the AUC thus recommended that white southern refugees be permitted to occupy abandoned lands in order to support themselves temporarily, and Schenck's original bill expressly proposed "the temporary use of abandoned lands and tenements" for the benefit of freedmen and refugees. [57] The second conference bill called for specific assignment of forty-acre plots and omitted the word "temporary," but, since Schenck was a member of the committee that drafted this proposal, it seems reasonable to suppose that it comported with his original purpose. Whether the conference committee intended anything more depended on the title that Congress could convey after three years, and this was a big question mark. [58]

It is nevertheless true that Congress proposed to assist the freedmen in ways that conceivably could lead to land redistribution. Equally, if not more, important than this potential economic support was the recognition of the status and rights of freemanship that land occupation, in contrast to contract labor arrangements, implied. The significance of this civil recognition can be seen in the position taken by the black New Orleans *Tribune* on the question of land and the freedmen. In condemning the Treasury Department's plantation leasing and contract labor policy, the *Tribune* proposed in early 1865 that black laborers join black and white managers in a system of associated farming. This system would allow emancipated slaves to feed and clothe themselves, go where they pleased, and become self-reliant, the *Tribune* explained. By receiving a low basic wage to cover necessities, the freed slaves would most importantly acquire a share of the crop and become partners in the enterprise.[59] Such a sharecropping arrangement would not only offer an economic incentive, but it would also recognize more clearly than contract labor the former slaves' status as freemen.[60] A recent study of southern freedmen confirms this finding by pointing out that blacks were more concerned with the form of their labor—that it be consistent with and reflect their status as freemen—than with the actual level of wages.[61] Thus, by providing for independent land occupation, albeit temporary, Schenck's bill and the second conference committee proposal contained a laissez-faire and civil rights dimension absent in earlier freedmen's bureau plans.

On March 3, 1865, the final day of the session, Congress enacted the second conference bill by voice vote. Senate approval came after very brief debate, while the House, having already agreed to substantially the same measure in the form of Schenck's bill, concurred with no discussion at all.[62] Two years after the first proposal had been introduced, Republican lawmakers had finally created a freedmen's bureau.

In analyzing congressional action, it appears that clearer recognition of the status of the former slaves as freemen was an important difference between the final bill and earlier versions. Even at the end disagreement persisted on this issue as a few members on both sides of the aisle objected to what they still regarded as undue coercion of the freedmen.[63] There can be no doubt, however, that the inclusion of white refugees in the bill was a decisive consideration in its enactment. This provision had not been present in any form in earlier freedmen's legislation. Its rapid acceptance in Schenck's bill, after the House had already approved the first conference committee report, suggests that it was of equal, if not greater, importance in creating the bureau than the abandonment of the guardianship idea.

Although they were not disinterested observers, there seems to be no reason to doubt the testimony of American Union Commission representatives that the inclusion of white refugees was decisive. A few months later, Joseph P. Thompson wrote to the commissioner of the Freedmen's Bureau, General O. O. Howard, stating that the principal objections to the first conference bill of Eliot and Sumner were fear of bureaucratic abuse in the creation of a new department and the bill's exclusive concern for blacks. The alternative proposal of Robert C. Schenck and the second conference bill based upon it, Thompson explained, attracted much wider support, including that of many Democrats, because it was not exclusive. "This accounts for the naming of the Refugees first; and but for this combination," Thompson averred, "*no* bill for Freedmen could have passed the last Congress." Lyman Abbott, also an officer of the AUC, wrote that prejudice against Negroes threatened to prevent any freedmen's bureau bill from passing until a broader approach that included white refugees was undertaken.[64]

The idea that government should make no distinction among people on the basis of color had been in the past, and in future was to become even more closely, associated with the blacks' attempt to secure political and civil equality. It was highly ironic that under this principle southern white refugees were brought under the protection of the Freedmen's Bureau. In 1866, the American Union Commission, which helped shape this outcome, endorsed the nondiscrimination idea in a way that throws light on its use in the formation of the bureau.

Early in 1866, the AUC and several freedmen's aid societies, run mainly by abolitionists, agreed to combine their organizations. They were unable to agree on the purpose of the merged association and thus could not decide on a name. According to Lyman Abbott, the freedmen's groups were reluctant to give up the advantage which their exclusive and limited purpose of assisting blacks (signified in the names of their organizations) gave them in the eyes of a large segment of the northern public. The AUC on the other hand, in order to allay sectional hostility and promote reunification, believed that whites should be aided and that race should not be a consideration in the operations of the new organization. The name of the body, AUC representatives held, should reflect this outlook by containing no reference whatever to race or to the freedmen.[65] The upshot was a compromise in which, though the name "freedmen" was retained, whites were to be included and distinctions of race and color were to be disregarded.[66] Abbott considered the result a vindication of his position. He later wrote: "the radical abolitionists, who had insisted on no distinction because of race or color when that principle was of benefit to the negro, could not deny it because it was of benefit to the white man."[67]

Just this kind of compromise seems to have been reached in Congress in February 1865. Robert C. Schenck said as much when he pointedly observed that the "peculiarity" of his refugees and freedmen's bureau bill was that it made "no discrimination on account of color—a favorite phrase, as is well understood, in these days among us all."[68]

The use of the nondiscrimination principle in the formation of the Freedmen's Bureau reflected at once resentment against blacks and commitment to the ideal of racially impartial legal equality. That both antislavery Republicans and Democratic lawmakers could be apprehensive lest blacks receive preferential treatment says much about the inability of Americans in the 1860s to comprehend the dimensions of the race question and the circumstances in which emancipation left the freed people. Even before the abolition of slavery had been fully accomplished, political representatives were sensitive to what has been described in more recent times as "reverse discrimination." At the same time, the use of the nondiscrimination principle in conjunction with the doctrine of laissez-faire legal equality represented a concession to racial egalitarianism. Republicans applied the egalitarian idea in opposing the Eliot-Sumner conference bill as a coercive and paternalistic system of guardianship which denied blacks status as freemen, and then in insisting that loyal white refugees had an equal right to any federal assistance to relieve the dislocation and suffering caused by the war.

Given the dominance of the idea of equality before the law in mid-nineteenth century America, the logic of the situation made the application and acceptance of the principle of no discrimination according to color irresistible. Yet, if it was true that including white refugees was the only way to secure the passage of freedmen's bureau legislation, as Thomas D. Eliot later conceded, [69] and if the bureau protected the rights and well being of the emancipated slaves, as most historical accounts agree it did, then ironic as the use of the nondiscrimination principle was in 1865, in a larger sense it was consistent with the historic purpose of the idea as an instrument for achieving black equality before the law.

NOTES

1. 38th Cong., 1st sess., *House Executive Documents*, No. 3, "Report of the Secretary of the Treasury on the State of the Finances for the Year 1864: General Regulations Concerning Commercial Intercourse, Abandoned Property, and the Employment and General Welfare of Freedmen," 321-324; *Liberator*, August 19, 1864, letter of "M. DuPays"; John Eaton, *Grant, Lincoln and the Freedmen: Reminiscences of the Civil War* (New York, 1907), 167-168; Thomas W. Conway to Nathaniel S. Banks, September 30, October 18, 27, 1864, Banks Papers, Library of Congress; Howard K. Beale, ed., *The Diary of Gideon Welles* (3 vols.; New York, 1960), II, 150; Paul S. Pierce, *The Freedmen's Bureau: A Chapter in the History of Reconstruction* (Iowa City, Ia., 1904), 24-25; George R. Bentley, *A History of the Freedmen's Bureau* (Philadelphia, 1955), 44-45.

2. Boston *Commonwealth*, April 8, 1864; Eaton, *Grant, Lincoln and the Freedmen*, 37-38; Pierce, *Freedmen's Bureau*, 31.

3. 38th Cong., 1st sess., *Senate Executive Documents*, No. 53, "Final Report of the American Freedmen's Inquiry Commission to the Secretary of War," May 15, 1864, 109; [Edward Atkinson], "The Future Supply of Cotton," *North American Review* 98 (April 1864): 497; Eaton, *Grant, Lincoln and the Freedmen*, 38.

4. [Lyman Abbott], *The American Union Commission: Its Origin, Operations and Purposes* (New York, 1865), 1-2; Lyman Abbott, "Southern Evangelization," *New Englander* 23 (October 1864): 699-708; *Report to the Contributors to the Pennsylvania Relief Association for East Tennessee* (Philadelphia, 1864), 26-27.

5. Circular of the American Union Commission (n.p., n.d.), National Archives, RG 105, M-752, roll 13.

6. Ibid.; American Union Commission, *Speeches of Hon. W. Dennison, J. P. Thompson, N. G. Taylor, J. R. Doolittle, J. A. Garfield . . . Washington, February 12, 1865* (New York, 1865), 19-22.

7. Petition of the Refugee Relief Commission of Ohio, National Archives, RG 233, 38A-B1.

8. [Abbott], *The American Union Commission*, 3-4, 23.

9. Bentley, *Freedmen's Bureau*, 46-48; Josephine S. Griffing to Lyman Trumbull, August 10, 1864, Trumbull Papers, Library of Congress.

10. The conference committee included Republicans Thomas D. Eliot, William D. Kelley, and Democrat Warren P. Noble from the House, and Republicans Charles Sumner, Jacob Howard, and Democrat Charles R. Buckalew from the Senate.

11. 38th Cong., H.R. No. 51, sec. 4, 6, 9, 12, Report of Conference Committee, *Congressional Globe*, 38th Cong., 2d sess., 563 (February 2, 1865).

12. H.R. No. 51, sec. 1, 4.

13. H.R. No. 51, sec. 5; *Congressional Globe*, 38th Cong., 2d sess., 564 (February 2, 1865); LaWanda Cox, "The Promise of Land for the Freedmen," *Mississippi Valley Historical Review* 45 (December 1958): 417.

14. New Orleans *Tribune*, December 10, 1864; Worcester *Daily Spy*, February 6, 24, 27, 1865; *Independent*, March 2, 1865.

15. Boston *Journal*, February 1, 1865, Washington correspondence; Washington

Chronicle, February 9, 1865, letter on freedmen's affairs.

16. Ibid., editorial on freedmen; *Independent*, February 9, 1865, editorial.

17. Ibid.

18. Eaton, *Grant, Lincoln and the Freedmen*, 224.

19. Washington *Chronicle*, February 8, 1865, letter on freedmen's affairs in Congress.

20. Ibid.; Louis S. Gerteis, *From Contraband to Freedman: Federal Policy Toward Southern Blacks, 1861-1865* (Westport, Conn., 1973), 169-171.

21. New Orleans *Tribune*, September 10, 24, 1864, January 28, 1865; New York Evening *Post*, January 26, 1865, report of National Freemen's Relief Association meeting.

22. Washington *Chronicle*, February 13, 1865, letter on freedmen's affairs; *Independent*, January 26, 1865, letter on the Freedmen's Bureau.

23. Gerteis, *From Contraband to Freedman*, 147-149.

24. John Eaton, Public Letter, February 6, 1864, enclosed in letter of Thomas D. Eliot to Charles Sumner, March 7, 1864, Sumner Papers, Harvard University Library; Eaton, *Grant, Lincoln and the Freedmen*, 226; New York *Times*, February 9, 1865, editorial; *Independent*, January 26, 1865, letter on Freedmen's Bureau by F.A.S.

25. Washington *Chronicle*, February 13, 1865, letter on freedmen's affairs.

26. *Independent*, January 12, 1865, letter on Freedmen's Bureau by F.A.S.

27. Washington *Chronicle*, February 8, 1865, letter on freedmen's affairs in Congress; Eaton letter, February 6, 1864, in Eliot to Sumner, March 7, 1864, Sumner Papers, Harvard University Library.

28. *Liberator*, December 9, 1864, letter of "M. DuPays"; Josephine S. Griffing to Charles Sumner (November 1864), Sumner Papers, Harvard University Library; Springfield *Weekly Republican*, February 11, 1865, editorial.

29. *Congressional Globe*, 38th Cong., 2d sess., 768 (February 13, 1865), remarks of Charles Sumner, 988 (February 22, 1865), remarks of Lot Morrill, 564 (February 9, 1865), remarks of Thomas D. Eliot.

30. Ibid., 988 (February 22, 1865), remarks of Lot M. Morrill, 689, 693 (February 9, 1865), remarks of Thomas D. Eliot and William D. Kelley, 961 (February 22, 1865), remarks of Charles Sumner.

31. Ibid., 689 (February 9, 1865), 959 (February 21, 1865).

32. Ibid., 985 (February 22, 1865), 960, 963 (February 21, 1865).

33. Cincinnati *Daily Commercial*, February 28, 1865, Washington letter from "Mack."

34. New Orleans *Tribune*, February 7, 1865, September 10, 18, 1864, January 8, March 12, 1865.

35. Philip S. Foner, ed., *The Life and Writings of Frederick Douglass* (4 vols.; New York, 1955), III, 188-189, IV, 164.

36. *Congressional Globe*, 38th Cong., 2d sess., 984-985 (February 22, 1865), 959, 962 (February 21, 1865); New York *Herald*, February 23, 1865, Washington correspondence.

37. *Congressional Globe*, 38th Cong., 2d sess., 694 (February 9, 1865), The vote was 64 to 62.

38. Resolution introduced by John Law of Indiana, January 5, 1865, National Ar-

chives, RG 233, 38A-B1. The resolution was referred to the Committee on Military Affairs.

39. 38th Cong., H.R. No. 698, sec. 1-2, MS, National Archives, RG 233, 38A-B1; *Congressional Globe*, 38th Cong., 2d sess., 691 (February 9, 1865).

40. Schenck, a former Whig, served as brigadier general of volunteers in 1861-1862. Injured at the second battle of Bull Run, he left the army and, partly at the request of Lincoln and Stanton, ran against Democrat Clement L. Vallandigham for a seat in the Thirty-eighth Congress. The correspondent of the Cincinnati *Gazette* characterized Schenck as "particularly hated of all Democrats, who make it a point sometimes not to listen to him, but after Thad Stevens and Winter Davis no Unionist is surer of attention to what he has to say." Kenneth W. Wheeler, ed., *For the Union: Ohio Leaders in the Civil War* (Columbus, Ohio, 1968), 24-25; Cincinnati *Gazette*, January 24, 1865, Washington correspondence.

41. *Congressional Globe*, 38th Cong., 2d sess., 691 (February 9, 1865).

42. Ibid.

43. Joseph P. Thompson to Robert C. Schenck, January 9, 1865, National Archives, RG 233, 38A-B1.

44. Joseph P. Thompson to O. O. Howard, May 20, 1865, Howard Papers, Bowdoin College Library.

45. American Union Commission, *Speeches . . . Feb. 12, 1865*, 6, 19; Henry Highland Garnet, *A Memorial Discourse . . . February 12, 1865* (Philadelphia, 1865), 85-86; Washington *Chronicle*, February 13, 1865; Boston *Journal*, February 13, 1865, Washington correspondence. Garnet spoke earlier in the day, Sunday, February 12, independently of the AUC meeting which was held in the evening.

46. John Eaton to Alice Eaton, February 3, 1865, Eaton Papers, University of Tennessee Library; Eaton, *Grant, Lincoln and the Freedmen*, 224.

47. *Congressional Globe*, 38th Cong., 2d sess., 693 (February 9, 1865), 908 (February 18, 1865), 989 (February 22, 1865), remarks of Reverdy Johnson; New York *Times*, February 9, 1865. During the Senate debate on the conference bill, Johnson stated that the vote in the House on Schenck's bill was almost unanimous.

48. Ibid., 768 (February 13, 1865).

49. Ibid., 959 (February 21, 1865), 989-990 (February 22, 1865). Republicans voting against the conference report were Cowan, Dixon, Doolittle, Grimes, Hale, Harlan, Harris, Henderson, Howe, Lane of Indiana, Ten Eyck, and Trumbull. Seven were westerners, five easterners.

50. The conference committee included Schenck and Boutwell, Republicans, and Rollins, a Democrat, from the House, and Republicans Wilson and Harlan and border state Unionist Willey of West Virginia from the Senate.

51. H.R. No. 51, sec. 1, 3-4, *Congressional Globe*, 38th Cong., 2d sess., 1182 (February 28, 1865).

52. *Congressional Globe*, 38th Cong., 2d sess., 689 (February 9, 1865), remarks of Thomas D. Eliot, 988 (February 22, 1865), remarks of Lot M. Morrill.

53. William Whiting, *War Powers Under the Constitution of the United States*, 43d ed. (Boston, 1871), 464.

54. Cox, "The Promise of Land for the Freedmen," 413-440; William S. McFeely, *Yankee Stepfather: General O. O. Howard and the Freedmen* (New York, 1968),

104-105; M. L. Benedict, *The Impeachment and Trial of Andrew Johnson* (New York, 1973), 38.

55. 38th Cong., H.R. No. 276, February 29, 1864, introduced by George W. Julian; *Congressional Globe*, 38th Cong., 1st sess., 1187-1188 (March 18, 1864), remarks of George W. Julian.

56. Ibid., 38th Cong., 2d sess., 961 (February 21, 1865).

57. American Union Commission, *Speeches . . . Feb. 12, 1865*, 20; H.R. No. 698, sec. 2, February 9, 1865.

58. Gerteis, *From Contraband to Freedman*, 187.

59. New Orleans *Tribune*, January 28, 29, February 2, 1865.

60. August Meier, "Negroes in the First and Second Reconstruction," *Civil War History* 13 (June 1967): 122, observes that sharecropping began as a compromise between the blacks' desire to own or rent land and the plantation owners' desire to have the freedmen work for wages under contract.

61. Gerteis, *From Contraband to Freedman*, 167.

62. *Congressional Globe*, 38th Cong., 2d sess., 1307-1308 (March 2, 1865), 1348, 1402 (March 3, 1865).

63. Conservative Lazarus Powell of Kentucky said the bill placed "overseers and negro-drivers" over the freedmen, while Republican Jacob Howard of Michigan criticized it for imposing a military government on the former slaves. Ibid., 1307-1308 (March 2, 1865).

64. Joseph P. Thompson to O. O. Howard, May 20, 1865, Howard Papers, Bowdoin College Library; [Lyman Abbott], *The Results of Emancipation in the United States of America* (New York, 1867), 18.

65. Lyman Abbott, *Reminiscences* (Boston, 1915), 251, 260-261.

66. *The American Freedman*, I (May 1866), 18, Constitution of the American Freedmen's Union Commission.

67. Abbott, *Reminiscences*, 261.

68. *Congressional Globe*, 38th Cong., 2d sess., 691 (February 9, 1865). Thomas D. Eliot denied that the first conference bill discriminated in favor of blacks. It merely recognized, Eliot said, that the time had come to pass legislation on their behalf. Ibid., 693 (February 9, 1865).

69. In 1868, Eliot said that it would have taken another year to create the Freedmen's Bureau had it not been for Schenck's suggestion that white refugees also be brought under the provisions of the bill. Ibid., 40th Cong., 2d sess., 1815 (March 11, 1868).

7

Civil rights, federalism, and the thirteenth amendment

By the beginning of 1865, ultimate Union victory seemed assured, but Republican lawmakers had yet to come to grips with the freedmen's question. The bill for creating a freedmen's bureau was deadlocked in conference committee, as we have seen. Meanwhile, an attempt to revive the Wade-Davis bill with a provision for limited Negro suffrage had failed, and with it the possibility, by recognizing the Hahn government in Louisiana, of reaching a compromise with the president on reconstruction.[1] This circumstance gave added importance to the last of the wartime measures in which Republicans dealt with the rights of emancipated slaves, the Thirteenth Amendment. Here was an opportunity to clarify the status of the freed people and contribute materially to the disposition of the reconstruction issue.

The obvious correlation between the defeat of the Confederacy and the abolition of slavery gives the Thirteenth Amendment an aspect of inevitability. Whereas the Fourteenth Amendment readily appears as the result of a political struggle that conceivably could have had a different outcome, it is difficult to think of the drive for emancipation having any other conclusion than the terse command that "Neither slavery nor involuntary servitude . . . shall exist within the United States." In fact, the passage of the Thirteenth Amendment in 1865 was far from inevitable. Strongly opposed by conservatives, its approval was in doubt until the final congressional vote was recorded.

Although the Wade-Davis reconstruction bill seemed to provide the most expedient course of antislavery action in 1864, there were incontrovertible reasons for pursuing the abolition of slavery by constitutional amendment. Foremost among them were the legal uncertainty and incompleteness of previous antislavery actions. The Confiscation Act of 1862 freed only the slaves of rebels and operated only in insurrectionary districts. The Emancipation Proclamation secured personable liberation where Union armies gave it practical effect, but, besides omitting the border states, it exempted large portions of the seceded region.[2] Referring to these two measures, Senator Daniel Clark of New Hampshire summarized the constitutional logic of the situation: "Whatever be their force and extent, no one pretends they altered or abolished the laws of servitude in any of the slave states."[3]

Accordingly, the Republicans introduced several propositions for an antislavery amendment at the start of the Thirty-eighth Congress. In April 1864, the Senate approved what eventually became the Thirteenth Amendment, but House Republicans were unable to secure the two-thirds majority needed to approve a constitutional change. Throughout the second half of 1864, the success of the amendment seemed to grow more doubtful, and with the failure of Grant's Virginia campaign a reaction against insisting on abolition as a condition of peace set in. This reaction was manifested in Secretary Seward's moderate speech on reconstruction of September, which contained no reference to the proposed abolition amendment. As Congress assembled in December, the fate of the proposal remained uncertain.[4]

So far from being a foregone conclusion, the passage of the Thirteenth Amendment on January 31, 1865, came only after an intense effort was undertaken to secure needed Democratic votes. Organized by the Republican Secretary of State, the Seward lobby for the amendment was part of an attempt to create a broad-based conservative Union party by repudiating both radical Republicans and Copperhead Democrats.[5] The amendment was particularly important for this purpose because, by abolishing slavery, it gave promise of eliminating the divisive Negro question from national politics. Radicals on the other hand could be counted on to support the measure, even if it did not go so far in protecting freedmen's rights as some of them might have preferred.

Unlike the Fourteenth Amendment in 1866, the framing of the Thirteenth Amendment occasioned little controversy among Republicans. This was owing to the consensus that prevailed on the meaning of slavery and abolition and to the almost universal disposition to rely on the Northwest Ordinance, the historic instrument of antislavery purpose, to accomplish the reform. While several proposals were submitted, the version that was overwhelmingly favored was explicitly based on the 1787 territorial ordinance. Introduced by Missouri Senator John B. Henderson, it declared: "Neither slavery nor involuntary servitude, except as a punishment for crime whereof the party shall have been duly convicted, shall exist within the United States, or any place subject to their jurisdiction." A second section stated: "Congress shall have power to enforce this article by appropriate legislation."[6]

The Northwest Ordinance had, of course, long occupied a preeminent place in antislavery history. Its words of prohibition went directly into the constitutions of five states and, in somewhat different form, into five others.[7] The Wilmot Proviso of 1846, which was intended to keep slavery out of territory acquired from Mexico, used the language of the ordinance, and when Congress legislated freedom for the national territories in 1862, it enacted the historic prohibition of 1787. As the Republican editor Horace White observed, the phraseology of the ordinance was "among the household words of the nation."[8] Hence, it was all but inevitable that the old territorial law would be used to abolish slavery.

As the culmination of the abolition movement, the Thirteenth Amendment was invested with a variety of meanings and purposes. Most pervasive, indeed so fundamental as hardly to require elaboration, was the belief that the amendment would remove what all Republicans agreed was the cause of the war. Speaking in this vein, Republicans referred not so much to slavery as an institution, but to the political power that the slave states had wielded.[9] A more specific purpose concerned the question of a negotiated peace. While publicly Lincoln's announced peace terms in 1864 included complete abolition of slavery, privately he broached the possibility that acceptable terms might allow slavery to continue in some attenuated form, as by a prospective ratification of the abolition amendment by the rebel states to take effect several years later. It was to head off any such compromise that many Republicans supported the amendment in December 1864.[10]

Still another specific purpose of the Thirteenth Amendment was to remove slavery and race from American politics.[11] Conservative

Unionists in particular anticipated this result. The Washington *Evening Star* hailed the passage of the amendment as enabling Americans to become a homogeneous people with common interests and views. Kentucky Unionist George Yeaman described it as the basis for a new political unity and argued that approval of the amendment would rob radicals of their power. "When the whole people can stand united on this amendment as an accomplished fact," Yeaman asserted in January 1865, "they will speedily abandon or indignantly reject the other dangerous schemes that are now associated with this in the public mind." Democrat Anson Herrick of New York, who condemned the amendment in 1864, now said in support that it would lead to a reorganization of political parties and would forever eliminate slavery and the Negro question from politics. [12]

More than specific political purposes, the Thirteenth Amendment was intended to accomplish the single great reform that would complete the American system of liberty. The Chicago *Tribune* said it would remove "the last moral stain from our national escutcheon—the only disgrace from our flag." According to William Lloyd Garrison, the amendment constitutionalized the Declaration of Independence, while the New York *Times* stated that the republic would now be "thoroughly *democratic*—resting on human rights as its basis." The black New Orleans *Tribune* drew similar conclusions in observing: "We no longer have classes or castes among us. We are made one people and one nation." [13]

The chief significance of the Thirteenth Amendment, viewed as the nation's consummate reform action, was its effect on the status and rights of emancipated slaves. In 1866, when federal legislation to protect the freedmen against discriminatory state laws and private injury seemed necessary, many Republicans regarded slavery as the denial of fundamental civil rights. Accordingly, they interpreted the Thirteenth Amendment as securing basic civil rights to freed blacks and as giving the federal government power to legislate directly on individuals to protect those rights. In 1864 and 1865, however, a more narrow conception of slavery and the consequences of abolition prevailed. Republicans in general viewed slavery as the holding of property in man, that is, as chattelism. Further, they held that the abolition amendment secured to freed persons a right not to be held as property and empowered the federal government to guarantee this right against denial by any state law or public or private individual action.

While many Republicans thought the right not to be held as chattel necessarily implied the possession of a wide array of other civil rights, the framers of the Thirteenth Amendment did not contend that it gave Congress a direct and plenary power to legislate on civil rights in general.

Whether in an attempt to allay conservative apprehensions or because it was their considered judgment, most Republicans took a narrow view of slavery and hence of the scope and purpose of the amendment. "We propose to say in the organic law of the land," declared Representative John Farnsworth of Illinois, "that there shall be no more involuntary servitude except as a punishment for crime." According to Frederick E. Woodbridge of Vermont, the amendment would prevent the states from allowing their people to hold slaves as property. It meant simply that "such property shall no longer exist as property." Nathaniel Smithers of Delaware concurred that the effect of the amendment was "to convert into a man that which the law declared as a chattel," while Green Clay Smith of Kentucky announced: "We intend to establish the great truth that man cannot hold property in man." [14]

It was not just border state Republicans, but also antislavery people in general who shared this narrow view of the amendment. Insisting on a distinction between slavery and other forms of oppression, abolitionist Henry C. Wright argued that a slave was a man turned into a chattel. It was precisely that condition, asserted Wright, that the Thirteenth Amendment was designed to prohibit. Wendell Phillips contended that further measures were needed to protect the freedmen, and he agreed that the principal effect of the amendment was to proscribe chattelism. [15] In January 1865, a group of black clergymen offered a similarly narrow view of abolition in discussing the condition of freedmen in Georgia with Secretary of War Stanton and General William T. Sherman. When asked what they understood by slavery and freedom, the group's spokesman stated: "Slavery is receiving by irresistible power the work of another man, and not by his consent," while freedom meant "taking us from under the yoke of bondage and placing us where we can reap the fruit of our own labor." [16]

Slavery was at bottom chattelism, but, as this piece of evidence shows, it was difficult to confine the effect of the amendment to a right not to be held as property. To talk about placing freedmen in a position where they could enjoy the fruit of their labor was to move toward a broader conception of rights secured by the Thirteenth Amendment, as a corollary of the prohibition of chattelism. In stating that the right of "personal freedom without distinction" should be secured to all citizens, Representative Godlove Orth of Indiana suggested that something more than merely the right not to be held as property was involved in abolition. The same implication appeared in the statement of Senator John B. Henderson that adoption of the amendment would require former slaves to be treated as freedmen. Daniel Morris of New York showed the connection between the most narrow and a broader view of the amendment in observing that blacks had been held as property and their "civil rights . . . wantonly trampled under foot." To prohibit their being held as property seemed necessarily to require protection of basic civil rights.[17]

A number of Republicans developed this insight in more explicit terms. Thus, Representative John R. McBride of Oregon stated that emancipation under the Thirteenth Amendment involved "a recognition of natural rights," while Orth of Indiana said it would result in a practical application of the principle that life, liberty, and the pursuit of happiness were inalienable rights of all men. Others were more specific in describing rights that they believed the amendment would secure. Ebon C. Ingersoll of Illinois emphasized the right to enjoy the rewards of labor; John A. Kasson of Iowa the right to marriage and family relationships; James Harlan of Iowa the right to own property, to bring suit and testify in court, and to speak and write freely. Senator Henry Wilson of Massachusetts said the amendment would obliterate every last vestige of slavery and its "degrading and bloody codes"; in effect, he claimed that freedmen would acquire fundamental civil rights.[18] Even the conservative jurist S. S. Nicholas of Kentucky held that emancipated slaves enjoyed more than simply the right not to be held as chattel. While they were not citizens, observed Nicholas, they were entitled to the basic protection of person and property guaranteed by the common law to all free inhabitants of a state.[19]

An emancipation bill introduced in December 1863 by radical Owen Lovejoy of Illinois illustrated the broader conception of rights beyond simple freedom from chattelism that many Republicans came to identify with the Thirteenth Amendment. Lovejoy's bill provided that, whereas all men were created equal and were endowed with the right to life, liberty, and the fruits of honest toil, all slaves were to be declared freedmen. Henceforth they were to be protected "as all other free citizens are protected from unreasonable searches and seizures" and to be permitted to sue and be sued and to testify as witnesses in U.S. courts in all cases in the same manner as free white citizens. [20] Taking the same general view of post-emancipation rights, the New York *Tribune* said that, with the passage of the Thirteenth Amendment, the freed slave "takes his place with others as a citizen of the Republic, endowed with the same feelings and rights, and subject to the same duties as other citizens." [21]

Freedmen's rights, however, formed but a part of the concern for liberty evinced by the framers of the Thirteenth Amendment. As opposition to slavery before the war often focussed on the injury done to the rights and interests of white persons, so in abolishing slavery Republicans looked forward to expanded liberty for white citizens. Especially significant in this respect was the belief that the amendment would vivify the privileges and immunities clause of the Constitution, which many Republicans regarded as the source of national citizenship. [22]

The guarantee that citizens of each state should enjoy all the rights and privileges of citizens of the several states, said James M. Ashley during debate on the Thirteenth Amendment, created "a universal franchise which cannot be confined to States, but belongs to citizens of the Republic." Although the precise content of this national citizenship was a matter of conjecture, at the very least it seemed to secure a right to travel, speak, and write freely in all the states. For more than thirty years, Representative William D. Kelley of Pennsylvania recalled, notwithstanding the specific guarantee provided in the privileges and immunities clause, southerners had denied critics of slavery the right of transit through their states. As described by legalist Henry Everett Russell, the result was a virtual nullification of the constitutional provision and a denial of the fundamental rights of U.S. citizens. The Thirteenth Amendment, however, would carry into operation this all-important part of the Constitution, and for that reason was necessary. [23]

James Wilson of Iowa provided the most elaborate explanation of the relationship between the privileges and immunities clause and the Thirteenth Amendment. According to Wilson, the clause made the United States "a nation of equals" and was therefore of vital importance to every citizen. Specifically, it protected against state violation the basic rights of freedom of speech, press, religious opinion, assembly, and petition—rights which the First Amendment guaranteed against federal violation. This was what the Constitution ought to do, said Wilson, yet slavery had led to the denial of all these rights, breaching "the bond which holds the Union together" and reducing twenty million freemen of the North to the condition of semi-citizens of the United States. It was this situation that Wilson had in mind when he declared, in his own formulation of the Thirteenth Amendment, that slavery was "incompatible with a free government." Its abolition, he insisted, would "make the future safe for the rights of each and every citizen." [24]

Outside Congress defenders of the Thirteenth Amendment also stressed its importance for securing the liberties of white citizens. Southern Unionist Andrew Jackson Hamilton told a Faneuil Hall audience in 1863 that he hated slavery more because of its despotic attack on free government than because it was unjust to the slave. Law writer Edward F. Bullard emphasized that white persons could never be secure in their constitutional rights as long as slavery existed. [25] Although antislavery people enumerated many rights that had been denied in order to protect slavery, their chief concern remained the fundamental right of unrestricted interstate movement. That a Massachusetts man might speak his opinion in South Carolina and vice versa, said Kentucky Unionist Congressman Green Clay Smith in support of the Thirteenth Amendment, "is a glorious principle to fight for." To secure this right would be to vindicate "the great principle of the freedom of man." [26] In similar vein, the New York *Tribune* stated that the Thirteenth Amendment gave "hope that we may yet live and die in a free country—one which we may quietly, inoffensively traverse in every part without foolhardy exposure to the bludgeons of ruffians or the pistols and dirks of assassins." [27]

Supporters of the Thirteenth Amendment believed, then, that it would give emancipated slaves at least a right not to be chattelized and perhaps additional basic rights of locomotion, labor, and security to person and property, while for white persons it would remove the obstacle which had prevented elementary rights of citizenship from being exercised on a truly national basis. Emphasis on one or the other of these consequences might vary, but in general Republicans agreed that this was the scope and effect of the amendment. Regarding analytical comment as superfluous, the Boston *Journal* in noting Congressional approval of the amendment merely printed the text of the constitutional change and declared: "This tells the whole story for itself. Every man understands what the new article means."[28]

While it was true that virtually everyone in 1865 understood slavery as chattelism, the consequences of abolition and the meaning of the amendment were by no means so self-evident as Republicans believed. Slavery might be doomed and the slave power fatally weakened, but from the standpoint of the defenders of state sovereignty there was vast significance in the manner by which it should be abolished. If abolition must come, it were better accomplished under state than federal authority. Furthermore, conservatives denied the contention of some Republicans and conservative Unionists that approval of the amendment would actually weaken radicalism and promote political harmony.[29]

Viewing the amendment in conjunction with freedmen's and reconstruction proposals, Democrats saw it as an attempt to promote Negro equality and revolutionize the federal system. Taken in connection with the revised reconstruction bill, argued Representative William S. Holman of Indiana in January 1865, it was "the entering wedge" for the idea that no one could be free who was not a U.S. citizen invested with the right of suffrage. Daniel W. Voorhees of Indiana pointed to the Negro suffrage provision of the revised Wade-Davis bill and discerned an intention on the part of the framers of the amendment to make emancipated blacks voters, jurors, and officeholders. Robert Mallory of Kentucky associated the amendment with the freedmen's bureau bill and said its purpose was to hold Negroes in the South, make them the civil, political, and social equals of whites, and thus maintain control of the federal government. The concepts of the Negro as a free citizen of the United States, protected everywhere in defiance of state constitutions and laws and eventually even as a voting citizen, were "all propositions logically involved in the proposed amendment," averred Joseph K. Edgerton of Indiana.[30] Democrats did not, however, contend that the amendment by itself, either as a self-enforcing measure or through congressional implementation, would secure the political and civil equality that they decried.

Because the Thirteenth Amendment was so soon overshadowed after the war by events that made explicit protection of civil rights necessary, as in the Fourteenth Amendment, we have tended to forget the tremendous constitutional significance it had, even when considered narrowly as a prohibition of chattelism. For Democrats, it was enough that the federal government should have power to interfere with the states' traditional jurisdiction over personal liberty and rights merely to the extent of guaranteeing a right not to be held as property. This provision promised sufficient change in federal-state relations to warrant the conservatives' strongest condemnation.

Indeed, the principal conservative argument against the Thirteenth Amendment was that it represented an unconstitutional use of the amending power. The slavery issue, insisted Representative Anson Herrick of New York, was legitimately merged with the higher issue of the right of the states to control domestic affairs and institutions and to fix the status of all persons dwelling within their borders. This power was so fundamental that it could not be taken away except by the actual consent of each state. For some states to use the amending power to deny other states this essential attribute of political equality, said Joseph Edgerton, was to destroy the very principle on which the Union was founded.[31] Contending that sovereignty was indivisible and possessed by the states alone, conservatives held that the Thirteenth Amendment proposed to change the nature of the Union by creating a consolidated government.[32]

A few Democrats expressed apprehension that under the Thirteenth Amendment slavery might be viewed broadly as a denial of all civil and political rights and that the enforcement power of section 2 might be construed as authorizing direct federal legislation on the entire range of personal rights and liberties. Declaring that slavery was not simply the exemption from personal servitude, William Holman said that freedom involved the right to participate in government. The denial of the suffrage was a form of slavery, Holman suggested, which Congress could reach through the power conferred by the amendment "to invade any State to enforce the freedom of the African in war or peace." Robert Mallory predicted that, if rebel states denied blacks the right to vote, Congress would pass federal laws under section 2 of the amendment setting aside any such policy, and S. S. Cox of Ohio asked apprehensively what laws Congress would pass to carry the amendment into effect.[33]

In general, however, conservatives objected that the amending power was abused in the very formulation of the Thirteenth Amendment, not that the amendment gave Congress a plenary power over civil rights.[34] Edgerton thus reasoned that, if the power to change the Constitution could be used to destroy and give the federal government power to legislate against property in man, it could be used to interfere with marital rights, the relations of parent and child, the rules of inheritance, property laws, and all manner of local institutions. "If you begin upon this domain," asked S. S. Cox, "where is the limit to the exercise of this plenary amendatory power in domestic affairs?" So, too, the New York *World* expressed alarm not so much at the abolition amendment, but at the prospect of additional amendments that would deprive the states of power to regulate Negroes with respect to trials, residence, schools, and other matters. Edgerton summarized the conservative position: "The principle of the proposed amendment is the principle of consolidation, and cannot be drawn into precedent without a final subversion of our constitutional Government." [35]

Republicans acknowledged that the Thirteenth Amendment altered the relationship between the states and the federal government in regard to personal liberty. They did not, however, conceive of it as revolutionizing the federal system. The amendment denied states the power to protect slavery, but the federal government, of course, acquired nothing of this power. Republicans adhered to the traditional theory of divided sovereignty, maintaining that the amendment gave the federal government power to legislate to protect personal liberty. Yet, rather than consolidate local legislative power, this change only made concurrent a power previously exercised by the states alone.

Suppose, suggested Theodore Thayer of Pennsylvania in response to the Democratic charge of a revolution in federalism, that the Thirteenth Amendment did interfere with the domestic institutions of the states. Was there anything in the Constitution prohibiting the use of the amending power when local institutions might be affected? John A. Kasson of Iowa pointed out that centralization meant taking power from the states and giving it to the federal government. "But when you take it both from the States and from the United States," he added, "there is not a particle of centralization of power." The amendment merely took from the states "one single subject more in addition to those which were withdrawn by the original Constitution," Kasson concluded. It did not interfere with or undermine state rights. [36]

Publicist Henry Everett Russell held that, if the power to protect slavery was a legitimate state right, its destruction by the Thirteenth Amendment could only be reckoned a positive good. Yet, Russell denied that the measure centralized power. Furthermore, reasoning that slavery did not exist by positive state law but rather was simply recognized in state legislation as a social fact, Russell said it violated state constitutions and bills of rights. Accordingly, by abolishing slavery the Thirteenth Amendment upheld "the only true doctrine of State rights, namely, that the legislation of a State shall conform to the fundamental law at once of the State itself and the nation." James G. Blaine of Maine aptly summarized the Republican outlook when he wrote later that, as a result of the Thirteenth Amendment, "the relation between the National and State Governments, respecting the question of Human Liberty, was radically changed." Freedom of the person thereafter became a matter of national concern. [37]

The Thirteenth Amendment thus enlarged national power, but, viewed in proper historical perspective, its significance was less to promote federal consolidation than to redress the imbalance in federalism created by the swollen pretensions and assertions of state sovereignty before the war. On the contrary, it was the slave power that threatened to centralize power. During the debate on the Thirteenth Amendment, Republicans underscored this concern in recalling the aggressions of the Nebraska Act, the Dred Scott case, the Lecompton Constitution, and the Fugitive Slave Law. "It may be said without exaggeration that [the slave power] owned the South, used the Government, and hired the North," declaimed Glenni W. Scofield of Pennsylvania. Scofield said that, rather than promote centralization, the amendment "will rid the country of this centralizing power." "What possible connection is there," he asked, "between centralization and emancipation? Why should one follow the other?" [38]

The Republicans, recognizing an augmentation of federal power, nevertheless regarded the Thirteenth Amendment as consolidating the power of local legislation in the general government no further than was necessary to secure the right not to be held in bondage. The principal ground for this conclusion is the fact that slavery was defined as chattelism rather than as a denial of all political and civil rights. Despite this narrow view, many, if not most, Republicans believed the right not to be held as property was intrinsically related to other civil rights. Yet they did not contend that the Thirteenth Amendment gave the federal government power by direct legislation to secure rights surrounding the elementary right of personal liberty. This fact becomes clear when we consider the meaning of section 2 of the amendment, which gave Congress power to enforce the prohibition of slavery.

If one considers section 1 of the amendment, that is, the declaration that slavery shall not exist, to be self-executing and thus to require no legislative implementation, the conclusion emerges that section 2 was superfluous unless it gave Congress power to protect freedmen's rights beyond a mere right against chattelization.[39] In 1866, when the consequences of adopting a narrow view of the amendment were apparent, many Republicans made this argument. In 1864 and 1865, however, they did not reach this conclusion. Indeed, no consideration was given to section 2 as something that might empower Congress to do other than prohibit the master-slave relationship.

It is possible that the need to gain Democratic votes caused Republicans to conceal their true opinion of congressional power under section 2 of the amendment. Perhaps Lyman Trumbull, James Wilson, Jacob Howard, and other framers in fact believed that it gave Congress either exclusive or concurrent power to legislate on civil rights but refrained from saying so for political reasons. On the other hand, it is possible that many Republicans did not feel constrained by the political situation to hide their real convictions. Radicals in particular, who did not share the viewpoint of the Seward lobby on the importance of attracting conservative support for the amendment, would seem to have had no reason to trim their views. Referring to conservative Republican efforts to secure Democratic votes, Josiah Grinnell of Iowa, for example, declared in January 1865: "I am in no coaxing mood." Let Democrats oppose the Thirteenth Amendment, said Grinnell; when the next Congress should assemble, elected for this very purpose, "We can pass the constitutional amendment . . . without coaxing."[40]

The scope of congressional power under section 2 depended fundamentally on the meaning assigned to slavery in section 1. The evidence examined thus far shows that most Republicans viewed slavery as chattelism or as the master-slave relationship strictly conceived. Further support for a narrow interpretation of the amendment lies in the history of the antislavery provision of the Northwest Ordinance that formed the substance of the constitutional change. If, as they said, Republicans used the ordinance because its meaning was clear beyond doubt, the conclusion that the amendment gave Congress no general power to legislate on civil rights becomes even more compelling.

The pertinent fact about the Northwest Ordinance is that it had been interpreted to prohibit only the master-slave relationship, not to confer civil or political rights on Negroes. Indeed, its effectiveness in dealing with slavery narrowly defined was at times dubious, for it had not prohibited indentured service contracts, which meant that de facto slavery existed in Illinois and Indiana for many years. Nor had it prevented peonage or debt slavery.[41] The conservative legalist S. S. Nicholas summarized the judicial history of the ordinance in writing that its legal force was to abolish slavery and convert slaves into free inhabitants. As such, Nicholas added, freed slaves received no civil rights beyond the minimal protection of person and property provided by the general law of each state for all free inhabitants. The important point was that the ordinance itself conferred no rights and left emancipated slaves within the jurisdiction of the states.[42]

Republican preference for a narrow view of the Thirteenth Amendment and congressional power was evident in the rejection of the constitutional amendment which Charles Sumner proposed to abolish slavery in 1864. Sumner's proposal stated: "All persons are equal before the law, so that no person can hold another as a slave; and the Congress shall have power to make all laws necessary and proper to carry this declaration into effect everywhere within the United States and the jurisdiction thereof."[43] Republicans Lyman Trumbull and Jacob Howard quickly objected to this proposition. When the clerk erroneously read Sumner's resolution as stating that all persons were free before the law and Sumner interjected that the correct words were "equal before the law," Howard said it made no difference which term was used. Referring to the phrase "equal before the law," he added," in a legal and technical sense that language is utterly insignificant and meaningless as a clause of the Constitution." It was not known at all in the courts, Howard said, and hence had no legal signification. Both Howard and Trumbull believed that rather than seeking precedent, as Sumner proposed, in French history, where equality before the law was asserted not to abolish slavery but to eliminate political and civil ranks and privileges, Congress should rely on the language of the Northwest Ordinance. That language had been adjudicated repeatedly, Howard explained, and was well understood by the public and by judicial authorities. In the face of this criticism, Sumner withdrew his resolution.[44]

Sumner's version of the Thirteenth Amendment contained an extraodinarily broad grant of power which could have been construed to guarantee full civil and political rights to Negroes. [45] While it is possible that the significance of Sumner's proposal was not perceived and that the critics merely quarreled over phraseology, [46] a more accurate conclusion is that the Republicans understood its revolutionary potential—both for the status of the freedmen and for federalism—and rejected it. Sumner would not only declare blacks equal to whites, but he would also give Congress power to guarantee Negro equality by direct legislation. Howard showed awareness of the radical nature of this change when, after dismissing the language of equality before the law as legally insignificant, he observed critically and apprehensively: "Besides, the proposition speaks of all men being equal. I suppose before the law a woman would be equal to a man, a woman would be as free as a man. A wife would be equal to her husband and as free as her husband before the law." [47] In rejecting a version of the amendment asserting equality before the law, which they associated with political and civil equality, Howard and Trumbull expressed the Republicans' more limited intention to abolish slavery as chattelism, not to establish equal civil and political rights under congressional guarantee.

The framers of the Thirteenth Amendment rejected Sumner's extremely broad amendment but also repudiated conservative proposals that would have left emancipated slaves with no rights whatever. The most explicit measure of this sort was a substitute amendment introduced by Senator Garrett Davis of Kentucky which stated that "no negro or person whose mother or grandmother is or was a negro, shall be a citizen of the United States, or be eligible to any civil or military office, or to any place of trust or profit under the United States." Other resolutions rejected by the Senate (also introduced by Davis) sought to prevent emancipation in states which forbade residence of free Negroes, unless the federal government provided for the removal of freedmen, and to distribute the liberated black population of the South throughout the country. [48] These propositions, as James G. Blaine observed later, reflected apprehension that freed slaves would enjoy civil rights and political power. [49] In rejecting them, Senate Republicans did not, of course, expressly affirm that freedmen were citizens of the United States with a right to remain in the states where they resided, but that was the implication of the legislative action. Nevertheless, in passing the Thirteenth Amendment, Congress made no express determination of freedmen's rights or of the scope of federal power over civil rights beyond protection of the right not to be held as chattel.

Observers of differing political ideas agreed on the nonrevolutionary character of the amendment. Though thankful for it, Wendell Phillips warned that, even with this change in the Constitution, blacks could still be "ground to powder by the power of State sovereignty." At most, he reasoned, the amendment abolished chattelism and gave the freed slave a right, if oppressed in one state, to remove to another. Accurately assessing the temper of Congress, Phillips stated that Republicans were reliable when it came to the technical liberty of blacks but not when more advanced issues of civil rights were at stake. It was obvious to radicals such as Phillips that further constitutional amendments were necessary to protect the freedmen against denials of rights by the states.[50]

While many conservatives, as we have seen, thought the amendment would subvert state power, others offered a more cautious evaluation of its consequences. In January 1865, Representative James S. Rollins of Missouri discounted the idea that it would lead to other dangerous measures or that Republicans were bent upon consolidating the power of local legislation in Congress. Secretary of the Navy Gideon Welles, ever vigilant in behalf of state rights, regarded the amendment as "a step towards the reestablishment of the Union in its integrity." Welles believed that under the amendment the states would resume their original position and act for themselves. Although S. S. Cox warned against revolutionary consequences growing out of further constitutional amendments, he also admitted to believing that the Thirteenth Amendment "would impair only for a brief time the checks and balances, the very substance and essence of our federative system."[51]

After Congress approved the Thirteenth Amendment on January 31, 1865, Senator Henry Wilson of Massachusetts introduced a bill which elucidates Republican conceptions of federal power at this time, as well as their ideas as to what seemed necessary to complete emancipation. Wilson's measure prohibited the exclusion, on account of color, of any person from travel on railroads or navigable waters within the United States by reason of any state law, municipal ordinance, or regulation or usage of any corporation or person. The bill further declared that colored passengers were subject to the same laws, ordinances, rules, regulations, and usages as white passengers.

Finally, it provided for trial in federal court and, upon conviction, punishment of $500 fine and six months' imprisonment for any company or person violating the act. [52]

Wilson's bill formed part of an antislavery effort to secure equal rights for Negroes in schools, courts, and public transportation in the North. [53] In relation to the Thirteenth Amendment, however, it showed what some Republicans thought was needed to complete the work of the amendment. The colored passenger bill, editorialized the New York *Tribune*, was "a fit corollary to the antislavery amendment." The *Tribune*, believing Negroes were citizens whose rights were already protected by law, said that, if they were not, then laws such as Wilson's were appropriate and necessary. In referring to Wilson's measure, the *National Anti-Slavery Standard*, observed: "The nation owes it to the people of color, whose citizenship is at length acknowledged, to protect them in their rights as travellers, whether in cars, steamboats or stages." [54]

Wilson's bill was an assertion of federal power in relation to civil rights, but its constitutional basis was unclear. Wilson may have based the bill on the Thirteenth Amendment, on the assumption that the latter would be speedily ratified. If so, it meant that the "right to ride" was part of the freedom secured by the amendment which the federal government could protect against any state or private individual who attempted to deny it. Furthermore, as the bill referred simply to travel on railroads and navigable streams, it was apparently intended to secure this right on intra- as well as interstate modes of transportation. It was understood in this sense by the New York *Tribune*, which saw it as dealing with the problem of segregated streetcars in northern cities, a major source of controversy in early 1865. [55] Viewed in this manner, the bill reflected a broad conception of Thirteenth Amendment power operating in a sphere hitherto reserved to the states.

On the other hand, since the Thirteenth Amendment was not yet part of the Constitution, Wilson may have based his bill on the war power. This explanation is more likely, for in 1862, Congress had passed legislation authorizing the president, when in his judgment the public safety required it, to take possession of all telegraph lines and railroads in the United States. Wilson probably saw his passenger bill as justified under this same broad emergency power. [56] Whatever view one takes of the precise constitutional basis of the bill, what

stands out is the concern for the right of free travel. This concern re-
flects the interest evinced during the debate on the Thirteenth Amendment in safeguarding free movement and free speech in all the states.
Moreover, insofar as Wilson's bill by its choice of subject matter implied that protection of the freedmen in other matters such as schools,
courts, contracts, and persons and property in general remained and
presumably would be provided for within state jurisdictions, it reflected a limited view of the scope and necessity of federal involve-
ment in post-emancipation civil rights problems.

Wilson's passenger bill was an isolated measure which died in committee. Therefore, it cannot tell us very much about the original intentions of the framers of the Thirteenth Amendment. The best answer to that question is provided by the debates in Congress and the
commentary of contemporary observers, which we have already examined.

It seems clear that for most Republicans the amendment gave freedmen a right not to be held as chattel, and probably additional civil
rights, though the evidence on the latter point is not conclusive. But
while the amendment might be viewed as self-enforcing, requiring no
federal legislation, section 2, to be other than mere surplusage, does
not necessarily have to be viewed as giving Congress broad power to
legislate on civil rights. The antislavery amendment was the first
which gave power to the federal government and took it away from the
states. It was also the first to deal with a matter of social reform. These
considerations, especially in view of the importance of the reform
undertaken, are sufficient to explain why the framers made an explicit
grant of power to Congress to enforce the amendment. Republicans
were understandably unwilling to rest content with the idea that the
abolition of slavery might be considered a self-enforcing provision.

While the Republicans believed that the Thirteenth Amendment at
the very least secured personal liberty and probably additional rights,
they made no clear determination as to whether these rights belonged
to emancipated blacks as national or state citizens. In relation to earlier emancipation and military legislation, antislavery congressmen
and publicists, as we have seen, posited a theory of national citizenship as attaching to persons by reason of birth on American soil rather
than as derivative of state citizenship. They reached no firm conclusion as to the scope, extent, or means by which federal power might be
exercised to protect the rights of citizenship, nor, despite many argu-

ments to this effect, did Congress definitively establish that blacks were citizens of the United States. Considering the prewar status of Negroes in American public law, epitomized in the Dred Scott decision, it was a significant achievement, by recruiting blacks into the army, to establish that they were persons or freemen under the Constitution and part of the people of the United States. In view of the preponderant importance of state citizenship before the war, it was enough to insist that national citizenship did not depend on state citizenship, that it was primary, not derivative, and that American citizenship was dual, that is, legitimate and effective in both state and federal forums. In short, Congress did not resolve the complex relationship between state and federal citizenship.[57]

The debate on the Thirteenth Amendment did nothing to clarify the question of citizenship. In general, contending as they did that the amendment would enlarge the liberties of all citizens, Republicans seem to have regarded emancipated slaves as American citizens, which meant citizens of the United States and the states in which they lived. The federal government would have a new power to protect the liberty of American citizens by enforcing the prohibition of slavery, but the states would still have the main responsibility of protecting and regulating citizens' ordinary civil rights. Moreover, as the proposed reconstruction legislation of 1864-1865 showed, Republicans thought of freedmen's rights primarily in relation to the state governments. Their failure to define Thirteenth Amendment rights as exclusive attributes of national citizenship is further evidence of their limited conception of the changes in federalism that the abolition of slavery would introduce.

While the idea of dual citizenship was usually implicit in references to "American citizenship," explicit formulations of it appeared throughout the war. Thus, in 1863 a correspondent of Charles Sumner suggested a constitutional amendment declaring that any person born in the United States or admitted to citizenship under federal law was entitled in each state "to all privileges and immunities of citizens of that State, or of the United States." Yet, it was in relation to the states that American citizenship had its most important practical meaning. Years later, George S. Boutwell wrote that the alternatives faced during the war were a permanently divided country, or a Union of states "with equality of citizenship in the States." During debate on the reconstruction bill in February 1865, Thaddeus Stevens recommended that the Union authorities enroll "citizens of the United States" and allow the states to determine who its citizens should be by deciding who should vote. [58]

Uncertainty concerning national citizenship, and hence national power to protect civil rights, occasionally provoked radical criticism. In May 1865, Wendell Phillips complained that the U.S. government "stands today in the abnormal position of not knowing who are its own citizens . . . . We do not know who are the basis of our government; that lies with the States." [59] To remedy the situation, Phillips proposed a constitutional amendment that would prohibit any state from making any distinction in civil rights on account of race or color among persons born on her soil—not, Phillips was careful to say, among her citizens, for that would allow states to determine citizenship. In effect, this proposal meant that all persons born in the United States would be citizens of the nation protected against discriminatory state legislation. Phillips too thought in terms of state-centered federalism, as when he concluded that liberty would be secure "when we have given the negro the ballot in his right hand, the land under his feet, and a State Constitution above him, that guarantees him his citizenship." [60] Radical Republican William D. Kelley placed a similar emphasis on the state side of the dual citizenship idea in stating: "We need not fear that even the existing generation of freedmen will not prove themselves abundantly able to take care of themselves, and maintain the power and dignity of the States of which we shall make them citizens." [61]

Thus, while the Thirteenth Amendment would alter federal-state relations on the all-important matter of personal liberty, Republicans generally adhered to traditional conceptions of federalism. The radical *Independent* observed in 1862 that, whereas the South held to state rights in contradistinction to the nation, in the North "a strong love of State Rights is united to an equally strong pride and affection for Nationality." In discussing the Thirteenth Amendment as a basis for reconstruction, Representative Samuel C. Pomeroy of Kansas said in 1864 that the objective of reunion policy should be "such subordination of the several States to the General Government as shall secure a homogeneous and undisputed nationality, while not destroying the rights reserved to the states." In 1865, Wendell Phillips demanded restrictions on state rights lest they be carried to the pernicious conclusions of state sovereignty. At the same time, he affirmed: "I love

State Rights; that doctrine is the cornerstone of individual liberty." Phillips therefore sought "to check it mid-way" by a constitutional amendment which would prohibit states from discriminating on the basis of color.[62]

Republican legalist Marvin Warren of Ohio presented a view of federal-state relations that struck the kind of balance Phillips desired. Without distinguishing between state and national citizenship, Warren argued that the federal government had legitimate power and responsibility to protect individual rights as guaranteed in the Constitution. This viewpoint did not mean that the national government should interfere to redress every violation of the rights of person and property between citizens. It was more convenient and appropriate, Warren held, for the states to do that. In cases where states were unwilling or unable to protect the rights of their citizens, however, Warren contended, the federal government should interpose its power. Most assuredly, it was "the duty of the National Government to stand between the authorities of a State and one or more of its citizens . . . whenever the constitutional rights of either of these parties is without any other redress," Warren wrote.[63] While the framers of the Thirteenth Amendment affirmed nothing so clear as this in express terms, their tendencies lay in this direction.

Before the war, the theory and practice of state sovereignty, according to which the federal government was the mere agent of the states without authentic sovereign power, threatened to supersede traditional federalism and the idea of divided sovereignty.[64] At the same time, northern antislavery people relied on state powers to protect personal liberty in opposing the Fugitive Slave Law. The great change produced by the war—and signified by the Thirteenth Amendment—was the assertion of national sovereignty and power, alongside state power, to protect personal liberty. A generation after the war, historian Francis N. Thorpe captured the essence of this development in writing that, while principles of national sovereignty were a force from the beginning of the government, it was only in the war and reconstruction that they were realized. The dual civil system of federalism, then, actually began to operate, Thorpe concluded, as "concurrent sovereignty" for the first time since the national government was established.[65] The Thirteenth Amendment was the first clear expression of this sovereignty in the nation's organic law.

While, in retrospect, the abolition amendment stands out as merely the first of three reconstruction constitutional changes, congressional framers regarded it as conclusive rather than initiatory. As the culmination of the antislavery movement, it was seen as resolving the reconstruction question. Henry Everett Russell wrote that, when the amendment was ratified, "there would be no longer reason for differences . . . as to the proper mode of reinvesting the States usurped by the rebellion with their rightful powers as kindred republics of the nation." James W. Patterson of New Hampshire optimistically declared in January 1865 that the amendment "will give an easy and ready solution to the difficult questions arising under the proclamation of emancipation and bills of reconstruction."[66]

These sanguine expectations were shattered when the southern states began to organize local affairs under President Johnson's reconstruction policy. It then became obvious that the historic instrument for excluding slavery from the territories was not apposite for uprooting it where it had long existed. Within a few months a new and far broader understanding of freedmen's rights and congressional power under the Thirteenth Amendment began to take hold. As emancipation early in the war preceded awareness of a civil rights problem, so the rapidity with which the expectations of the framers of the Thirteenth Amendment were superseded after the war showed a failure to appreciate the difficulties involved in achieving equality before the law.

NOTES

1. Herman Belz, *Reconstructing the Union: Theory and Policy During the Civil War* (Ithaca, 1969), 244-276. Negro suffrage was advocated principally on the grounds that it would strengthen the interest of the Republican party and unionism in general in postwar southern politics and would enable the freed people to protect themselves and to enjoy civil rights without the necessity of extensive, continuing federal intervention in state affairs. Although Congress twice rejected limited proposals for Negro voting in legislation concerning Montana territorial government and elections in the District of Columbia, the issue at this time was in process of being reconnoitered rather than disposed of decisively.

2. *Congressional Globe*, 38th Cong., 1st sess., 1313-1314 (March 28, 1864), remarks of Lyman Trumbull, 1419-1422 (April 5, 1864), remarks of Reverdy Johnson.

3. Ibid., 1369 (March 31, 1864).

4. LaWanda Cox and John H. Cox, *Politics, Principle and Prejudice, 1865-66: Dilemma of Reconstruction America* (New York, 1963), 3-6; *Independent*, October 13, 1864, speech of Theodore Tilton.

5. Cox and Cox, *Politics, Principle and Prejudice*, 6-30, 39-40.

6. *Congressional Globe*, 38th Cong., 1st sess., 1312 (March 28, 1864).

7. The states in the first category were Ohio, Indiana, Illinois, Michigan, and Wisconsin, and in the second, Iowa, California, Minnesota, Oregon, and Kansas. Charles Fairman, *Reconstruction and Reunion: 1864-88, Part One* (New York, 1971), 1118-1119.

8. Horace White, *The Life of Lyman Trumbull* (Boston and New York, 1913), 224.

9. *Congressional Globe*, 38th Cong., 1st sess., 142, 144-146 (January 6, 1864), remarks of Godlove Orth and Glenni Scofield, 1320 (March 28, 1864), remarks of Henry Wilson, 38th Cong., 2d sess., 39 (December 14, 1864), remarks of George S. Boutwell and Thaddeus Stevens, 191 (January 10, 1865), remarks of John Kasson.

10. Ludwell H. Johnson, "Lincoln's Solution to the Problem of Peace Terms, 1864-1865," *Journal of Southern History* 34 (November 1968): 577-582; *Congressional Globe*, 38th Cong., 2d sess., 221 (January 11, 1865); New York *World*, February 1, 1865; New York *Times*, February 4, 1865; letter of John B. Henderson, *Harvard Law Review* 15 (December 1901): 301.

11. *Congressional Globe*, 38th Cong., 1st sess., 1314 (March 28, 1864), remarks of Lyman Trumbull.

12. Washington *Evening Star*, February 1, 1865; *Congressional Globe*, 38th Cong., 2d sess., 170-171 (January 9, 1865), remarks of George Yeaman, 526 (January 31, 1865), 38th Cong., 1st sess., 2616 (May 31, 1864), remarks of Anson Herrick.

13. Chicago *Tribune*, February 1, 1865; New York *Times*, February 1, 8, 1865; *Liberator*, February 10, 1865, speech of William Lloyd Garrison; New Orleans *Tribune*, February 23, 1865.

14. *Congressional Globe*, 38th Cong., 2d sess., 200 (January 10, 1865), 244 (January 12, 1865), 216 (January 11, 1865), 120 (January 5, 1865), 236 (January 2, 1865).

15. *Liberator*, February 17, 1865. See also *National Anti-Slavery Standard*, February 11, 1865; Henry Wilson, *History of the Rise and Fall of the Slave Power in America* (3 vols.; Boston, 1872-1877), III, 646.

16. William T. Sherman, *Memoirs* (2 vols.; Bloomington, Ind., 1957), II, 245-246.

17. *Congressional Globe*, 38th Cong., 2d sess., 143 (January 6, 1865), 38th Cong., 1st sess., 1463 (April 7, 1864), 38th Cong., 2d sess., 487 (January 28, 1865).

18. Ibid., 202 (January 11, 1865), 142 (January 6, 1865), 38th Cong., 1st sess., 2990 (June 15, 1864), 38th Cong., 2d sess., 193 (January 10, 1865), 38th Cong., 1st sess., 1439 (April 6, 1864), 1324 (March 28, 1864).

19. S. S. Nicholas, *Conservative Essays, Legal and Political* (4 vols.; Louisville, 1863-1869), III, 37.

20. 38th Cong., H.R. No. 21, December 14, 1863, MS, National Archives, RG 233, 38A-B1.

21. New York *Tribune*, February 6, 1865.

22. Article IV, sec. 2 of the Constitution states: "The Citizens of each State shall be entitled to all Privileges and Immunities of Citizens in the several States."

23. *Congressional Globe*, 38th Cong., 2d sess., 139 (January 6, 1865); Henry Everett Russell, "The Constitutional Amendment," *Continental Monthly* 6 (September 1864): 321; *Congressional Globe*, 38th Cong., 2d sess., 193 (January 10, 1865).

24. Ibid., 38th Cong., 1st sess., 1199, 1202-1203 (March 19, 1864).

25. A. J. Hamilton, *Speech at Faneuil Hall, April 18, 1863* (Boston, 1863), 33, 45-46; Edward F. Bullard, *The Nation's Trial: The Proclamation: Dormant Powers of the*

Government (New York and Albany, 1863), 47-48.

26. *Congressional Globe*, 38th Cong., 2d sess., 237 (January 12, 1865).

27. New York *Tribune*, February 1, 1865.

28. Boston *Journal*, February 1, 1865.

29. *Congressional Globe*, 38th Cong., 2d sess., 219 (January 11, 1865), 179 (January 9, 1865), remarks of James Cravens and Robert Mallory.

30. Ibid., 219 (January 11, 1865) 179, 181 (January 9, 1865), 38th Cong., 1st sess., 2987 (June 15, 1864). See also ibid., 2957 (June 14, 1864), remarks of Lewis W. Ross, and 38th Cong., 2d sess., 216 (January 11, 1865), remarks of C. A. White.

31. Ibid., 38th Cong., 1st sess., 2616 (May 31, 1864), 2986 (June 15, 1864). See also ibid., 1441 (April 6, 1864), remarks of Willard Saulsbury, 38th Cong., 2d sess., 223 (January 11, 1865), remarks of George Pendleton.

32. Ibid., 38th Cong., 1st sess., 2940-2941 (June 14, 1864).

33. Ibid., 2962 (June 14, 1864), 38th Cong., 2d sess., 180 (January 9, 1865), 242 (January 12, 1865).

34. Jacobus ten Broek, *Equal Under Law* (New York, 1965), 162, suggests that conservative fears that Thirteenth Amendment power would be used to guarantee full civil rights to the freedmen are evidence that Republicans intended to revolutionize the federal system. Aside from the consideration that their opponents' criticism does not necessarily prove anything about Republican intentions, the fact is that most Democrats who expressed an opinion on the matter did not accept the view that the amendment gave Congress plenary power over civil rights.

35. *Congressional Globe*, 38th Cong., 1st sess., 2986 (June 15, 1864), 38th Cong., 2d sess., 242 (January 12, 1865); New York *World*, January 9, 1865, quoted in Cox and Cox, *Politics, Principle and Prejudice*, 5.

36. *Congressional Globe*, 38th Cong., 2d sess., 246 (January 13, 1865), 239 (January 12, 1865), 191 (January 10, 1865).

37. Russell, "The Constitutional Amendment," 324; James G. Blaine, *Twenty Years of Congress: From Lincoln to Garfield* (2 vols.; Norwich, Conn., 1884), I, 539.

38. *Congressional Globe*, 38th Cong., 2d sess., 146 (January 6, 1865).

39. See Howard Devon Hamilton, "The Legislative and Judicial History of the Thirteenth Amendment," *National Bar Journal* 9 (March 1951): 80.

40. *Congressional Globe*, 38th Cong., 2d sess., 200 (January 10, 1865).

41. Hamilton, "Legislative History of the Thirteenth Amendment," 49-51; Eugene H. Berwanger, *The Frontier Against Slavery: Western Anti-Negro Prejudice and the Slavery Extension Controversy* (Urbana, 1967), 7-14.

42. S. S. Nicholas, *Conservative Essays*, III, 36-37, 53-54.

43. *Congressional Globe*, 38th Cong., 2d sess., 1482-1483 (April 8, 1864). Sumner cited several documents from revolutionary France as the source of his idea of equality before the law. He objected to the version of the amendment favored by the Judiciary Committee because it seemed to allow slavery as a punishment for crime.

44. Ibid., 1488-1489 (April 8, 1864).

45. Hamilton, "Legislative History of the Thirteenth Amendment," 31, states that Sumner's proposal would have been as comprehensive as the Thirteenth, Fourteenth, and Fifteenth Amendments combined. For a similar contemporary view, see *The Principia*, July 14, 1864, editorial.

46. This is the view of Hamilton, "Legislative History of the Thirteenth Amendment," 31.

47. *Congressional Globe*, 38th Cong., 1st sess., 1488 (April 8, 1864).

48. Ibid., 1370 (March 31, 1864), 1425 (April 5, 1864).

49. Blaine, *Twenty Years of Congress*, I, 505.

50. *Liberator*, February 3, 17, 1865.

51. *Congressional Globe*, 38th Cong., 2nd sess., 242 (January 12, 1865), remarks of S. S. Cox, 262 (January 13, 1865), remarks of James S. Rollins; Howard K. Beale, ed., *The Diary of Gideon Welles* (3 vols.; New York, 1960), II, 234.

52. 38th Cong., S. No. 427, February 4, 1865, introduced by Henry Wilson; 38th Cong., 2d sess., *Senate Journal*, 132.

53. James M. McPherson, *The Struggle for Equality: Abolitionists and the Negro in the Civil War and Reconstruction* (Princeton, 1964), 221-237.

54. New York *Tribune*, February 6, 1865; *National Anti-Slavery Standard*, February 11, 1865.

55. New York *Tribune*, February 6, 1865.

56. *U.S. Statutes at Large*, XII (Boston, 1863), 334.

57. See above, Ch. 2, pp. 25-31.

58. Henry M. Parkhurst to Charles Sumner, December 16, 1863, Sumner Papers, Harvard University Library; George S. Boutwell, "The Career of Abraham Lincoln," *The Magazine of History*, No. 193 (1895; reprinted, New York, 1934): 175; *Congressional Globe*, 38th Cong., 2d sess., 1002 (February 22, 1865).

59. Phillips presumably referred to the Dred Scott decision and the proposition, asserted by Justice Curtis, that persons born on American soil were citizens of the United States, provided that the state in which they were born or lived recognized them as state citizens.

60. *National Anti-Slavery Standard*, May 13, 1865.

61. William D. Kelley, et al., *The Equality of All Men Before the Law Claimed and Defended* (Boston, 1865), 25.

62. *Independent*, August 14, 1862; *Congressional Globe*, 38th Cong., 1st sess., 1026 (March 10, 1864); *National Anti-Slavery Standard*, May 13, 1865.

63. [Marvin Warren], *A Solution of Our National Difficulties, and the Science of Republican Government* (Cincinnati, 1863), 49-50.

64. Arthur Bestor, "State Sovereignty and Slavery: A Reinterpretation of Proslavery Constitutional Doctrine, 1846-1860," *Journal of the Illinois State Historical Society* 54 (Summer 1961): 117-180.

65. Francis N. Thorpe, *The Constitutional History of the United States, 1765-1895* (3 vols.; Chicago, 1901), III, 523, 529-530.

66. Russell, "The Constitutional Amendment," 323-324; *Congressional Globe*, 38th Cong., 2d sess., 485 (January 28, 1865). See also ibid., 38th Cong., 1st sess., 1314 (March 28, 1864), remarks of Lyman Trumbull; Harold M. Hyman, *A More Perfect Union: The Impact of the Civil War and Reconstruction on the Constitution* (New York, 1973), 284, 287, 289, 301.

8

Equality before the law

Influenced by Jacksonian democratic thought, mid-nineteenth century America made the doctrine of equal rights a convenient caption and symbol of the civil and political order. Wartime emancipation, however, by interjecting race into American politics in a way that had no previous parallel, severely challenged this egalitarian outlook. While the Republicans, no less than other Americans, rejected the notion of inherent racial equality, they yet believed that emancipation affirmed and extended the civil and legal equality of all persons. The meaning of the seemingly simple, but elusive, concept of equality before the law in the Civil War era forms the subject of the present chapter.

Conservatives took a dubious view of equality before the law in relation to emancipated slaves. Referring to language in the revised reconstruction bill of January 1865, Democrat Joseph K. Edgerton asked the meaning of the phrase "equality of civil rights before the law for all persons." Edgerton feared that, if the right to vote were considered a civil right, the clause might be used to extend suffrage to women, blacks, and aliens.[1] Attorney General Edward Bates, similarly apprehensive, seized on Charles Sumner's version of the Thirteenth Amendment, which declared all persons equal before the law, and asked: "What is equality before the law?" Upon learning of a state legislative resolution which would confer the rights of citizens on Negroes, Bates skeptically remarked: "Five cents reward for a definition of the phrase, 'full rights of citizenship.'"[2]

Conservatives, hostile to blacks, feared that even minimal recognition of equal civil rights would lead to denial of the states' power to classify persons according to race. When Sumner tried to block the readmission of Louisiana in February 1865 with a requirement that its constitution declare all persons equal before the law, Reverdy Johnson of Maryland asked whether this meant that a state could not legislate for each race separately. If so, said Johnson, it took from the state "all the authority that everybody from the time the Constitution was adopted to the present hour, has supposed to be the especial right of the State."[3] In his assessment of the political situation in December 1864, Montgomery Blair warned against radical efforts to promote the doctrine of equality before the law on behalf of Negroes. Blair regarded the radicals' equal rights campaign as a plain attempt to deprive white southerners of their power of municipal legislation.[4]

Skepticism about Republican motives in employing the idea of legal equality was in part justified, for interest in freedmen's rights rested upon political and economic as well as ideological and humanitarian considerations. Thus, when Charles Sumner wrote in March 1865, "Our last battle approaches. Its countersign will be equality before the law," he probably referred to the larger question of a reconstruction settlement that would establish northern hegemony over the South.[5] Nevertheless, equality before the law was not simply a political tool conceived at the war's end for carrying on the sectional struggle by other means. The idea of legal equality was rooted in practical as well as ideological concerns and engaged Republican attention throughout the war as a corollary of emancipation.

The first and most fundamental meaning of equality before the law was universal freedom. That is, by making all persons free emancipation would make them all equal before the law. In order to understand the force and significance of this idea, it is necessary to recall that before the Civil War slavery was not universally regarded, by very definition, as a negation of equality before the law. When Edward Bates questioned the meaning of equality before the law in 1864, he went on to ask: "Does *that equality* necessarily prevent the one from becoming the slave of the other?"[6] What Bates apparently meant is that when different classes in the community—men, women, adults, minors, aliens, citizens, blacks, whites, freemen, slaves—were secured in the rights assigned to each class by the legislative or judicial power, each could be said to enjoy equality before the law. Moreover, slave trials before the Civil War show that many southern states extended to slaves a substantial measure of equality with respect to criminal law procedures.[7] Thus equality before the law might mean not only giving each class its due, but also recognizing that some rights, such as criminal trial procedures, applied equally to all classes. In either case, the point was that equality before the law was compatible with the classification of persons as freemen and slaves.

Republicans rejected this proposition as early as the 1850s when they argued that blacks should be recognized as equal before the law at least in respect of the right of personal liberty.[8] Wartime emancipation secured this elementary equality. The abolition of slavery in the District of Columbia, declared John Bingham in 1862, "will illustrate . . . that principle of your constitution which is its chief glory—that all are equal before the law." Proclaiming a new nation to be the result of the Thirteenth Amendment, Isaac Arnold of Illinois said: "Liberty, equality before the law is to be the great cornerstone." In like manner, the New York *Times* argued that the Thirteenth Amendment meant that "all men under the American flag are then 'free' and 'equal' in the sight of the law." Another Unionist writer, reasoning that slavery had perverted and brutalized the law, held that equal protection of the law would result from abolition.[9]

As noted in examining the origins of the Thirteenth Amendment, a few Republicans formulated abolition proposals in explicit equality-before-the-law terms. John P. Hale of New Hampshire introduced a bill declaring that, because all persons within the United States were equal before the law, all claims to personal service were abolished.[10] Better known was Sumner's version of the Thirteenth Amendment which stated that "all persons are equal before the law, so that no person can hold another as a slave."[11] While critical of Sumner's resolution, Republican Jacob Howard seemed to accept the equation of freedom and equality. At the same time, he seemed to recognize that equality before the law could be interpreted to mean far more than the right of personal liberty.[12]

As emancipation proceeded, Republicans enlarged the meaning of legal equality beyond the minimum equality that theorists recognized as present in all liberty.[13] In essence, equality before the law came to comprise the same basic civil rights that many Republicans saw as a necessary corollary of the Thirteenth Amendment right not to be held as chattel. Publicist Henry Everett Russell expressed the idea in asserting that, because the basis of American government was the equality of all men before the law, the manhood or citizenship of the Negro must be accepted. Also equating manhood with citizenship, James Russell Lowell wrote that democratic legal equality meant making one person's manhood as good as another's and giving every one the right of unlimited free trade in all his faculties. Others held that after emancipation, blacks would equally enjoy all the moral rights of humanity or universal natural rights. [14]

In more specific terms, equality before the law referred to guarantees of legal process for the protection of person and property. Republican Senator James Harlan explained in 1862 that emancipated slaves would be equal to white men in their right to justice and the protection of the laws. According to the Washington *Chronicle*, the civil equality of blacks meant that they would be subject to the same standard of equity and justice and the same privileges which the law accorded to others. Publicist Charles Lord similarly concluded that Negroes would enjoy "equality in the obvious sense of one man having the natural right as truly of the use of his time, and property, as another, and justice before the civil tribunal," while legalist James Alexander Hamilton stated that the equality of all men meant that "all men are equal before the law, and equally entitled to protection for their lives, their liberty, and in pursuit of happiness." [15]

The Republican conception of equality before the law was very different from what later generations would consider true equality. Reflecting the almost universal prejudice against blacks in American society, theorists adopted a defensive and apologetic tone in arguing for Negro equality. Thus, Henry Everett Russell advised that it was not necessary to assert the Negro's equality in any comprehensive sense. All that was desired, Russell observed, was not a metaphysical theory of his perfect equality, nor a belief that he was by nature inferior, but rather the simple recognition of black manhood. According to James Russell Lowell, the point was not to attempt the impossibility of making one person equal in all respects to another; it was merely to acknowledge the Negro's manhood as equal to that of whites. A writer in the moderate Unionist *Continental Monthly* explained that the choice was not, as many supposed, between slavery and total equality for blacks. All that blacks needed was equal protection in the moral rights of humanity. [16]

Legal equality was distinct from political and social equality, as well as from the modern idea of the inherent equality of all persons or races. "Equality cannot be conferred on any man, be he white or black," asserted James Russell Lowell. John Bingham observed that the equality of all men did not refer to intellectual ability, wealth, social position, or political privileges. In answering Democratic critics who charged him with radical egalitarian beliefs, Thaddeus Stevens announced in 1865: "I have never held to that doctrine of negro equality." Not in any general sense, but only in respect of the law, said Stevens, were all men equal. [17]

Disavowal of social equality was commonplace among Republicans and antislavery people in general. The conventional view, as explained by the abolitionist Theodore Tilton, was that social equality regulated itself apart from public policy. Whether blacks became equal to whites, reasoned radical Henry Winter Davis, was not something that the law could decide. Representative James Patterson of New Hampshire advised Republicans that the black man would determine for himself his place in the social scale, while Unionist Timothy T. Davis of New York at once affirmed the equality of all men before the law and subscribed to the prevailing belief in the fundamental distinction between the races. "I would make every race free and equal before the law," said Davis, "permitting to each the elevation to which its own capacity and culture should entitle it." Thus, instead of reflecting a fundamental belief in the inherent equality of all people, as is characteristic of the mid-twentieth century approach to the subject, equality before the law was asserted in the absence of any such view. "*Human Rights do not depend on the equality of Man or Races*," declared the New York *Tribune*, "but are wholly independent of them." [18]

While political rights have been absorbed in the modern idea of equality before the law, the distinction drawn between legal and social equality continues to exist in constitutional law, as in the delineation of public and private spheres of action. [19] The difference, and it is a great one, is that the public sphere in which legal equality is guaranteed has been enlarged far beyond the limits placed upon it a century ago. When analyzing the Negro question in 1865, for example, the moderate Washington *Chronicle* held that highways and railways were public places where discrimination against blacks should not be permitted. In private relations, however, that is, in churches, places of amusement, and voluntary associations, the social law based on individual choice was paramount. [20] Antislavery opinion on this matter differed. Some abolitionists, for example, tried to bring employment, housing, churches, hotels, restaurants, and places of recreation within the sphere of legal equality. [21] Segregated schools were another contentious issue which radicals believed inconsistent with the doctrine of equal rights. Yet, moderates thought schools came under the rule of society which allowed discrimination. Though it looked forward to the eventual disappearance of the prejudice that made separate schools necessary, the Washington *Chronicle* defended segregated schools as not inconsistent with the general proposition that all should "stand equal before the law." [22]

During the war, Republicans formulated legislation intended to express the idea of equality before the law. While these proposals betrayed a lack of appreciation for the intractable nature of the civil rights problem in the context of racial prejudice, they did contain the essential ideas of the major constitutional landmarks of legal equality, the Civil Rights Act of 1866 and the Fourteenth Amendment.

The first enactment of legal equality, introduced as a corollary to the abolition of slavery in the District of Columbia in 1862, declared that all persons of color in the District were subject to the same laws, were to be tried in the same manner, and were liable to the same punishment as white persons. Perhaps because the number of blacks involved was small, the measure aroused little interest and produced no debate. With Senator Henry Wilson describing it as a logical corollary of emancipation and cautiously advising that it could do no harm, the Senate approved the guarantee of legal equality. [23] The act was important mainly as a foreshadowing of the subsequent direction of public policy, and it enlarged the economic and social avenues available to blacks in the federal city. [24]

In addition to the straightforward argument that blacks should be governed by the same rules as whites, a more narrow conception of equality before the law centered on the right of blacks to testify in federal courts. This issue was first broached in 1862 in connection with a bill for removing the disqualification of color for U.S. mail carriers. The Senate passed the bill, but the House opposed it on the ground that, as blacks were not permitted to testify in many states and as state rules of evidence and testimony applied in federal courts, blacks as postal officials would be unable to testify against mail depredators. [25] Indeed, rather than remove the restrictions on black testimony, Congress did the opposite by making state rules concerning the competency of witnesses in common law trials, equity, and admiralty—which in many states excluded Negroes—applicable also in federal courts. [26] In 1864, Charles Sumner led a successful effort to reverse this legislation. A rider that Sumner tacked on to an appropriation bill declared that in the courts of the United States there should be no exclusion of any witness on account of color. [27] According to his friend and biographer Edward L. Pierce, Sumner regarded the right to testify as "the most important of all in establishing the manhood and citizenship of the colored people." [28]

Reconstruction legislation of 1863-1865 asserted equality before the law in the same general terms that characterized the District of Columbia Act of 1862. Conservative Republican Ira Harris of New York first inserted in a reconstruction measure the requirement that in the trial and punishment of Negroes the same rules should be used as applied to whites. [29] The Wade-Davis plan passed by Congress in 1864 similarly provided that in occupied rebel states the laws for the trial and punishment of white persons should extend to all persons. [30] Henry Winter Davis, forced to defend the bill against the charge that it did not give adequate protection against black codes, said it was "the shortest possible declaration that all men should be equal before the law." [31]

Others sought to express the idea of equality before the law in still broader terms. Radical Republican Thomas D. Eliot, a critic of Davis's measure, introduced an amendment in 1865 which would require the rebel states to form new state constitutions "guaranteeing to all persons freedom and equal rights before the law." [32] James M. Ashley offered a similar proposal demanding that reorganized loyal governments guarantee to all persons "equality of civil rights before the law." [33] These were exceedingly broad formulations designed to provide a more effective and comprehensive guarantee of legal equality than the trial and punishment provision of the original Wade-Davis plan. [34]

As Negro suffrage became an issue in 1864, some antislavery people held that equality before the law comprised political as well as civil rights. At the urging of Wendell Phillips, the radical Cleveland convention in May 1864 approved a platform demanding equality before the law for all men, which was understood to mean Negro suffrage. Radicals also tried unsuccessfully to enfranchise blacks under the

Wade-Davis reconstruction bill. After Lincoln pocketed the measure, Wendell Phillips Garrison rebuked those who criticized the president for preventing the establishment of equality before the law. "This is just what the bill did not do," Garrison argued, "except in the single item of personal liberty, for it prohibited the negro element from entering at all into the reconstruction of the disloyal States." In February 1865, Charles Sumner used the debate over the readmission of Louisiana as a forum for further asserting that political rights were part of legal equality. Reunion must not be permitted, Sumner vowed, until the seceded states formed governments based "on the consent of the governed and Equality before the law." [35]

This broader conception of legal equality remained a minority view among antislavery people. While radicals might complain that the Thirteenth Amendment accomplished but half of what was needed to create equality before the law, [36] most Republicans were satisfied that the national guarantee of personal liberty, combined perhaps with some kind of executive or legislative requirement of equal laws for the trial and punishment of all persons, would secure the requisite legal equality.

It is important to note that equality before the law, like the ordinary civil rights that were seen as a corollary of personal liberty under the Thirteenth Amendment, was substantially within the jurisdiction of states. Even the Wade-Davis bill, which is often viewed as a nationalizing measure that derogated from state rights, did not propose to nationalize civil rights in the sense of making the federal government permanently responsible for protecting legal equality. (The exception was the *habeas corpus* jurisdiction by which federal courts could guarantee the right of personal liberty.) Rather, it allowed the states to retain power and responsibility over civil rights protection. After the ratification of the Thirteenth Amendment, Republicans anticipated the need for little, if any, federal intervention in order to establish equality before the law. [37]

It is apparent from this inquiry that a great discrepancy existed between what seemed to be demanded in 1865 with respect to equality before the law and what proved to be necessary a year later. Indeed, the whole issue of civil rights equality seemed strangely unproblematic. In part, this was the result of the Republicans' preoccupation with military matters and a natural tendency to put off that which could be put off, especially if it involved a controversial political issue.

More important, however, the discrepancy between 1865 expectation and 1866 actuality concerning equality before the law reflected a failure to appreciate the depth and scope of the race question in the United States.

Generally, this failure of understanding can be attributed to the racism of the society. More specifically, it was based on the misapprehension that racial prejudice was rooted in slavery and would gradually disappear after slavery was abolished. [38] Although in retrospect it is apparent that emancipation gave rise to new modes of discrimination and prejudice based on physical rather than social distance and separation, [39] the impression received from the wartime experience was that hostility toward blacks was on the wane. [40] The enlistment of blacks in the army seemed to signify a decrease in anti-Negro prejudice, and the prospect of a political role for the freedmen further encouraged the belief that the stigma of color would in time be removed. These considerations led the *Independent* in December 1863 to conclude that, in spite of former prejudice, Negroes were being "admitted into the great brotherhood of men." This was not done with an enthusiastic spirit of fraternity, the radical journal added, but for common sense, practical reasons. [41]

As a result of these attitudes, Republicans only rarely anticipated the difficulties that might be encountered in securing equality before the law. Yet, upon occasion questions were raised and the issue probed. The attempt to pass the revised Wade-Davis bill in January 1865 provided one such opportunity and revealed disagreement among Republicans. Although they had approved virtually the same measure at the previous session, a few antislavery members now questioned the efficacy of the Wade-Davis stipulation that laws for the trial and punishment of white persons should apply to all persons. Henry L. Dawes and Thomas D. Eliot, both of Massachusetts, argued that, despite this provision, black laws would be revived through the requirement that occupying Union authorities enforce presecession state laws. Dawes and Eliot contended that only slavery would be prohibited and that blacks would not even be allowed to testify in courts. [42]

Henry Winter Davis regarded this intraparty criticism as political in motivation and thus treated it scornfully. If blacks had to be tried by the same court, under the same law, upon the same evidence, and for the same crime, Davis declared, the black laws were more effectively annihilated than they would be by the lengthiest conceivable statute. Nevertheless, Davis seemed to concede something to the critics when he agreed to amend the bill to provide that the laws for the *government*, as well as for the trial and punishment, of all persons should be the same. The Maryland radical reasoned that, inasmuch as the term *government* referred to the provisions and execution of the law which defined the rights of persons and property, blacks would certainly be assured equal protection. [43] While the attack on the bill does appear to have been politically inspired, the question of an effective legislative formula to secure equality before the law was more important and more problematic than Davis seemed to assume.

Implementation of equality before the law was also at issue in wartime debate over whether ordinary civil suits at common law would be sufficient to protect the freed people or whether special legislation would be required. The exclusion of Negroes from Washington streetcars provoked discussion of the issue in February 1864. At the urging of Charles Sumner, the Senate Committee on the District of Columbia was charged with considering the expediency of a legislative ban on the exclusion of blacks from municipal railways. Sumner and Henry Wilson favored legislation affirming that the streetcar company had no right to make racial distinctions. The District committee, however, including five Republicans and a border Unionist, reported in the negative.

According to chairman James Grimes, the railway company had no authority to discriminate against persons on the basis of race. If it did discriminate, the proper remedy was a civil suit. Grimes stated that "every person has a right to ride in the cars, and . . . a colored person has the same remedies open to him for any infringement of his rights by the Company as anybody else." Waitman T. Willey of West Virginia held that the law was as open to one race as to another, so that blacks with grievances could apply for redress to the courts just as white persons did. Grimes's position on this issue was consistent with his demand for laissez-faire equality and disregard of racial distinctions in freedmen's bureau legislation. He concluded that Negroes were better off bringing suit at common law than they would be if special legislation were passed on their behalf. [44]

Racial subordination as reflected in the practice of streetcar segregation was so thoroughly established that it was patently false to think that blacks could achieve equality before the law merely by ordinary litigation unaided by legislation. Thus, when the streetcar question came up later in the same session and again in 1865, Congress rejected the view of the Senate District of Columbia committee and prohibited railways in the federal city from excluding any person from any car on account of color. [45]

Three positions were taken on the streetcar segregation issue in these subsequent deliberations. The first defended the right of streetcar companies to discriminate on racial grounds. [46] The second denied a right to discriminate but held that the proper remedy for injury of this sort was a civil suit. [47] The third position was that Congress should affirm the right of all persons to ride free of discrimination by enacting positive legislation prohibiting exclusion because of color. In this view, a Negro who was discriminated against would still have to go to law for redress of grievances, but his ability to vindicate his rights would be greatly enhanced by a positive statute declaring what those rights were. [48] Many Republicans insisted that equality before the law could be achieved by civil suits and that legislation *for* blacks as a special group could lead to special legislation *against* them. [49] A majority, however, accepted the view that failure to legislate was tantamount to endorsing an exclusionary policy against the blacks. [50] "Shall we never pass *positive* laws for the defence of the poor and oppressed," asked an antislavery correspondent, "for fear of being charged with *'special'* legislation'?" [51]

Reliance on civil suits by aggrieved persons was the time-honored remedy in Anglo-American law for the redress of injury or the vindication of rights, and in general it remained the favored means of achieving equality before the law. This fact could be seen in an analysis of the freedmen's question by the black New Orleans *Tribune* in early 1865. Situations marked by the absence or iniquity of law, the *Tribune* observed, called for the application of political pressure to change existing rules and statutes or to make new ones. Where freedmen's rights were not recognized, this kind of action was needed. But where laws existed and were violated, the injured person could apply in his private capacity to a court of justice. "Individuals go to law, unaided, isolated, singly,—and receive redress," the *Tribune* optimistically stated. "In every well regulated community every man or woman is fully protected, in all his or her civil rights, no matter how feeble, humble, or isolated one may be." [52] Thus, while conservatives might rail against radical impatience with the civil law, [53] Republicans in

general assumed that existing legal processes would adequately protect freedmen's rights. Even after civil rights laws were enacted in
1866, individual legal action remained the principal mode of securing
equality before the law. [54]

Implicit in the question of protecting freedmen's rights by ordinary
legal process or by special legislation was the issue of whether race was
a reasonable classification consistent with equality before the law.
Blacks had for so long been dealt with as a separate group for the purpose of systematic denial of rights that it seemed natural, in order to
protect and assist them, to continue to regard them as a distinct class.
Thus, whereas the Confiscation Act of 1862 freed slaves, it authorized
Negroes to be employed in military labor. Similarly, the Militia Act of
1862 and the Enrollment Act of 1864 referred to blacks as a distinct
class, apart from male citizens eligible for military service. [55] This approach did not seem to deny equality before the law. In January 1863,
for example, Thaddeus Stevens introduced legislation to equalize the
treatment of Negro troops with respect to pay, allowances, equipment,
and protection. Blacks should be protected, punished, and governed
by the same rules as white soldiers, argued Stevens. Yet, the bill, as a
fellow Republican pointed out, did not place blacks on precisely the
same footing as whites. Aside from the fact that it designated blacks
as a class, it subjected them to such rules and regulations as the president might prescribe, in addition to the rules and articles of war which
alone governed the regular army and volunteers. Stevens's bill would
also require five years' service from black soldiers rather than the customary three years for white troops. Even so, Stevens regarded the
measure as giving blacks "equality of rights" as soldiers. [56]

Thomas D. Eliot, arguing for the relevance of race, criticized the revised Wade-Davis bill of 1865 on the ground that it gave Negroes the
right to vote, "not because of their complexion, but because of their
condition in the service." [57] If blacks left the army, they would lose the
right to vote. More satisfactory to Eliot was the freedmen's bureau bill
passed by the House in 1864, which rested upon a racial classification.
The Freedmen's Bureau was to supervise and assist all persons of
African descent as well as emancipated slaves. Hence, many Republicans believed that to ignore race, as those did who argued that blacks
could go to law to secure their rights just like white persons, was to
confirm existing patterns of race discrimination.

The conservative point of view, to which many Republicans subscribed, held that recognizing blacks as a separate class, or introducing race into legislation even for the purpose of preventing discrimination, was inconsistent with equality before the law. Attorney General Edward Bates, for example, protested legislation for the enlistment of Negroes when no law provided specifically for the enlistment of whites.[58] Senator Reverdy Johnson of Maryland, insisting that he wished to give Negroes all the rights necessary for the protection of life and property, objected to the act prohibiting District of Columbia railroads from excluding persons on account of color.[59] As an alternative to what he considered special legislation on the streetcar segregation question, Republican Robert C. Schenck proposed that railroads be required to furnish all fare-paying passengers with a seat. He believed this proposal would eliminate the "unnecessary excitement about the distinction between blacks and whites." Ignoring race in a formal sense, Schenck would allow private social judgments to regulate the relations between persons on railways.[60] Schenck's approach on this issue was similar to his stand on the freedmen's bureau question on which, by proposing to assist freedmen and white refugees rather than either freedmen or blacks alone, he was able to set aside the exclusive racial basis that had defined earlier freedmen's bills.[61]

The problem of racial classification and equality before the law was raised in somewhat different form by General Sherman's famous order of January 1865 for the voluntary settlement of freedmen along the southern coast from Charleston, South Carolina, to Jacksonville, Florida. When faced with the specific problem of aggressive state agents who were trying to recruit blacks, as well as the larger matter of the disposition of the freed blacks, Sherman, in conjunction with Secretary of War Stanton and after consultation with Negro leaders, set aside abandoned lands for the exclusive use of the former slaves. Heads of families were to receive forty acres under possessory titles, and the "sole·and exclusive management of affairs" was to be left to blacks, subject only to Union military supervision. No white persons, except for army officials, were to be allowed to enter the designated area.[62]

Many antislavery people approved Sherman's order because it offered blacks protection against rapacious whites, a means of self-support without apprenticeship or forced labor, and unconditional recognition of freedom. The New York *Evening Post* regarded it as a significant change from General Banks's supervised labor system in the Mississippi Valley. It stated with laissez-faire enthusiasm that the order "throws the blacks entirely on their own resources—which should have been done, in our opinion, long ago." The Boston *Journal* praised Sherman's directive for constituting "a series of colored communities, which are endowed with all the rights and responsibilities of American citizenship just as fully and as fast as the nature of their antecedents will allow." Though they would be separated from whites and their self-governing status would be qualified by military supervision, the freedmen's liberty and rights seemed to have been recognized.[63]

Other antislavery people, however, pronounced Sherman's order a form of colonization that denied blacks equality before the law. While some objected that separation would deprive blacks of civilizing and edifying contact with whites,[64] the more telling argument attacked the principle of racial classification implicit in the policy. "What true citizenship is it," asked radical General Benjamin F. Butler, "to be deprived of their equal rights, in the land their arms have helped to save?" The New York *Tribune* believed racial prejudice was at the bottom of the plan. "We shall not begin to solve the problem of emancipation," admonished the *Tribune*, "till we aim at making the Southern blacks American citizens, with all the privileges, rights, and enlightment that a Republican Government can bestow, and abandon the notion that he is only a black man who has ceased to be a slave."[65]

The abolitionist Elizur Wright went to the root of the problem raised by Sherman's Negro settlement order when he stated in March 1865: "We have got to decide pretty soon—little as we may like it—whether they shall have a nation of their *own* or a fair share in ours."[66] Obviously, in retrospect blacks were not given a fair share, and this fact has often caused the alternative of separate nationhood to appear attractive. At the time, pessimism about race relations led many antislavery people to favor plans such as Sherman's.[67] To some extent also, blacks themselves supported separation proposals, including Sherman's order.[68] Nevertheless, the imperative of integration, which derived from the belief that racial classification was inconsistent with true equality before the law, overcame the tendency toward separation. The black New Orleans *Tribune* summarized the case against separation or, what it regarded as the same thing, internal colonization. Blacks could not be treated as Indians and gathered in any section of the country, the *Tribune* declared. Warning that such a policy would plant the seeds of race war in the future, the *Tribune* criticized efforts by Negro groups to obtain a land grant from Congress "and become 'a people'!" [69]

Legal equality in general referred to rights and privileges marking out new spheres of power and ability for freed slaves. It also referred to regulations and restraints that defined the ordered liberty under law which was considered an essential part of republican government. Army freedmen's official John Eaton called attention to the regulative aspect of legal equality when he described the transition from slavery to freedom. In local communities in the South, Eaton explained, blacks freed under national authority were treated merely as escaped chattel. They were subjected to harsh punishment and personal abuse and experienced the law in capricious forms. The remedy for such arbitrary treatment, however, said Eaton, was to bring Negroes under the army's pass system. Just as whites within military lines were required to carry passes, so too must the freed people. While the pass system was useful for promoting social order and discipline, Eaton also believed it helped blacks above all to "escape and rise above the general wreck of old slavocratic municipal statues, ordinances, and customs social and civil." Eaton concluded that after being brought under the military pass system, Negroes came to stand on an equal footing with the white man. [70]

The New Orleans *Tribune* also recognized the element of restraint in equality before the law. Adopting a laissez-faire point of view, the *Tribune* emphasized the importance of leaving the freedmen alone to form their own labor arrangements in the competitive market place. At two points only, reasoned the black journal, must the government intervene: to set up labor courts for the resolution of industrial disputes and to enact effective vagrancy laws. The regulative element inherent in legal equality was contained in the latter. The best liberal principles, stated the *Tribune*, required the indifferent application of the law of vagrancy to both black and white races to protect society against the idle and irresponsible. "A good law on vagrancy," announced the *Tribune*, "equally applicable to the whole population, giving power to set to work the man who has no means of existence, will effectively protect the general interest of society." [71]

At a minimal level, the Thirteenth Amendment established equality before the law in providing a guarantee of personal liberty. By the end of the war, moreover, a consensus was forming among Republicans on the need for more explicit guarantees of legal equality, assuring equal access to courts of law and requiring the application of the same laws for the protection of person and property to both races. Yet, it was by no means clear how equality before the law could most effectively be expressed and implemented. As late as the spring of 1866, the Republican Bangor *Daily Whig and Courier* observed that, while the people demanded a government of equal rights, they were indifferent to the exact form which legislation or constitutional amendment for this purpose might take. Only "let the principle be attained," said the *Whig and Courier*, "and they are satisfied." [72] Building on the wartime experience, Republicans in the Civil Rights Act of 1866 and the Fourteenth Amendment were at this very time fixing the fundamental terms and forms in which the idea of equality before the law was expressed in the reconstruction period. It is to these measures that we now turn.

NOTES

1. *Congressional Globe*, 38th Cong., 2d sess., App., 78 (February 20, 1865).

2. Howard K. Beale, ed., *The Diary of Edward Bates, 1859-1866* (Washington, D.C., 1933), 330, 517.

3. *Congressional Globe*, 38th Cong., 2d sess., 1105 (February 25, 1865).

4. Montgomery Blair to Abraham Lincoln, December 6, 1864, Lincoln Papers, Library of Congress.

5. Charles Sumner to William Lloyd Garrison, March 29, 1865, Garrison Papers, Boston Public Library.

6. Beale, ed., *Diary of Edward Bates*, 330.

7. Daniel J. Flanigan, "Criminal Procedure in Slave Trials in the Antebellum South," *Journal of Southern History* 40 (November 1974): 537-564.

8. Harry V. Jaffa, *Crisis of the House Divided: An Interpretation of the Issues in the Lincoln-Douglas Debates* (New York, 1959).

9. *Congressional Globe*, 37th Cong., 2d sess., 1639 (April 11, 1862), 38th Cong., 1st sess., 2989 (June 15, 1864); New York *Times*, February 8, 1865; *Address of the Democratic League: The Real Motives of the Rebellion* (New York, 1864), 12.

10. 38th Cong., S. No. 3, December 14, 1863.

11. *Congressional Globe*, 38th Cong., 1st sess., 1482 (April 8, 1864).

12. Ibid., 1488 (April 8, 1864). Cf. above Ch. 7, pp. 126-127.

13. Francis Lieber, *On Civil Liberty and Self-Government*, 3d ed. (Philadelphia, 1891), 282.

14. H. E. Russell, "Negro Troops," *Continental Monthly* 6 (August 1864): 196-198; [J. R. Lowell], "Reconstruction," *North American Review* 100 (April 1865): 554; Anon., "The Destiny of the African Race in the United States," *Continental Monthly* 3 (May

1863): 603; *Congressional Globe*, 37th Cong., 2d sess., 1639 (April 11, 1862).

15. *Congressional Globe*, 37th Cong., 2d sess., App., 322 (July 11, 1862); Washington *Chronicle*, March 2, 1865; James Alexander Hamilton, *The Constitution Vindicated: Nationality, Secession, Slavery* (New York, 1864), 12.

16. H. E. Russell, "Negro Troops," 195; [Lowell], "Reconstruction," 554; "Destiny of the African Race," 602-603.

17. [Lowell], "Reconstruction," 559; *Congressional Globe*, 37th Cong., 2d sess., 1639 (April 11, 1862), 38th Cong., 2d sess., 125 (January 5, 1865).

18. Washington *Chronicle*, February 27, 1865, speech of Theodore Tilton; Henry Winter Davis, *Speeches and Addresses* (New York, 1867), 363; *Congressional Globe*, 38th Cong., 2d sess., 484 (January 28, 1865), 154-155 (January 7, 1865); New York *Tribune*, October 7, 1862, quoted in Robert F. Durden, "Ambiguities in the Antislavery Crusade of the Republican Party," in Martin Duberman, ed., *The Antislavery Vanguard: New Essays on the Abolitionists* (Princeton, 1965), 390.

19. See Charles L. Black Jr., "The Constitution and Public Power," *Yale Review* 52 (October 1962): 54-66.

20. Washington *Chronicle*, March 2, 1865.

21. James M. McPherson, *The Struggle for Equality: Abolitionists and the Negro During the Civil War and Reconstruction* (Princeton, 1964), 222-230.

22. Washington *Chronicle*, March 8, 1865.

23. *Congressional Globe*, 37th Cong., 2d sess., 2020 (May 8, 1862); *U.S. Statutes at Large*, XII, 407; Henry Wilson, *History of the Antislavery Measures of the Thirty-seventh and Thirty-eighth United States Congresses, 1861-65* (Boston, 1865), 419.

24. Constance McLaughlin Green, *The Secret City: A History of Race Relations in the Nation's Capital* (Princeton, 1967), 60.

25. *Congressional Globe*, 37th Cong., 2d sess., 1626 (April 11, 1862), 2231-2232 (May 20, 1862).

26. Ibid., 3261 (July 11, 1862), 3354-3357 (July 15, 1862); *U.S. Statutes at Large*, XII, 588-589. Prior to this time, state rules were applicable only in common law cases.

27. *Congressional Globe*, 38th Cong., 1st sess., 3259-3260 (June 25, 1864); *U.S. Statutes at Large*, XIII, 351; Edward L. Pierce, *Memoir and Letters of Charles Sumner* (4 vols.; Boston, 1877-1894), IV, 181; Sumner to Henry W. Longfellow, April 24, 1864, Sumner to George W. Curtis, April 13, 1864, Sumner Papers, Harvard University Library.

28. Pierce, *Memoir and Letters of Sumner*, IV, 181.

29. 37th Cong., S. No. 200, sec. 3, January 30, 1863; S. No. 538, sec. 2, February 17, 1863.

30. 38th Cong., H.R. No. 244, sec. 10, February 15, 1864.

31. *Congressional Globe*, 38th Cong., 2d sess., 935 (February 20, 1865), 970 (February 21, 1865).

32. 38th Cong., H.R. No. 602, January 12, 1865, amendment of Thomas D. Eliot.

33. H.R. No. 602, sec. 12, January 7, 1865.

34. *Congressional Globe*, 38th Cong., 2d sess., 300 (January 17, 1865), remarks of Thomas D. Eliot.

35. William F. Zornow, *Lincoln and the Party Divided* (Norman, Okla., 1954), 72-86; *Liberator*, August 19, 1864, letter of "M. DuPays"; *Congressional Globe*, 38th

Cong., 2d sess., 1099 (February 25, 1865); Sumner to Carl Schurz, July 11, 1865, Sumner Papers, Harvard University Library.

36. Giles Rease to Charles Sumner, February 27, 1865, Sumner Papers, Harvard University Library.

37. Harold M. Hyman, *A More Perfect Union: The Impact of the Civil War and Reconstruction on the Constitution* (New York, 1973), 284.

38. George M. Fredrickson, *The Black Image in the White Mind: The Debate on Afro-American Character and Destiny, 1817-1914* (New York, 1971), 39-40; Boston *Commonwealth*, October 18, 1862; *Liberator*, June 24, 1864, New England Freedmen's Report; New Orleans *Tribune*, December 1, 1864, report on colored people's rights on railways.

39. C. Vann Woodward, *American Counterpoint: Slavery and Racism in the North-South Dialogue* (Boston, 1971), 234-260.

40. Fredrickson, *The Black Image in the White Mind*, 167-168.

41. *Independent*, December 24, 1863.

42. *Congressional Globe*, 38th Cong., 2d sess., 298 (January 17, 1865), 935 (February 20, 1865).

43. Ibid., 970 (February 21, 1865).

44. Ibid., 38th Cong., 1st sess., 553-554 (February 10, 1864), 786 (February 24, 1864), 817-818 (February 25, 1864); 38th Cong., 1st sess., *Senate Reports*, No. 17, February 24, 1864.

45. *U.S. Statutes at Large*, XIII, 329, act of July 1, 1864, 537, act of March 3, 1865.

46. *Congressional Globe*, 38th Cong., 1st sess., 1141 (March 16, 1864), remarks of Willard Saulsbury, 1159 (March 17, 1864), remarks of James Doolittle.

47. Ibid., 1156 (March 17, 1864), remarks of Reverdy Johnson.

48. Ibid., 1158-1159 (March 17, 1864), remarks of Charles Sumner and Lot M. Morrill.

49. Ibid., 38th Cong., 2d sess., 1027 (February 23, 1865), remarks of James Patterson, 994 (February 22, 1865), remarks of Thomas Davis. Six Republicans opposed Sumner's motion to bar racial exclusiveness from streetcars in March 1864. Ibid., 38th Cong., 1st sess., 1161 (March 17, 1864).

50. Ibid., 38th Cong., 2d sess., 1026 (February 23, 1865), remarks of Thaddeus Stevens.

51. *National Anti-Slavery Standard*, March 18, 1865, Washington correspondence.

52. New Orleans *Tribune*, January 7, 1865.

53. Beale, *The Diary of Edward Bates*, 331-332 (February 10, 1864).

54. Hyman, *A More Perfect Union*, 263-281, 457, 467-468, 476, 529.

55. William Whiting, *War Powers Under the Constitution of the United States*, 43d ed. (Boston, 1871), 493, 509-510. See above, Ch. 2, pp. 21-23.

56. *Congressional Globe*, 37th Cong., 3d sess., 557 (January 27, 1863), 598-599 (January 29, 1863).

57. Ibid., 38th Cong., 2d sess., 299 (January 17, 1865).

58. Beale, ed., *Diary of Edward Bates*, 395.

59. *Congressional Globe*, 38th Cong., 1st sess., 1156 (March 17, 1864).

60. Ibid., 38th Cong. 2d sess., 1027-1028 (February 23, 1865).

61. See above, Ch. 6, pp. 101-108.

62. Proposed Order of General Sherman, Military Division of the Mississippi, January 1865, Stanton Papers, Library of Congress; Lloyd Lewis, *Sherman: Fighting Prophet* (New York, 1932), 481-482; William T. Sherman, *Memoirs* (2 vols.; Bloomington, Ind., 1957), II, 246.

63. Worcester *Daily Spy*, January 30, 1865; New York *Evening Post*, January 28, 1865; Boston *Journal*, February 3, 1865.

64. New York *Times*, February 26, 1865; Boston *Commonwealth*, February 4, 1865; [J. R. Lowell], "Reconstruction," 555.

65. Cincinnati *Daily Commercial*, February 8, 1865, speech of General B. F. Butler; New York *Tribune*, January 30, 1865.

66. Elizur Wright to Charles Sumner, March 6, 1865, Sumner Papers, Harvard University Library.

67. Frank Blair, Sr., to Andrew Johnson, November 14, 1864, in William E. Smith, *The Francis Preston Blair Family in Politics* (2 vols.; New York, 1933), II, 338; 38th Cong., S. No. 45, January 13, 1864, bill for colonizing Negroes in Texas introduced by James H. Lane of Kansas; *Congressional Globe*, 38th Cong., 1st sess., 672-675 (February 16, 1864), remarks of James H. Lane; Wilbert H. Ahern, "The Cox Plan of Reconstruction: A Case Study in Ideology and Race Relations," *Civil War History* 16 (December 1970), 293-308.

68. Sherman, *Memoirs*, II, 246; Edward M. Stanton to William Lloyd Garrison, February 12, 1865, Garrison Papers, Boston Public Library.

69. New Orleans *Tribune*, September 22, 1864.

70. John Eaton, *Grant, Lincoln and the Freedmen: Reminiscences of the Civil War* (New York, 1907), 136-137.

71. New Orleans *Tribune*, February 7, 1865.

72. Bangor *Daily Whig and Courier*, March 19, 1866.

9

The civil rights settlement of 1866

The optimism with which Republicans viewed the question of freedmen's rights in early 1865 was abruptly dispelled by the course of events following Lincoln's assassination. Under dispensation from President Johnson, southern legislatures enacted codes of law which from the southern white point of view were intended to delineate civil rights not previously available to blacks as well as to protect society against dislocation and upheaval arising from emancipation. In the eyes of Republicans, however, these laws—the famous black codes—if not an attempt to reenslave the freedmen were patently intended to deny them equality before the law and equal rights.[1] Numerous acts of injury and abuse against Negroes by private individuals further convinced Republicans of the need for more effective protection of civil rights than the army and the Freedmen's Bureau were able to provide. The Civil Rights Act of 1866 and the Fourteenth Amendment, which together summarized the evolution of Republican civil rights ideas and established the framework for protection of Negro rights in the reconstruction period, were the result of this postwar reaction to executive policy.

Three fundamental considerations came together in the settlement of the civil rights issue after Appomattox. The first was the basic Republican conception of civil rights. Although it now stood out with greater clarity, it remained essentially what it had been during the war. Distinguishing between political and social equality on the one hand and legal equality on the other, Republicans defined legal equality as consisting of the rights of personal liberty and locomotion, property ownership, free labor and liberty of contract, freedom of speech and religious worship, the sanctity of family and home, the right to bring suit and testify in court, and generally the protection of person and property that belonged to all freemen or citizens. The motivation behind civil rights legislation, the second element in the situation, also remained as it was during the war—a blend of humanitarian idealism and pragmatic political and economic concerns, tempered by sensitivity to northern racial prejudice. If the strategic position of the freedmen in reconstruction politics was more apparent, so too was the sense that guaranteeing the results of the war required effective protection of the freedmen's liberty. The third part of the civil rights settlement of 1866 was the theory of federalism. Unlike the other two elements, however, this one took on considerably greater importance than it had during the war.

Although ideas about federalism were by no means irrelevant to wartime policy making, to a considerable extent they were superseded by the doctrine of emergency war powers. Under this theory, the federal government might invade spheres of power traditionally reserved to the states, as in conscription and internal security matters. Republicans, however, employed the grasp of war theory not in derogation of federalism but as a temporary alternative to it.[2] Both the Freedmen's Bureau and reconstruction bills, for example, while they were extraordinary assertions of national power, assumed that the states would resume principal responsibility—under a federal guarantee of personal liberty—for individual civil rights.

In 1866, widespread civil disorder directed against blacks made the grasp of war theory still relevant for civil rights protection.[3] This was apparent in the passage of the second freedmen's bureau bill, which extended the life of the military protective agency. In framing the Civil Rights Act of 1866 and the Fourteenth Amendment, however, Republicans acted within the framework of federalism rather than the war powers doctrine. The principal aim of these measures was to place the protection of freedmen's rights on a permanent basis, consistent with the view that the states should remain the principal centers of republicanism.

While the Thirteenth Amendment clearly changed the federal system by giving the national government power to protect personal liberty, the extent of this new federal authority was uncertain. In 1864 and 1865, Republicans had been content vaguely to assume that the freedmen would enjoy the basic rights of citizenship surrounding personal liberty, without clarifying the scope and nature of federal power to secure those rights. Southern treatment of blacks in 1865-1866 led to a consideration both of the rights that were necessarily, if only inferentially, guaranteed by the prohibition of slavery, and of the power of Congress to protect them. The Civil Rights Act of 1866 and the Fourteenth Amendment were the result of this reconsideration.

Conservative apprehensions of 1864-1865 foreshadowed the Republicans' new view of the Thirteenth Amendment after Appomattox. While Democrats in the Thirty-eighth Congress had objected to the use of federal power to protect personal liberty, southern whites in 1865 feared the more drastic possibility that a general legislative power over the freedmen might be derived from the antislavery amendment. Jefferson Davis, for example, told the Confederate Congress that the Thirteenth Amendment asserted a federal right to legislate on the relations between Negroes and whites. Others believed it would be interpreted to authorize laws establishing political and social equality for blacks. In ratifying the Thirteenth Amendment, therefore, the legislatures of South Carolina, Florida, Alabama, Louisiana, and Mississippi expressed the opinion that it gave Congress no power to legislate on the political status or civil relations of former slaves.[4]

This opinion carried to its logical conclusion the congressional view of 1864-1865 that the amendment prohibited slavery, narrowly defined, and gave Congress power to protect personal liberty, also narrowly defined. Republicans had not contended for federal power to legislate directly on civil rights, and when after the war white southerners questioned the scope of the Thirteenth Amendment, Secretary of State Seward stated that the enforcement section restrained rather than enlarged congressional power.[5] Nor was Seward the only Republican to hold this view. When, in January 1866, a Republican representative sought to place the House on record in support of congressional power to legislate broadly on civil rights under section 2, Thaddeus Stevens objected. "I dislike to," the radical leader said, "but I rather think it is in conflict with the opinion of the Secretary of State. We all know that the second section is restraining."[6]

Although Stevens blocked the resolution, the attempt to maintain party unity on this issue was unsuccessful, for by 1866 a large number of Republicans believed the amendment did in fact enlarge federal legislative power over civil rights. The freedom promised in the Thirteenth Amendment was not a mere nominal freedom, wrote William M. Grosvenor. "It involves full protection in all rights of person and property—absolute equality before the law." [7] In the summer of 1865, Congressman James A. Garfield of Ohio anticipated the views of fellow lawmakers in asking: "What is freedom? Is it the bare privilege of not being chained,—of not being bought and sold, branded and scourged?" Liberty was a tangible reality, Garfield argued, that could not exist without protection in the rights of property, contract, and access to courts of law. [8] Republicans furthermore discovered an abundance of federal power in the Thirteenth Amendment. Whereas personal liberty and civil rights were previously held under state authority, the New York *Tribune* observed in a commentary on the amendment, "hereafter they are to be upheld and guarded by the Nation." [9]

Republicans in the Thirty-ninth Congress were quick to express this new conception of the Thirteenth Amendment. They reasoned that, as slavery consisted in a deprivation of natural rights, its prohibition at once guaranteed all the rights of freemen. Although it was difficult to say theoretically where the line between slavery and freedom should be drawn, Lyman Trumbull declared, the practical issue was that the restraints on liberty necessary in civil society should affect all persons equally, regardless of race. The discriminatory laws that the southern states were enacting, Trumbull said, were an infringement on liberty and a badge of servitude prohibited by the Thirteenth Amendment. [10]

To most Republicans, moreover, it now seemed clear that Congress could legislate to protect rights guaranteed by the amendment. The enlarged operations of the Freedmen's Bureau, for example, though still primarily military and justified under the war powers doctrine, were seen by many as a legitimate exercise of congressional power under the Thirteenth Amendment. [11] Several Republicans insisted that this broad interpretation of the amendment expressed the true intention of the framers in the previous Congress. Thus, Trumbull said he had never doubted that under section 2 Congress could protect every person in the United States in all the civil rights belonging to a free citizen. [12] Conservatives professed astonishment at this interpretation of the Thirteenth Amendment. It is perhaps revealing that, when a critic asked whether he had offered this view in the Thirty-eighth Congress, Trumbull replied: "I do not know that I stated it to the Senate."[13]

While congressional representation and the political status of former rebels were being considered in the Joint Committee on Reconstruction, created by Congress in December 1865 to formulate a plan of reunification, a more immediate focus of legislative attention was on the need to protect the freedmen against state discrimination and private injury and abuse in the South.[14] The second freedmen's bureau bill of February 1866, which extended indefinitely the life of the agency and gave bureau agents jurisdiction over violations of freedmen's rights, provided a military response to this problem. But because they desired to restore the rule of civil law as soon as possible, Republicans at the same time formulated a measure for peacetime, nonmilitary protection of civil rights. This was the civil rights bill of 1866.

Introduced by Lyman Trumbull in January 1866, the civil rights bill contained a definition of citizenship that included Negroes, enumerated basic civil rights in which blacks were to be protected equally with whites, and instructed federal officials in the enforcement of these rights. All persons born in the United States, except Indians not taxed, were declared to be citizens of the United States. Regardless of race, color, or previous condition of servitude, citizens were to have the same right in each state or territory to make and enforce contracts; to sue, be parties, and give evidence in courts; to inherit, lease, or own property; and generally to have the full and equal benefit of all laws for the security of person and property as was enjoyed by white persons. In addition, the bill declared in more sweeping terms "that there shall be no discrimination in civil rights or immunities" among the inhabitants of any state on account of race, color, or previous slavery.

The rights thus specified were given sanction by section 2 of the bill, which stated that any person who under color of any law, statute, ordinance, regulation, or custom deprived any inhabitant of rights secured by the act was guilty of a misdemeanor. Punishment upon conviction was to be $1,000 and/or one-year imprisonment. The bill gave U.S. district courts exclusive jurisdiction over crimes committed against the act and concurrent jurisdiction to district and circuit

courts over civil and criminal cases involving persons who were unable
to enforce in state courts rights secured by the act. Finally, the bill required a variety of federal officers to institute proceedings against
violators of the act.[15]

Although the general prohibition of discrimination in civil rights or
immunities which the bill proposed proved to be controversial, the
conception of rights that informed the measure was not really at issue.
Since emancipation began, a consensus had been forming among
Republicans that the freed people should be protected in the basic
rights of property, contract, free labor, family, religion, access to
courts—all that was suggested by the appeal to life, liberty, and the
pursuit of happiness. The bill clearly expressed this consensus more
broadly and forthrightly than the Thirteenth Amendment or the debate upon it in the Thirty-eighth Congress had.[16] At the same time,
the bill was narrowly conceived in that it retained the customary distinction between civil rights and political and social rights. To satisfy
apprehensions on this point, Republicans deleted the general ban on
discrimination on civil rights, which conservatives feared would be
interpreted to secure equal political rights for blacks or to prevent
states from making any distinctions whatever among persons on the
basis of race.[17]

It was not so much the scope of civil rights but rather the question of
which government—state or federal—would have jurisdiction in
relation thereto that was at issue. Before the war, states regulated personal liberty and civil rights. The Thirteenth Amendment gave Congress a degree of authority in this sphere, and the civil rights bill attempted specifically to define the extent of this power. Although
racial attitudes and political desires provided motivation, in a proxi-
mate sense the controversy concerned the distribution of power in the
federal system.

The question of Negro citizenship provided an opportunity to deal
with the problem of federalism, on the ground that if blacks were citizens of the nation the federal government had authority to protect
their rights.

As we have seen in an earlier chapter, the Dred Scott ruling that
blacks were not citizens of the United States in the sense of the Constitution resolved the antebellum dispute over Negro citizenship. Although Republicans repudiated this doctrine during the war, they
failed to give Negro citizenship the kind of authoritative affirmation

necessary to change constitutional law. Consequently, in the debate on the civil rights bill in 1866, conservatives invoked the 1857 ruling and held that only by a constitutional amendment could Negroes become citizens. [18] Arguing that state and federal citizenship were separate and distinct legal entities, each of which was protected against interference from the other, conservatives objected to the attempt by Congress in the civil rights bill to make Negroes citizens of states as well as the nation and to regulate their rights as state citizens. [19]

The central idea in the Republican theory of citizenship was that all persons born or naturalized in the United States were citizens of the United States and of the state in which they resided. In their review of antebellum precedents, Republicans pointed out that Negroes were subjects of the British Crown; became state citizens in 1776 and national citizens in 1789; and thereafter were recognized as citizens in some states and occasionally for certain purposes as citizens of the United States. [20] In the Republican view, national citizenship was primary, which meant that state citizenship depended upon or derived from it. In contrast, the constitutional law of the Dred Scott case held either that state and national citizenship were exclusive and distinct, or that state citizenship was primary in the sense that persons born in the United States were citizens of the nation only if they were recognized as citizens of the state in which they resided.[21]

The more significant fact was that American citizenship was dual. Furthermore, it was coterminous and cooperative rather than bifurcated and conflicting. What is a citizen of the United States, asked Lyman Trumbull, if he is not a citizen of a state? Trumbull declared that if American citizenship conferred no rights in the states its worth was dubious indeed. The Philadelphia *North American* criticized the conservative idea that state and national citizenship were entirely separate and observed that "The two things are essentially the same." The publicist Samuel Spear similarly reasoned that a citizen of the United States was of necessity a citizen of the state in which he resided, "since the same terms of citizenship apply equally to both." [22]

Considering that in the antebellum era state sovereignty and compact theories of the Union denied the very notion of allegiance to and hence citizenship in the federal government, the historical significance of the Republican theory was to establish beyond peradventure the duality of American citizenship. [23] Senator John Conness of California apprehended the point when he wrote that the war led to "the going out and end of Virginian, South Carolinian, Mississippian . . . and the coming in of American citizenship of the freest of republics." What Conness meant was not that state citizenship no longer existed, but that national citizenship had become a reality. [24] Observing that it was a mark of sovereign power to define and determine citizenship, Union publicist Samuel F. Foot wrote in 1865 that the question was whether the states possessed unrestricted sovereignty in this matter. Republicans denied it, and in the civil rights bill they asserted a concurrent and, in the sense described above, a primary power over citizenship. The practical importance of the dual citizenship doctrine, Foot wrote, was to prevent the states from refusing to recognize the freedmen as state citizens. [25] In explaining that the Republican purpose was to place citizenship on unquestionable ground, James G. Blaine perceived the necessity of invading what had been the states' virtually exclusive domain. The point to be secured, he wrote, was that citizenship must not be given different constructions in different states. [26]

Although their rhetoric of national citizenship might imply a body of nationally uniform law regulating the exercise of specific rights as in local or municipal law, Republicans in actuality contended only that within diverse states all persons, regardless of race, must enjoy equally the benefit of whatever laws existed for the protection of person and property. Thus, the purpose of the civil rights bill was to guarantee intrastate equality before the law. This could be seen in the very structure of the measure, which after determining who were national citizens, declared them to be entitled to certain rights in the states, in effect as state citizens. Underscoring this theme, Representative Samuel Shellabarger of Ohio said the bill did not confer or define civil rights; it simply required that in conferring rights and obligations a state must make no distinction of race. William Lawrence of Ohio and Lyman Trumbull agreed that the bill merely insisted on the equal protection of civil rights existing among citizens of the same state. [27]

In apparent contradiction to the demand for intrastate equality, some Republicans posited exclusive rights of national citizenship based on the privileges and immunities clause of the Constitution. Trumbull and Lawrence, for example, said the clause protected the right to acquire property, to enjoy life, liberty, and the pursuit of happiness, and to travel into and be protected in any state. [28] They believed, moreover (though others disagreed), that the civil rights bill, which they regarded as in part based on the privileges and immunities clause, accomplished the purpose of protecting citizens when traveling outside their own states. [29]

This conception of exclusive rights of national citizenship was not so broad as it appeared, for whatever privileges the clause comprehended—a matter on which no agreement was ever reached—federal power was effective only in relation to travel or sojourn in another state. This, beyond the guarantee of personal liberty in the Thirteenth Amendment, was the essential meaning and the extent of direct federal responsibility for civil rights. Half the territory of the United States had been *terra incognita* to nearly half its citizens, Samuel Shellabarger said in support of his bill for the protection of the privileges and immunities of national citizens. While Shellabarger thought his measure was more effective than Trumbull's civil rights bill, he saw both as attempts to protect citizens from other sections of the republic against outrages while in the South. The objective, he wrote to Trumbull in April 1866, was for "the Nation to throw its shield over all its children in their free intercourse and enjoyment of these privileges in all the States." [30] The same interstate concern was evident in the query of another correspondent of Trumbull's: "what is a government worth that cannot protect its own citizens? I want to travel in Mississippi with as much feeling of personal safety as in Massachusetts." [31]

This limited direct federal responsibility for civil rights notwithstanding, intrastate equality for persons who were at once national and state citizens was the principal concern of the Civil Rights Act. Rather than consisting in rights, the exclusive source and guarantor of which was the federal government, the idea of American citizenship was more typically expressed in the decentralist notion of equality before the law within diverse states. Of necessity perhaps this development must be described as the nationalization of civil rights. Yet, rather than taking the form of centralized uniformity, as in a unitary government, it followed the peculiar pattern of American federalism. It did so because of the Republicans' attachment to state-centered federalism and, in a more immediate sense, because of the black codes. The result of the initiative which President Johnson's policy allowed the southern states—an initiative which itself, of course, was a much stronger reflection of the state-centered constitutionalism within which American politics operated—the black codes relieved Republicans of the need positively to define national civil rights.

Instead, the Republicans could protect the rights of citizenship in the negative form of prohibiting intrastate inequities. [32]

More than the rights pertaining to citizenship, the nature and scope of federal legislative power was the main issue in the civil rights bill debate. Conservatives, pursuing the doctrine expressed by several southern legislatures in ratifying the Thirteenth Amendment, held that the new article of the Constitution prohibited property in man and gave Congress power only to prevent chattelization. They were willing to support, and in fact did support, legislation for this purpose. [33] But measures like the civil rights bill, which went beyond this narrow view, were regarded as a revolutionary attempt to consolidate the power of local legislation in Congress. [34] In particular, conservatives objected that the civil rights bill would subject state officers (persons acting "under color of law") to criminal punishment for enforcing state laws that might be in conflict with the federal statute. [35] Summarizing the conservative position, the Washington *National Intelligencer* said the question was not whether the nation was bound to protect southern Negroes against all injury, but whether the wrongs done to blacks were within the limits of federal power. Was the federal government, which protected citizens abroad, "to stand aloof in apathy and indifference when its citizens [were] oppressed at home?" The *Intelligencer*'s answer was an emphatic "yes." [36]

Although it represented an extension of federal power scarcely conceivable before the war, in the historical context of 1866 the most significant characteristic of the civil rights bill was its constitutional restraint. While it obviously dealt with matters previously within exclusive state jurisdiction, the critical question was to what extent the act allowed federal power to intrude in local affairs. The debate in Congress and journalistic commentary show that Republicans adopted a moderate position which called for the intrusion of federal power only part of the way into the civil rights field. Republican lawmakers intended to redress and place restrictions upon state actions in relation to Negroes, not supersede state power over private actions that violated the blacks' rights. Subject to the conditions in the civil rights bill, which were designed to prevent the kind of flagrant discrimination passing beyond mere diversity that the black codes represented, states would remain the principal centers of republican government. The bill thus embodied a theory of state action as a limitation on federal power.

Although the Civil Rights Act was intended to replace the temporary procedures of military power, the state action theory in fact led Republicans to hold that the law would cease to operate when the states enacted laws of their own protecting freedmen's rights. Even the Civil Rights Act, in other words, was looked on as a temporary expedient. Thus, Senator William M. Stewart of Nevada, reasoning that Congress under the Thirteenth Amendment could legislate only against discriminatory state acts, said that states could avoid the effect of the Civil Rights Act by passing fair statutes recognizing Negroes' rights. According to William Lawrence of Ohio, the state action with which Congress was legitimately concerned under the Thirteenth Amendment might take the form of either discriminatory laws or a failure to provide laws protecting certain citizens. Lawrence believed the federal government could not, nor did the civil rights bill attempt, to punish ordinary private offenses against the rights of person and property in the states. And though he defended the civil penal enactments of the Civil Rights Act as preferable to military tribunals, he too described it as a temporary measure that might be abandoned when the necessity for it ended. [37]

Explaining the state action theory further, Representative Samuel Shellabarger emphasized that the civil rights bill did not reach "mere private wrongs" but only those done "under color of state authority." It did not usurp the states' power generally to punish offenses against citizens' rights. [38] James Wilson of Iowa, chairman of the Judiciary Committee and manager of the bill in the House, stated that the entire structure of the measure rested on the states' discrimination in civil rights on account of color. When asked why the bill did not apply penal sanctions to other than state officers, that is, "to the whole community" instead of only those acting under color of law, Wilson replied: "We are not making a general criminal code for the States." [39]

Outside Congress, many observers agreed that the state action criterion defined the scope of federal power in the Civil Rights Act. The act did not secure social rights or guard against private discrimination. Antislavery clergyman David A. Wasson pointed out that the bill was not only limited to protecting person and property, but it also provided safeguards "only against *legalized* and *formal* unfairness." According to the Philadelphia *North American*, the act secured neither political rights nor social rights pertaining to streetcars, hotels, churches, or public places. It protected only person and property

against unfriendly state legislation and executive and judicial practices. The Baltimore *American* similarly viewed the congressional
purpose as that of dealing with state laws and other state acts that
denied blacks' rights. [40]

In addition to discriminatory acts of states, southern Negroes met
injury and abuse at the hands of private individuals after the war. In
recent years this fact has provided the basis for an historical and legal
argument that Congress in the Civil Rights Act intended to proscribe
private as well as official state acts directed against Negroes. [41] In this
view, particular importance attaches to the word "custom" in section
2 of the act, the argument being that the criminal punishment of any
person who "under color of any law, statute, ordinance, regulation, or
custom" deprives another person of civil rights was meant to comprehend private acts of discrimination. [42]

Little contemporary evidence exists to support this interpretation.
Some conservative opponents of the Civil Rights Act did argue that it
would displace state power over civil rights and confer social rights by
which blacks would be protected against private discrimination. [43]
Yet, for the most part critics viewed the criminal sanctions against
state officers as sufficiently revolutionary to warrant condemnation,
without assuming that Congress was trying to regulate all crimes
against freedmen. [44] Among supporters of the measure, a few expressions of opinion outside Congress went beyond the state action limitation, but only the most vague and tenuous suggestions came from lawmakers. [45] It seems clear, moreover, that the word "custom" in
section 2 of the Civil Rights Act did not have the connotation of private conduct given it by critics of the state action theory. In its legislative context, it was another way of describing state actions or procedures. [46]

The Civil Rights Act would have a bearing on crimes committed
against blacks but not a direct impact in the sense of authorizing
federal prosecution of ordinary crimes. The Baltimore *American* illustrated the anticipated effect of the law when it decried the widespread murder and robbery of blacks. Such acts were committed with
impunity "and there is no law to punish the criminals!" the *American*
protested. The gravamen of the charge, however, was that under existing law the testimony of black witnesses to crimes against freedmen
could not be received in state courts. By forcing the admission of
Negro testimony, the Civil Rights Act would enable criminals to be
punished, but the expected forum was the state courts. [47]

Lyman Trumbull's views on the state action question command particular attention as he was author of the Civil Rights Act. On the one hand, Trumbull seemed to endorse the state action theory when he explained that the purpose of the bill was to secure equal civil rights when they were denied by state authorities; all that was required, he added, was racially impartial state laws. [48] On the other hand, in declaring that "any person who shall deprive another of any right . . . in consequence of his color or race will expose himself to fine and imprisonment," Trumbull seemed to support federal jurisdiction over private acts. [49] Clarification came in Trumbull's interpretation of the phrase "under color of law." If these words were omitted, he reasoned, the persons to whom they applied would still be affected by the act, on the theory that Congress could punish any one who violated U.S. law. Presumably, this punishment could affect either state officials or private persons. Because the main trouble blacks experienced came from discriminatory state laws and acts performed thereunder, Trumbull explained, the term "under color of law" was inserted. And this phrase, he went on to say, was intended as a limitation. [50] The evident meaning is that the criminal sanctions of section 2 were to be confined to state officers.

Trumbull said further that, if a state law on its face guaranteed equal rights for blacks, a Negro whose rights were violated could not go into federal court. It must be assumed in such a situation, Trumbull declared, that a state court would fairly enforce the state law. Even if a state law discriminated against blacks, it did not follow that a Negro would have the right to go directly into federal court, again because the presumption was that a state judge would invalidate the law as inconsistent with U.S. law. But if a freed person was unable to enforce his right under state law in a state court, or if a discriminatory state law was not voided in a state court, the Civil Rights Act would authorize removal of the case to federal court. [51] According to Trumbull, therefore, federal intervention was directed against state action that either discriminated against or failed to uphold the freedmen's rights.

The state action theory of federal power in the Civil Rights Act was less nationalistic than the rhetoric of federal sovereignty with which several Republicans defended the measure. James Wilson, for example, said: "we possess the power to do those things which Governments are organized to do . . . . we may protect a citizen of the United States against a violation of his rights." [52] The Columbus *Morning*

Journal asserted that the Civil Rights Act rested on "the right and duty of this great Nation to guarantee the liberties of the citizen everywhere within its boundaries . . . independent of all constitutions and laws [and] inherent in all governments.[53] Inconsistency disappears, however, when the dual character of American citizenship and the state-centered nature of the Republican theory of federalism are taken into consideration.

The Thirteenth Amendment nationalized freedom, and the Civil Rights Act extended national protection of citizens' rights. But these measures did not create exclusive federal jurisdiction over both state and private actions, as the rhetoric of nationalism might imply. Instead, they gave expression to the national idea of citizenship and civil rights, in the form of equal protection of the law within diverse states. The language of nationalism was real enough, signifying as it did the vindication of federal power against the destructive theory of secession. The decisive result, however, at least in the sphere of civil liberty and citizenship, was the repudiation of state sovereignty (expressed in exclusive state jurisdiction before the war) and the elevation of federal power to a position of equal importance with the states as the ultimate guarantor of civil rights. The states would have the primary, and the federal government the ultimate, responsibility to protect civil rights.

Governor John A. Andrew of Massachusetts expressed the interdependent character of the Republican view of federalism when he emphasized the vested interest that the nation had in the life of the states and that the states had in the life of the Union. "It seems to me," he declared, "that the stream of life flows through both State and Nation from a double source: which is a distinguishing element of its vital power." Representative John A. Bingham summarized the peculiarly American idea that nationality was best realized in local institutions when he stated that the American system was "centralized government, decentralized administration." Before the civil rights bill was passed, Richard H. Dana, Jr., a prominent Union legalist, aptly characterized the point of view from which most Republicans later regarded it. "We do not mean to exercise sovereign civil jurisdiction over them in our Congress," he said of the former Confederate states.

Our system is a planetary system; each planet revolving around its orbit, and all round a common sun. This system is held together by a balance of powers—centripetal and centrifugal forces. . . . Let not that balance be destroyed.

Only as a last resort would Dana urge sovereign civil jurisdiction over the states.[54]

Circumstances in the South in 1866 seemed to require Dana's last resort remedy, and the civil rights bill provided it. But it did so only in partial measure. The sovereign civil jurisdiction of the federal government was distinctly limited to persons acting under color of law. This restriction distinguished the Republican interpretation of congressional power under the Thirteenth Amendment.

The civil rights bill was enacted by Congress in March, vetoed by President Johnson, and passed over the executive veto on April 9, 1866. Meanwhile, the Joint Committee on Reconstruction was preparing a constitutional amendment that would complete the civil rights settlement in the early postwar period. Originally concerned with congressional representation and the political status of former Confederates, the scope of the Fourteenth Amendment was enlarged by the addition of a citizenship and civil rights section that placed the new civil rights law beyond both legislative repeal and doubt concerning its constitutional legitimacy.

The question of its constitutional legitimacy was of particular interest to John Bingham, a member of the Joint Committee on Reconstruction. Bingham believed the Thirteenth Amendment did not give Congress power to impose criminal sanctions against state officers as the Civil Rights Act proposed. Therefore, on several occasions he formulated versions of a constitutional amendment supplying this want.[55] Bingham's principal effort in this direction, introduced into the House in February 1866, stated: "Congress shall have power to make all laws which shall be necessary and proper to secure to the citizens of each State all privileges and immunities of citizens in the several States, and to all persons in the several States equal protection in the rights of life, liberty, and property."[56]

Objection to this proposal came not only from Democrats, but also from several Republicans who opposed the transfer of sovereignty over civil rights to the federal government that the bill seemed clearly to authorize.[57] The House postponed Bingham's measure, and when the reconstruction committee made its report in April, it abandoned the direct national power approach in favor of a state action formula. [58] The point was to devise a way of enabling Congress to oversee or guarantee equal civil rights within states without assuming direct sovereign jurisdiction. Bingham himself provided the needed formulation—section 1 of the Fourteenth Amendment as it stands today: "No State shall make or enforce any law which shall abridge the privileges or immunities of citizens of the United States; nor shall any State deprive any person of life, liberty, or property without due process of law; nor deny to any person within its jurisdiction the equal protection of the laws."

The main questions about Bingham's new formulation were whether it merely affirmed the conception of civil rights and federal power embodied in the Civil Rights Act or whether it went beyond it in both respects. In debate, several Republicans regarded section 1 as the constitutional equivalent of the civil rights bill, expressed in a form that prevented subsequent legislative repeal. [59] Others saw its merit in removing any doubts about the constitutionality of the recently enacted law. [60] Since that measure had been discussed so thoroughly, however, there was little inclination to explore the precise meaning of the terms contained in section 1. [61]

Conservative critics interpreted section 1 as a guarantee of civil rights in the most comprehensive sense. In their apprehensive view, it erased the distinction between social and political rights and civil rights. [62] A similarly broad interpretation has been adduced by several historians who have held that the due process, privileges and immunities, and equal protection clauses had a sweeping, radical humanitarian meaning which derived from the abolition movement and was understood and appreciated, though for political reasons not loudly proclaimed, by the framers of the Fourteenth Amendment. [63] That a consensus existed among Republicans in favor of this radical view of the amendment may be doubted, however, for the words of section 1 were too vague and general to permit any such conclusion. [64] Apposite in this regard was the recollection of George S. Boutwell, a radical Republican and member of the Joint Committee on Reconstruction. In explaining Bingham's preference for the privileges and immunities clause in the Fourteenth Amendment, Boutwell wrote: "Its euphony and indefiniteness of meaning were a charm to him." [65]

Although the exceedingly broad term *civil rights* was rejected by the Joint Committee on Reconstruction (just as it was deleted from the civil rights bill) because it was too latitudinarian, [66] the due process,

privileges and immunities, and equal protection clauses reached far-
ther than the civil rights law. The most accurate assessment of their
import is that they provided a compromise formulation that might in
the future be interpreted in the expansive mode desired by some radicals but did not disavow or contradict—indeed, in the judgment of
most observers seemed to ratify and confirm—the more limited scope
of the Civil Rights Act.[67]

Even if the rights of American citizens[68] were defined broadly, it
did not follow that the legislative power of Congress was similarly extensive.[69] It was a pertinent question, then, whether Congress possessed plenary legislative power to protect civil rights against individual private actions, or whether it was limited by the state action
theory. Although for purposes of advocacy at constitutional law it is
possible to argue a sovereign national power over civil rights,[70] the
preponderance of evidence supports the conclusion that the framers
of the Fourteenth Amendment intended the states to remain the
primary protectors of civil rights against private wrongs. The federal
government, they believed, could intervene legislatively only when
states denied rights by passing discriminatory laws or by failing to
protect citizens.[71]

The clearest indication of this purpose was the abandonment of
Bingham's original constitutional amendment giving Congress power
in express terms to legislate to protect civil rights. Although the alternative negative method of placing limitations on the states can lead
to varying interpretations of the scope of federal power,[72] federal
intervention in one way or another is keyed to state action. This state
action point of view was so strong that, amidst criticism that his proposal would give Congress general legislative power over individual
civil rights, Bingham offered a state action interpretation of even his
original grant of plenary power to Congress. Arguing that the issue
was whether Congress would have power to punish state officials, not
private individuals, for violating civil rights, he said his proposal conferred upon Congress "power to see to it that the protection given by
the laws of the States shall be equal in respect to life and liberty and
property to all persons."[73] Thaddeus Stevens also suggested that
Bingham's measure "simply provide[d] that, where any State makes a
distinction in the same law between different classes of individuals,
Congress shall have power to correct such discrimination and inequality."[74] If Bingham and Stevens, in response to pressure from fellow

Republicans, were willing to place this limited construction on an express grant of power to Congress, the final form of the amendment seems inescapably to signify a state action qualification on federal power.

Indeed, one searches in vain for evidence of any substantial or widespread desire to give plenary power over civil rights to the federal legislature. Even the most radical organs of opinion outside Congress favored placing restrictions on the states. [75] Furthermore, if the Thirteenth and Fourteenth Amendments and the Civil Rights Act reached private as well as state action, it is remarkable that conservatives did not protest. [76] Rather than protest, they condemned the encroachment on exclusive state jurisdiction which the moderate state action theory imported.

In June 1866, Congress approved the Fourteenth Amendment. All of the former Confederate states except Tennessee rejected it and only two years later, as a condition of the Military Reconstruction Act of 1867, did the Fourteenth Amendment become part of the Constitution. Nevertheless, the Civil Rights Act and the Fourteenth Amendment laid down the fundamental principles by which the nation would be guided in integrating the freed slave population into the civil order. Enforcing the 1866 guarantees of civil rights equality presented difficulties that made the original problem of conceptualization and definition seem easy by contrast. More far-reaching federal intervention was soon necessary, in the form of the Reconstruction Act of 1867, which instituted Negro suffrage in the former Confederate states; the Fifteenth Amendment, guaranteeing the right not to be excluded from voting on account of color; and the acts of 1870-1871 to enforce the Fourteenth and Fifteenth Amendments, which were aimed at private injuries to Negroes that states had not prevented. [77] Rather than alter the civil rights settlement of 1866, these actions were an outgrowth and confirmation of the constitutional logic of the immediate postwar measures. They represented a further attempt to secure equal rights for Negroes within the political and constitutional assumptions of state-centered federalism. [78]

Frederick Douglass showed how the more advanced issue of Negro suffrage derived from and reinforced existing constitutional assumptions. Voting as a means of self-protection for blacks was necessary, Douglass wrote in December 1866, because the Thirteenth and Fourteenth Amendments and the Freedmen's Bureau and Civil Rights

Acts were not fully adequate for the task of guaranteeing freedmen's rights. Nor could they ever be truly adequate, Douglass said, "unless the whole structure of the government is changed from a government by States to something like a despotic central government, with power to control even the municipal regulations of States." Douglass accurately described the moderate nature of the change in federal-state relations embodied in the measures of 1866, observing that the arm of the federal government was long, but it was still too short effectively to protect the rights of individuals in the states. The idea of local control and decentralized power was so thoroughly embedded in popular attitudes that it was impossible to change the character of the government. Neither, however, was it desirable to abandon state-centered federalism, Douglass added significantly. The solution—the way to protect blacks and make states' rights compatible with human rights—was to give every citizen the ballot. [79] Following this course of reasoning, Republicans in the Reconstruction Act of 1867 and the Fifteenth Amendment made Negro suffrage the final element in the civil rights settlement. [80]

The law of equal citizenship and civil rights ran far ahead of the actual social practices and civil relationships of Reconstruction era Americans. Equal in law, blacks were not equal in fact. But changes of vast moment had taken place in the status and rights of American Negroes. The revolution in personal status began when freed slaves, at first regarded as contraband of war, were employed in Union military service. Though not determinative of citizenship, this signified that Negroes were part of the people of the United States and contradicted the Supreme Court's assertion to the contrary in the Dred Scott case. Military service also placed blacks in a position to claim the rights of American citizenship. As the number of freed slaves increased, an ideological and humanitarian concern for the rights of emancipated slaves emerged alongside the pragmatic political and military interest manifested in the Confiscation Act of 1862 and Lincoln's Emancipation Proclamation. This dual concern lay behind radical antislavery criticism of the Lincoln administration's freedmen's labor policies in the occupied South and the president's plan of reconstruction, with its willingness to accept whatever white southern Unionists thought expedient in relation to the status and rights of freed slaves. Political as well as ideological considerations also informed the Wade-Davis reconstruction bill, which prohibited slavery in state constitutions and extended federal *habeas corpus* jurisdiction as a guarantee of the freed slaves' personal liberty.

The status and rights of emancipated slaves, along with emergency welfare assistance, was a major concern of Congress in creating the Freedmen's Bureau in 1865. After wrestling with the conflict between post-emancipation government supervision of blacks and recognition of the former slaves' free status, Congress chose to emphasize the free status consideration as much as possible within a framework of lais-sez-faire legal equality. At the same time, with the help of War Demo-crats, Republicans in Congress approved the Thirteenth Amendment prohibiting slavery and guaranteeing personal liberty against infringement by state or individual private action. The Republicans initially viewed the amendment as ample security for freedmen's rights and were naively optimistic about the blacks' ability to achieve legal equality within state jurisdictions. By the end of 1865, the wholesale discrimination and injury to the freed people led them to discover within the confines of the Thirteenth Amendment the necessary federal power to protect the civil rights that were now seen as surrounding and inextricably connected to personal liberty. This protection the Civil Rights Act of 1866 provided against discriminatory state action, while the Fourteenth Amendment supplied an unquestionable constitutional basis for national legislative guarantees of fundamental civil rights. The Fourteenth Amendment also placed restrictions on state-centered federalism that were intended to safeguard the equal rights of Negro citizens under the laws of the several states. Judicial interpretation consistent with the moderate constitutional outlook of the framers of the Civil Rights Act and the Fourteenth Amendment culminated in the Slaughterhouse and other Supreme Court decisions of the 1870s, which underscored the state action limitations on federal power to protect civil rights.

A century later, with the decline of the modern civil rights movement in the 1960s, the defects, weaknesses, and, as it seemed, the ultimate failure of Republican Reconstruction dominated the historiography of the period. In a broad sense, the failure of reconstruction was seen as owing to the racism of American society, but this was rather a precondition than a precise cause. What seemed even more decisive was the flawed nature of the Republican conception of equality. It was, after all, only civil and legal, and eventually political, equality that congressional policy insisted upon. Historians pointed out that

Republicans all but ignored land reform and economic equality. The basis of the Republicans' civil rights demands for the freedmen, moreover, was not a belief in "true equality," that is, the inherent racial equality of blacks. Republicans desired equal rights for Negroes, one historian wrote, only because they believed all should be equal before the law, not because they believed in true equality. The commitment to equality before the law thus appeared to be a limitation that doomed reconstruction policy from the outset.[81]

It is difficult to agree with this judgment, not so much because it pretends to know what true equality is as because it employs a present-day view of the problem as a basis for evaluating the events of the 1860s. Much as we may wish that Civil War Republicans had believed in the inherent equality of all races, it is unhistorical to judge reconstruction policy by this standard. The really significant fact is that Republicans asserted equality before the law as the foundation of national policy toward the freedmen, in conscious despite of the contemporary belief in inherent racial differences and Negro inferiority. While civil and political equality may be inadequate for reform purposes in the late twentieth century, in the perspective of the nineteenth century equality before the law was a radical doctrine which seemed eminently relevant and sound.[82] That it was not successfully incorporated in social practices and political institutions affecting blacks is no evidence that it was flawed or insignificant or that another conception of equality would have been more widely accepted. The question of success or failure aside, the civil rights settlement of Republican reconstruction policy marked significant gains for blacks and provided a rationale and framework within which the rights and interests of Negroes and other citizens could in subsequent years be more fully and effectively protected.

NOTES

1. The black codes generally sought to induce freedmen to work, while protecting their liberty and rights in a minimal sense. The laws dealt with property-holding, employment, vagrancy, apprenticeship, contracts, domestic relations, and testimony in courts and procedures for litigation, among other things. The central idea was that blacks, as before the war, were subject to and required special legislation. See Theodore B. Wilson, *The Black Codes of the South* (University, Ala., 1965).

2. M. L. Benedict, "Preserving the Constitution: The Conservative Basis of Radical Reconstruction," *Journal of American History* 61 (June 1974): 72-76.

3. *Congressional Globe*, 39th Cong., 1st sess., 319 (January 19, 1866), remarks of Lyman Trumbull.

4. Robert F. Durden, *The Gray and the Black: The Confederate Debate on Emancipation* (Durham, N.C., 1972), 186; Cincinnati *Daily Commercial*, February 25, 1865, letter from Frankfort, Ky.; *Documentary History of the Constitution of the United States of America, 1786-1870* (5 vols.; Washington, D.C., 1894), II, 606, 610; Francis N. Thorpe, *The Constitutional History of the United States, 1765-1895* (3 vols.; New York, 1901), III, 159.

5. Seward presumably meant that federal legislative power was confined to preventing chattel slavery and did not extend to the protection of civil rights in general. Edward McPherson, *A Political Manual for 1866* (Washington, D.C., 1866), 23.

6. *Congressional Globe*, 39th Cong., 1st sess., 130 (January 5, 1866).

7. William M. Grosvenor, "The Rights of the Nation, and the Duty of Congress," *New Englander* 24 (October 1865): 769.

8. Burke A. Hinsdale, ed., *The Works of James Abram Garfield* (2 vols.; Boston, 1882), I, 86, 89.

9. New York *Tribune*, November 17, 1865.

10. *Congressional Globe*, 39th Cong., 1st sess., 588 (February 1, 1866), remarks of Ignatius Donnelly, 504 (January 30, 1866), remarks of Jacob Howard, 1124 (March 1, 1866), remarks of Burton C. Cook, 474 (January 29, 1866), remarks of Lyman Trumbull.

11. Ibid., 110 (December 21, 1865), 297-298 (January 18, 1866), remarks of William M. Stewart, 630 (February 3, 1866), remarks of Asahel W. Hubbard, 631 (February 3, 1866), remarks of Samuel W. Moulton, 656 (February 5, 1866), remarks of Thomas D. Eliot. The second Freedmen's Bureau bill of 1866 gave bureau agents jurisdiction over violations of freedmen's civil rights and also of cases in which freedmen were discriminated against in rights specified and secured by the bill. This jurisdiction was posited on the interruption of ordinary judicial proceedings and was military in nature. The rights guaranteed in the freedmen's bureau bill were the same as in the Civil Rights Act, to be considered below.

12. Ibid., 503 (January 30, 1866), remarks of Jacob Howard, 1151 (March 2, 1866), remarks of M. Russell Thayer, 1159 (March 2, 1866), remarks of William Windom, 77 (December 19, 1865), remarks of Lyman Trumbull.

13. Horace White, *The Life of Lyman Trumbull* (Boston and New York, 1913), 250.

14. A constitutional amendment dealing with representation in Congress was reported by the joint committee in January 1866. In April, after the civil rights bill was passed, this subject was combined with the political status of former rebels and civil rights in what eventually became the Fourteenth Amendment. See Joseph B. James, *The Framing of the Fourteenth Amendment* (Urbana, 1956), 55-66.

15. *Congressional Globe*, 39th Cong., 1st sess., 211-212 (January 12, 1866).

16. Ibid., 475 (January 29, 1866), remarks of Lyman Trumbull, 632 (February 3, 1866), remarks of Samuel W. Moulton; O. J. Hollister, *The Life of Schuyler Colfax* (New York, 1886), 271.

17. *Congressional Globe*, 39th Cong., 1st sess., 504-505 (January 30, 1866), remarks of Reverdy Johnson, 603-604 (February 2, 1866), remarks of Edgar Cowan; Alfred H. Kelly, "The Fourteenth Amendment Reconsidered: The Segregation Decision,"

Michigan Law Review 54 (June 1956): 1066-1069.

18. *Congressional Globe*, 39th Cong., 1st sess., 497, 504 (January 30, 1866), remarks of Peter G. Van Winkle and Reverdy Johnson.

19. Ibid., 1268-1269 (March 8, 1866), remarks of Michael C. Kerr, 1776-1777, 1780 (April 5, 1866), remarks of Reverdy Johnson.

20. Ibid., 1115-1117 (March 1, 1866), remarks of James Wilson, 3031 (June 8, 1866), remarks of John B. Henderson.

21. The former opinion was Chief Justice Taney's, the latter Justice Curtis's. Taney actually held that there were two kinds of state citizenship: one exclusively for state purposes and another for national purposes subsumed under the federal Constitution.

22. *Congressional Globe*, 39th Cong., 1st sess., 1781 (April 5, 1866), remarks of Lyman Trumbull; Philadelphia *North American*, April 11, 1866; Samuel T. Spear, *The Citizen's Duty in the Present Crisis* (New York, 1866), 16.

23. In 1866, according to the constitutional historian Alfred H. Kelly, "it was not at all clear whether any such thing as national citizenship existed." "The Fourteenth Amendment Reconsidered," 1058.

24. John Conness, *Some Men and Measures of the War and Reconstruction Period* (Boston, 1882), 10.

25. Samuel A. Foot, *Republican Form of Government* (n.p. [1865]); Samuel A. Foot, *Autobiography* (2 vols.; New York, 1872), I, 415.

26. James G. Blaine, *Twenty Years of Congress: From Lincoln to Garfield* (2 vols.; Norwich, Conn., 1884), II, 189.

27. *Congressional Globe*, 39th Cong., 1st sess., 1293 (March 9, 1866), 1832 (April 7, 1866), 1760 (April 4, 1866).

28. Ibid., 1835 (April 7, 1866), remarks of William Lawrence, 474-475 (January 29, 1866), remarks of Lyman Trumbull.

29. Samuel Shellabarger of Ohio disagreed that the civil rights bill accomplished this end. He therefore introduced a bill to protect national citizens in their privileges and immunities when traveling, sojourning, or taking up residence in another state. Shellabarger's bill provided that every U.S. citizen could go freely into any state, own or lease property, transact business, enjoy access to courts of law, and receive the benefit of all other privileges and immunities which citizens of the state enjoyed under like circumstances. The bill differed from Trumbull's civil rights bill mainly in applying criminal sanctions to private individuals who denied the rights of U.S. citizens as well as to persons acting under color of law, that is, state officers. 39th Cong., H.R. No. 437, April 2, 1866; *Congressional Globe*, 39th Cong., 1st sess., App., 293 (July 25, 1866), remarks of Samuel Shellabarger.

30. Ibid., 295 (July 25, 1866).

31. Charles D. Cleveland to Lyman Trumbull, April 7, 1866, Trumbull Papers, Library of Congress.

32. Harold M. Hyman, *A More Perfect Union: The Impact of the Civil War and Reconstruction on the Constitution* (New York, 1973), 424-425.

33. See, for example, 39th Cong., S. No. 232, March 27, 1866, introduced by James Doolittle. This bill declared all slaves free persons, abolished laws and customs establishing the right of property in slaves, punished any person who restrained anyone of his liberty, and authorized federal officers to secure freedmen's liberty by the use of the writ

of *habeas corpus*. Provoked by reports of the seizure and removal of freedmen in certain states, Congress in May 1866 passed an anti-kidnapping act without any conservative opposition. *Congressional Globe*, 39th Cong., 1st sess., 852 (February 15, 1866).

34. Ibid., 318 (January 19, 1866), remarks of Thomas Hendricks, 372 (January 23, 1866), remarks of Reverdy Johnson, 601 (February 2, 1866), remarks of James Guthrie, 1268, 1271 (March 8, 1866), remarks of Michael C. Kerr, App., 158 (March 8, 1866), remarks of Columbus Delano.

35. Ibid., 1154 (March 2, 1866), remarks of Nathaniel B. Eldridge, 1265 (March 8, 1866), remarks of Thomas T. Davis, 1809 (April 6, 1866), remarks of Willard Saulsbury.

36. Washington *National Intelligencer*, March 29, 1866.

37. *Congressional Globe*, 39th Cong., 1st sess., 445 (January 26, 1866), 1785 (April 5, 1866), remarks of William M. Stewart, 1833-1837 (April 7, 1866), remarks of William Lawrence.

38. Ibid., 1294 (March 9, 1866). Shellabarger's civil rights bill, referred to above, was intended in his own words to punish "every violation of the rights of free intercourse travel transit change of abode &c &c as between among and in the several states [*sic*]." "Yours," he wrote to Trumbull, "punishes *discriminations* 'under *color of law*,' and none others." Shellabarger to Trumbull, April 7, 1866, Trumbull Papers, Library of Congress.

39. *Congressional Globe*, 39th Cong., 1st sess., 1118-1120 (March 1, 1866). For other expressions of state action views, see the remarks of Josiah Grinnell, ibid., 651-652, Samuel McKee, 654 (February 5, 1866), John Sherman, 744 (February 8, 1866), Henry Wilson, 603 (February 2, 1866).

40. Boston *Commonwealth*, April 7, 1866; Philadelphia *North American*, April 10, 1866; Baltimore *American*, April 3, 1866. See also Toledo *Blade*, March 28, April 7, 1866; Philadelphia *Press*, April 9, 10, 1866; Chicago *Tribune*, March 17, 29, 1866; Bangor *Daily Whig and Courier*, April 2, 1866; B. F. Butler, *The Status of the Insurgent States* (n.p., n.d.), 11; New York *Tribune*, February 3, 1866; Boston *Evening Transcript*, April 9, 1866; Worcester *Daily Spy*, March 29, 1866; Springfield *Weekly Republican*, April 28, 1866.

41. The U.S. Supreme Court in the case of Jones *v.* Alfred H. Mayer Co. (392 *U.S.* 409 [1968]) ruled that a Negro family could not be excluded from purchasing a home in a housing development. Holding that such exclusion was a violation of the Civil Rights Act of 1866, the Court in an elaborate historical argument interpreted the Thirteenth Amendment and the Civil Rights Act as prohibiting both state officers and private individuals from discriminating against Negroes or denying them civil rights. Similar historical conclusions have been advanced by Robert L. Kohl, "The Civil Rights Act of 1866, Its Hour Come Round at Last: Jones *v.* Alfred H. Mayer Co.," *Virginia Law Review* 55 (March 1969): 272-300; Arthur Kinoy, "Jones *v.* Alfred H. Mayer Co.: An Historic Step Forward," *Vanderbilt Law Review* 22 (April 1969): 475-483; and "The Constitutional Right of Negro Freedom Revisited: Some First Thoughts on Jones *v.* Alfred H. Mayer Company," *Rutgers Law Review* 22 (Spring 1968): 537-552; Robert J. Kaczorowski, "The Nationalization of Civil Rights: Constitutional Theory and Practice in a Racist Society, 1866-1883," Ph.D. dissertation, University of Minnesota, 1971, and "Searching for the Intent of the Framers of the Fourteenth Amendment," *Connecticut Law Review* 5 (Winter 1973): 368-398.

42. 392 *U.S.* 422-424; Robert J. Kaczorowski, "Race, Law and Politics: Congress and Civil Rights After the Civil War," unpublished paper, 58-59, n. 88.

43. Howard K. Beale, ed., *The Diary of Gideon Welles* (3 vols.; New York, 1960), II, 460-461; Baltimore *Sun*, March 29, 1866; Cincinnati *Commercial*, March 27, 30, 1866; Washington *National Intelligencer*, March 24, 1866.

44. Charles Fairman, *Reconstruction and Reunion, 1864-88, Part One* (New York, 1971), 1219.

45. William Whiting, *War Powers Under the Constitution*, 43d ed. (Boston, 1871), 399; New York *Evening Post*, April 2, 10, 1866; New York *Tribune*, March 28, 1866, speech of Horace Greeley; *Congressional Globe*, 39th Cong., 1st sess., 631 (February 3, 1866), remarks of Samuel W. Moulton, 745 (February 8, 1866), remarks of John B. Henderson, 602 (February 2, 1866), remarks of Henry S. Lane; Benedict, "Preserving the Constitution," 80-81, n. 34.

46. Fairman, *Reconstruction and Reunion*, 1239-1241.

47. Baltimore *American*, April 2, 1866.

48. *Congressional Globe*, 39th Cong., 1st sess., 1760 (April 4, 1866). See also ibid., 600 (February 2, 1866).

49. Ibid., 475 (January 29, 1866).

50. Ibid., 1758 (April 4, 1866).

51. Ibid., 1759 (April 4, 1866).

52. Ibid., 1119 (March 1, 1866).

53. Columbus *Morning Journal*, March 29, 1866. See also New York *Evening Post*, March 26, 28, 1866; Philadelphia *North American*, April 9, 1866; Bangor *Daily Whig and Courier*, March 29, 1866; *Congressional Globe*, 39th Cong., 1st sess., 1262-1263 (March 8, 1866).

54. Albert G. Browne, *Sketch of the Official Life of John A. Andrew* (New York, 1868), 171-172; *Congressional Globe*, 39th Cong., 1st sess., 1292 (March 9, 1866), R. H. Dana, Jr., *Reorganization of the Rebel States, Speech at Faneuil Hall, June 21, 1865* (n.p., n.d.), 4.

55. James, *The Framing of the Fourteenth Amendment*, 81-90.

56. *Congressional Globe*, 39th Cong., 1st sess., 1034 (February 26, 1866).

57. Ibid., 1063 (February 27, 1866), remarks of Robert S. Hale, 1095 (February 28, 1866), remarks of Giles Hotchkiss.

58. Alexander Bickel, "The Original Understanding and the Segregation Decision," *Harvard Law Review* 69 (November 1955): 40-47; James, *The Framing of the Fourteenth Amendment*, 103-115.

59. *Congressional Globe*, 39th Cong., 1st sess., 2462, 2464 (May 8, 1866), remarks of James A. Garfield, M. Russell Thayer, 2498 (May 9, 1866), remarks of John M. Broomall.

60. Ibid., 2498, 2511 (May 9, 1866), remarks of John M. Broomall and Thomas D. Eliot, 2961 (June 5, 1866), remarks of Luke P. Poland.

61. Bickel, "The Original Understanding," 47, 52.

62. *Congressional Globe*, 39th Cong., 1st sess., 2467 (May 8, 1866), remarks of Benjamin M. Boyer, 2538 (May 10, 1866), remarks of Andrew J. Rogers.

63. Jacobus ten Broek, *Equal Under Law* (New York, 1965); Howard Jay Graham, *Everyman's Constitution: Historical Essays on the Fourteenth Amendment, The 'Conspiracy Theory,' and American Constitutionalism* (Madison, 1968), 152-265; Kelly,

"The Fourteenth Amendment Reconsidered," 1051-1057.

64. Fairman, *Reconstruction and Reunion*, 1283-1300.

65. George S. Boutwell, *Reminiscences of Sixty Years in Public Affairs* (2 vols.; New York, 1902), II, 42.

66. Bickel, "The Original Understanding," 57.

67. Ibid., 57-63; Kelly, "The Fourteenth Amendment Reconsidered," 1071, 1079-1085.

68. Section 1 of the Fourteenth Amendment stated that all persons born or naturalized in the United States were citizens of the United States and of the state in which they resided.

69. Section 5 gave Congress power to enforce the provisions of the amendment by appropriate legislation.

70. Cf. Arthur Kinoy, "The Constitutional Right of Negro Freedom," *Rutgers Law Review* 21 (Spring 1967): 387-441.

71. Benedict, "Preserving the Constitution," 76-77; Laurent B. Frantz, "Congressional Power to Enforce the Fourteenth Amendment Against Private Acts," *Yale Law Journal* 73 (July 1964): 1352-1384.

72. Frantz, "Congressional Power to Enforce the Fourteenth Amendment." At one extreme would be complete congressional displacement of state power over civil rights, at the other extreme congressional action only when there was positive and overt injury or denial of rights by state law. The middle position was congressional legislation based on state action, defined as either acts of positive discrimination or of omission in the form of a failure to protect blacks from injury.

73. *Congressional Globe*, 39th Cong., 1st sess., 1090, 1094 (February 28, 1866).

74. Ibid., 1063 (February 27, 1866).

75. *National Anti-Slavery Standard*, February 24, 1866; New Orleans *Tribune*, December 24, 1865. The constitutional amendment preferred by each of these radical journals declared: "No State shall make any distinction in civil rights and privileges among the naturalized citizens of the United States residing within its limits, or among persons born on its soil of parents permanently resident there, on account of race, color, or descent."

76. Fairman, *Reconstruction and Reunion*, 1219.

77. Hyman, *A More Perfect Union*, 516-542.

78. Benedict, "Preserving the Constitution," 83-90.

79. Frederick Douglass, "Reconstruction," *Atlantic Monthly* (December 1866): 761-762. See also *National Principia*, April 12, 1866, editorial.

80. Benedict, "Preserving the Constitution," 83-84.

81. V. Jacque Voegeli, *Free But Not Equal: The Midwest and the Negro During the Civil War* (Chicago, 1967), 182; Herman Belz, "The New Orthodoxy in Reconstruction Historiography," *Reviews in American History* 1 (March 1973): 106-113.

82. Bernard Schwartz, *A Commentary on the Constitution of the United States: Rights of the Person* (2 vols.; New York, 1968), II, 488-489; Hyman, *A More Perfect Union*, 546.

Bibliography

PRIMARY SOURCES

Manuscripts

American Union Commission Papers, House of Representatives File of Printed Bills,
    Record Group 233, National Archives, Washington, D.C.
Bird, Francis W., Papers, Harvard University Library, Cambridge, Mass.
Chase, Salmon P., Papers, Library of Congress, Washington, D.C.
Curtis, George W., Papers, Harvard University Library, Cambridge, Mass.
DuPont, Samuel F., Papers, Eleutherian Mills Historical Library, Greenville, Del.
Garrison, William Lloyd, Papers, Boston Public Library, Boston.
Howe, Samuel Gridley, Papers, Harvard University Library, Cambridge, Mass.
Norton, Charles Eliot, Papers, Harvard University Library, Cambridge, Mass.
Pierce, Edward L., Papers, Harvard University Library, Cambridge, Mass.
Sumner, Charles, Papers, Harvard University Library, Cambridge, Mass.
Stanton, Edwin M., Papers, Library of Congress, Washington, D.C.
Trumbull, Lyman, Papers, Library of Congress, Washington, D.C.
United States House of Representatives, Papers of Committees and unprinted bills,
    Record Group 233, National Archives, Washington, D.C.

Newspapers

Baltimore *Daily American*
Boston *Commonwealth*
Boston *Journal*
Chicago *Tribune*
Cincinnati *Commercial*
Cincinnati *Gazette*

Congressional Globe
Independent
Liberator
National Anti-Slavery Standard
National Principia
New Orleans *Tribune*
New York *Evening Post*
New York *Herald*
New York *Times*
New York *Tribune*
New York *World*
Philadlephia *North American*
Springfield *Weekly Republican*
Washington *Chronicle*
Washington *National Intelligencer*
Worcester *Daily Spy*

Pamphlets, Speeches, Books, Articles

Abbott, Lyman. *The American Union Commission: Its Origins, Operations and Purposes.* New York, 1865.
———. *The Results of Emancipation in the United States of America.* New York, 1867.
———. "Southern Evangelization," *New Englander* 23 (October 1864): 699-708.
Address of the Democratic League: The Real Motives of the Rebellion. New York, 1864.
Agnew, Daniel. *Our National Constitution: Its Adoption to a State of War or Insurrection,* 2d ed. Philadelphia, 1863.
Aikman, William. *The Future of the Colored Race in America.* New York, 1862.
Anon. "The Destiny of the African Race in the United States," *Continental Monthly* 3 (May 1863): 600-610.
Atkinson, Edward. "The Future Supply of Cotton," *North American Review* 98 (April 1864): 477-497.
Bacon, Leonard. "Reply to Professor Parker," *New Englander* 22 (April 1863): 221-254.
Baird, Thomas H. *Memorial Praying for the Enactment of Measures to Preserve the Constitution and the Union.* Pittsburgh, 1864.
Barnes, Albert. *The Conditions of Peace.* Philadelphia, 1863.
Bates, Edward. *Opinion on Citizenship.* Washington, D.C., 1863.
Beecher, Henry Ward. *Universal Suffrage and Complete Equality in Citizenship.* Boston, 1865.
Bishop, Joel P. *Secession and Slavery: Or the Effect of Secession on the Relation of the United States to the Seceded States and to Slavery.* Boston, 1864.
———. *Thoughts for the Times.* Boston, 1863.
Blair, Montgomery. *Speech on the Causes of the Rebellion and In Support of the President's Plan of Pacification.* Baltimore, 1864.

————. *Speech on the Revolutionary Schemes of the Ultra-Abolitionists, and in Defense of the Policy of the President*. New York, 1863.

Broom, W. W. *Great and Grave Questions for American Politicans*. Boston, 1865.

Bullard, Edward F. *The Nation's Trial: The Proclamation: Dormant Powers of the Government*. New York and Albany, 1863.

Burnett, Peter. *The American Theory of Government*. New York, 1861.

Butler, Benjamin F. *The Status of the Insurgent States*. n.p., n.d.

Chase, S. P. *Letter to the Loyal National League*. Washington, D.C., 1863.

Chase, Warren. *The American Crisis; or, Trial and Triumph of Democracy*. Boston, 1862.

Cobb, Thomas R. R. *An Inquiry into the Law of Negro Slavery in the United States of America*. New York, 1968; orig. pub. 1858.

Combs, J. J. *Speech at the Union League of Washington*. Washington, D.C. 1863.

Crosby, Alpheus. *The Present Position of the Seceded States*. Boston, 1865.

Curtis, Benjamin R. *Executive Power*. Boston, 1862.

Dana, R. H., Jr. *Reorganization of the Rebel States, Speech at Faneuil Hall, June 21, 1865*. n.p., n.d.

Davis, Henry Winter. *Speeches and Addresses*. New York, 1867.

Dean, Gilbert. *Speech on the Governor's Annual Message*. Albany, 1863.

de Gasparin, Agenor. *A Letter to President Johnson*, 2d ed. New York, 1865.

Dickson, William M. *The Absolute Equality of all Men Before the Law, the Only True Basis of Reconstruction*. Cincinnati, 1865.

Dostie, A. P. *Address Before the Republican Association of New Orleans, May 9, 1866*. n.p., n.d.

Douglass, Frederick. "Reconstruction," *Atlantic Monthly* 18 (December 1866): 761-765.

Drake, Charles D. *Union and Anti-Slavery Speeches*. Cincinnati, 1864.

Edmonds, J. W. *Reconstruction of the Union*. New York, 1867.

Emancipation League. *Facts Concerning the Freedmen*. Boston, 1863.

Farrar, Timothy. "States Rights," *New Englander* 21 (October 1862): 695-724.

Fisher, George P. "Of the Distinction Between Natural and Political Rights," *New Englander* 23 (January 1864): 1-27.

Foot, Samuel A. *Republican Form of Government*. n.p. [1865].

Gardner, Daniel. *A Treatise on the Law of the American Rebellion*. New York, 1862.

Garnet, Henry Highland. *A Memorial Discourse*. Philadelphia, 1865.

Gibson, James. *Reconstruction*. Albany, 1867.

Grosvenor, William M. "The Rights of the Nation, and the Duty of Congress," *New Englander* 24 (October 1865): 755-777.

Hahn, Michael. *What Is Unconditional Unionism?* New Orleans, 1863.

Hamilton, Andrew Jackson. *Letter to the President of the United States*. New York, 1863.

————. *Speech at Faneuil Hall*. Boston, 1863.

Hamilton, James A. *The Constitution Vindicated: Nationality, Secession, Slavery*. New York, 1864.

————. *State Sovereignty*. New York, 1862.

Hurd, John C. *The Law of Freedom and Bondage*. 2 vols. Boston, 1858-1862.

Ingersoll, Joseph Reed. *Secession: In the Future*. Philadelphia, 1862.

Jay, John. *The Great Issue: An Address Delivered Before the Union Campaign Club of East Brooklyn.* New York, 1864.

Kelley, William D., et al. *The Equality of All Men Before the Law Claimed and Defended.* Boston, 1865.

Kimball, William H. "Our Government and the Blacks," *Continental Monthly* 5 (April 1864): 431-435.

Kirkland, Charles P. *The Destiny of Our Country.* New York, 1864.

Kroeger, Adolph E. *The Future of the Country.* n.p., 1864.

Lieber, Francis. *On Civil Liberty and Self-Government,* 3d ed. Philadelphia, 1891.

Lintz, Frederick G. *Letters from an Adopted Citizen of the Republic to His Mother in Germany.* n.p., 1864.

Livermore, George. "An Historical Research Respecting the Opinions of the Founders of the Republic on Negroes as Slaves, as Citizens, and as Soldiers," *Proceedings of the Massachusetts Historical Society* 6 (1862-1863).

Lord, Charles E. *Slavery, Secession and the Constitution.* Boston, 1864.

Loring, George B. *Safe and Honorable Reconstruction.* South Danvers, Mass., 1866.

Lowell, J. R. "Reconstruction," *North American Review* 100 (April 1865): 540-559.

Lowrey, Grosvenor P. *The Commander-in-Chief: A Defence Upon Legal Grounds of the Proclamation of Emancipation.* New York, 1863.

McKaye, James. *The Mastership and Its Fruits: The Emancipated Slave Face to Face with his Old Master.* New York, 1864.

Nicholas, S. S. *Conservative Essays, Legal and Political.* 4 vols. Louisville, Ky., 1863-1869.

Norton, Charles Eliot. "American Political Ideas," *North American Review* 101 (October 1865): 550-565.

Nott, C. C. *The Coming Contraband.* New York, 1862.

Owen, Robert Dale. "The Claims to Service or Labor," *Atlantic Monthly* 12 (July 1863): 116-125.

———. *The Cost of Peace: Letter to S. P. Chase.* n.p., 1862.

———. *The Policy of Emancipation.* Philadelphia, 1863.

———. *The Wrong of Slavery, the Right of Emancipation, and the Future of the African Race in America.* Philadelphia, 1864.

Parker, Joel. *Letters to Rev. Henry M. Dexter and to Rev. Leonard Bacon.* Cambridge, Mass., 1863.

———. *The War Powers of Congress and the President.* Cambridge, Mass., 1863.

Pierce, Edward L. "The Contrabands at Fortress Monroe," *Atlantic Monthly* 8 (November 1861): 626-640.

Pomeroy, John Norton. *An Introduction to Municipal Law.* 2d ed. San Francisco, 1886.

Raymond, Henry J. *The Administration and the War.* n.p., 1863.

Redfield, Isaac F. "On American Secession and State Rights," *Monthly Law Reporter* 26 (December 1863): 70-85.

Report by the Committee of the Contrabands' Relief Commission of Cincinnati, Ohio, Proposing a Plan for the Occupation and Government of Vacated Territory in the Seceded States. Cincinnati, 1863.

Report to the Contributors to the Pennsylvania Relief Association for East Tennessee. Philadelphia, 1864.

Russell H. E. "The Constitutional Amendment," *Continental Monthly* 6 (September 1864): 315-326.

————. "Negro Troops," *Continental Monthly* 6 (August 1864(: 191-198.

Scovel, James M. *Our Relations with the Rebellious States.* Trenton, N.J., 1866.

Seward, William H. *The Great Issues. Speech at Auburn, New York, September 3, 1864.* n.p., 1864.

Smith, Truman. *Considerations on the Slavery Question, Addressed to the President of the United States.* New York, 1863.

Spear, Samuel T. *The Citizen's Duty in the Present Crisis.* New York, 1866.

Stanton, F. P. "The Freed Men of the South," *Continental Monthly* 2 (December 1862): 730-734.

Tarbox, I. N. "Universal Suffrage," *New Englander* 24 (January 1865), 151-167.

Thompson, Joseph P. *Christianity and Emancipation.* New York, 1863.

————. *Revolution Against Free Government Not a Right But a Crime.* New York, 1864.

————. *Speech at Washington, February 12, 1865.* New York, 1865.

Throop, Montgomery. *The Future: A Political Essay.* New York, 1864.

Twining, Alexander C. "President Lincoln's Proclamation of Freedom to the Slaves," *New Englander* 24 (January 1865): 178-186.

Ward, Charles. *Contrabands: Suggesting an Apprenticeship Under the Auspices of the Government to Build the Pacific Railroad, January 8, 1863.* Salem, Mass. 1866.

Warren, Marvin. *A Solution of Our National Difficulties, and the Science of Republican Government.* Cincinnati, 1863.

Wheat, Marvin T. *The Progress and Intelligence of Americans: Collateral Proof of Slavery.* 2d ed., Louisville, Ky., 1863.

Whipple, E. P. "Reconstruction and Negro Suffrage," *Atlantic Monthly* 16 (August 1865): 238-247.

Whiting, William. *War Powers Under the Constitution of the United States.* 43d ed., Boston, 1871.

Willard, Emma. *Via Media: A Peaceful and Permanent Settlement of the Slavery Question.* Washington, D.C., 1862.

Yates, William. *Rights of Colored Men to Suffrage, Citizenship and Trial By Jury.* Philadelphia, 1838.

Yeatman, James E. *A Report on the Conditions of the Freedmen of the Mississippi, Presented to the Western Sanitary Commission, December 17, 1863.* St. Louis, 1864.

Memoirs, Diaries, Reminiscences, Collected Writings

Abbott, Lyman. *Reminiscences.* Boston, 1915.

Basler, Roy P., et al., eds. *The Collected Works of Abraham Lincoln.* 9 vols. New Brunswick, N.J., 1953-1955.

Beale, Howard K., ed. *The Diary of Edward Bates, 1859-1866.* Washington, D.C., 1933.

————. *The Diary of Gideon Welles.* 3 vols. New York, 1960.

Blaine, James G. *Twenty Years of Congress: From Lincoln to Garfield.* 2 vols. Norwich, Conn., 1884.

Blair, Montgomery. "The Republican Party As It Was and Is," *North American Review* 131 (November 1880): 422-430.

Boutwell, George S. "The Career of Abraham Lincoln," *The Magazine of History,* No. 193 (1895).

————. *Reminiscences of Sixty Years in Public Affairs.* 2 vols. New York, 1902.

Brown, Albert G. *Sketch of the Official Life of John A. Andrew.* New York, 1868.

Conness, John. *Some Men and Measures of the War and Reconstruction Period.* Boston, 1882.

Dana, R. H., Jr. "Nullity of the Emancipation Edict," *North American Review* 131 (July 1880): 128-134.

Dennett, Tyler, ed. *Lincoln and the Civil War in the Diaries and Letters of John Hay.* New York, 1939.

Donald, David H., ed. *Inside Lincoln's Cabinet: The Civil War Diaries of Salmon P. Chase.* New York, 1954.

Eaton, John. *Grant, Lincoln and the Freedmen: Reminiscences of the Civil War.* New York, 1907.

Ferris, Aaron A. "The Validity of the Emancipation Edict," *North American Review* 131 (December 1880): 551-576.

Foner, Philip S., ed. *The Life and Writings of Frederick Douglass.* 4 vols. New York, 1952.

Foot, Samuel A. *Autobiography.* 2 vols. New York, 1872.

Hinsdale, Burke A., ed. *The Works of James Abram Garfield.* 2 vols. Boston, 1882.

Hollister, O. J. *The Life of Schuyler Colfax.* New York, 1886.

Long, John D. *The Republican Party: Its History, Principles, and Policies.* New York, 1888.

Marshall, Jessie Ames, ed. *Private and Official Correspondence of General Benjamin F. Butler.* 5 vols. Norwood, Mass., 1917.

Nicolay, John G., and Hay, John. *Abraham Lincoln: A History.* 10 vols. New York, 1890.

Perry, Thomas Sergeant, ed. *The Life and Letters of Francis Lieber.* Boston, 1882.

Pierce, Edward L. *Memoir and Letters of Charles Sumner.* 4 vols. Boston, 1877-1894.

Salter, William. *The Life of James W. Grimes.* New York, 1876.

Sherman, William T. *Memoirs.* 2 vols. Bloomington, Ind., 1957.

Thorndike, Rachel Sherman, ed. *The Sherman Letters: Correspondence Between General and Senator Sherman from 1837 to 1891.* New York, 1894.

Welling, James C. "The Emancipation Proclamation," *North American Review* 130 (February 1880), 163-85.

White, Horace. *The Life of Lyman Trumbull.* Boston and New York, 1913.

SECONDARY WORKS

Books

Arieli, Yehoshua. *Individualism and Nationalism in American Ideology.* Baltimore, 1966.

Bartlett, I. H. *Wendell Phillips: Brahmin Radical.* Boston, 1961.

Belz, Herman. *Reconstructing the Union: Theory and Policy During the Civil War.* Ithaca, N.Y., 1969.

Bentley, George R. *A History of the Freedmen's Bureau.* Philadelphia, 1955.

Brock, W. R. *An American Crisis: Congress and Reconstruction, 1865-1867.* New York, 1963.

Brown, Ira V. *Lyman Abbott, Christian Evolutionist: A Study in Religious Opinion.* Cambridge, Mass., 1953.

Cain, Marvin R. *Lincoln's Attorney General: Edward Bates of Missouri.* Columbia, Mo., 1965.

Cornish, Dudley T. *The Sable Arm: Negro Troops in the Union Army, 1861-1865.* New York, 1956.

Cox, LaWanda, and Cox, John. *Politics, Principle and Prejudice, 1865-66: Dilemma of Reconstruction America.* New York, 1963.

Curry, Leonard P. *Blueprint for Modern America: Nonmilitary Legislation of the First Civil War Congress.* Nashville, 1968.

Degler, Carl N. *Neither White Nor Black: Slavery and Race Relations in Brazil and the United States.* New York, 1971.

Donald, David H. *Charles Sumner and the Rights of Man.* New York, 1970.

Durden, Robert F. *The Gray and the Black: The Confederate Debate over Emancipation.* Duham, N.C., 1972.

Fairman, Charles. *Reconstruction and Reunion, 1864-88, Part One.* New York, 1971.

Flack, Horace E. *The Adoption of the Fourteenth Amendment.* Baltimore, 1908.

Foner, Eric. *Free Soil, Free Labor, Free Men: The Ideology of the Republican Party Before the Civil War.* New York, 1970.

Fredrickson, George M. *The Black Image in the White Mind: The Debate on Afro-American Character and Destiny, 1817-1914.* New York, 1971.

————. *The Inner Civil War: Northern Intellectuals and the Crisis of the Union.* New York, 1965.

Gerteis, Louis S. *From Contraband to Freedman: Federal Policy Toward Southern Blacks, 1861-1865.* Westport, Conn., 1973.

Gettys, Luella. *The Law of Citizenship in the United States.* Chicago, 1934.

Graham, Howard Jay. *Everyman's Constitution: Historical Essays on the Fourteenth Amendment, the "Conspiracy Theory," and American Constitutionalism.* Madison, Wis., 1968.

Hopkins, Vincent C. *Dred Scott's Case.* New York, 1951.

Howell, Roger. *The Privileges and Immunities of State Citizenship.* Baltimore, 1918.

Hyman, Harold M. *A More Perfect Union: The Impact of the Civil War and Reconstruction on the Constitution.* New York, 1973.

————, ed. *New Frontiers of the American Reconstruction.* Urbana, Ill., 1966.

Jaffa, Harry V. *Crisis of the House Divided: An Interpretation of the Issues in the Lincoln-Douglas Debates.* New York, 1959.

James, Joseph B. *The Framing of the Fourteenth Amendment.* Urbana, Ill., 1956.

Litwack, Leon F. *North of Slavery: The Negro in the Free States, 1790-1860.* Chicago, 1961.

McPherson, James M. *The Struggle for Equality: Abolitionists and the Negro in the Civil War and Reconstruction.* Princeton, 1964.

Morris, Thomas D. *Free Men All: The Personal Liberty Laws of the North, 1780-1861.* Baltimore and London, 1974.

Niven, John. *Gideon Welles, Lincoln's Secretary of the Navy.* New York, 1973.

Perman, Michael. *Reunion Without Compromise: The South and Reconstruction: 1865-1868.* Cambridge, England, 1973.

Pierce, Paul S. *The Freedmen's Bureau: A Chapter in the History of Reconstruction.* Iowa City, Iowa, 1904.

Quarles, Benjamin. *Lincoln and the Negro.* New York, 1962.

Randall, James G. *Constitutional Problems Under Lincoln.* Rev. ed. Urbana, Ill., 1951.

Roche, John P. *The Early Development of United States Citizenship.* Ithaca, N.Y., 1949.

Rose, Willie Lee. *Rehearsal for Reconstruction: The Port Royal Experiment.* Indianapolis, Ind., 1964.

ten Broek, Jacobus. *Equal Under Law.* New York, 1965; orig. publ. as *The Antislavery Origins of the Fourteenth Amendment,* 1951.

Thomas, Benjamin P., and Hyman, Harold M. *Stanton: The Life and Times of Lincoln's Secretary of War.* New York, 1962.

Thomas, John L. *The Liberator: William Lloyd Garrison.* Boston, 1963.

Thorpe, Francis N. *The Constitutional History of the United States, 1765-1895.* 3 vols. Chicago, 1901.

Voegeli, V. Jacque. *Free But Not Equal: The Midwest and the Negro During the Civil War.* Chicago, 1967.

Wiecek, William M. *The Guarantee Clause of the U.S. Constitution.* Ithaca, N.Y., 1972.

Williams, George W. *A History of the Negro Troops in the War of the Rebellion.* New York, 1969; orig. publ. 1888.

Wilson, Theodore B. *The Black Codes of the South.* University, Ala., 1965.

Wood, Forrest G. *Black Scare: The Racist Response to Emancipation and Reconstruction.* Berkeley and Los Angeles, 1968.

Woodward, C. Vann. *American Counterpoint: Slavery and Racism in the North-South Dialogue.* Boston, 1971.

Zornow, William Frank. *Lincoln and the Party Divided.* Norman, Okla., 1954.

Articles and Dissertations

Abbott, Richard H. "Massachusetts and the Recruitment of Southern Negroes, 1863-1865," *Civil War History* 14 (September 1968): 197-210.

Ahern, Wilbert H. "The Cox Plan of Reconstruction: A Case Study in Ideology and Race Relations," *Civil War History* 16 (December 1970): 293-308.

Anon. "The 'New' Thirteenth Amendment: A Preliminary Analysis," *Harvard Law Review* 82 (April 1969): 1294-1321.

Ansell, S. T. "Legal and Historical Aspects of the Militia," *Yale Law Journal* 26 (April 1917): 471-480.

Belz, Herman. "The New Orthodoxy in Reconstruction Historiography," *Reviews in American History* 1 (March 1973): 106-113.

Benedict, M. L. "Preserving the Constitution: The Conservative Basis of Radical Reconstruction," *Journal of American History* 61 (June 1974): 65-90.

Bickel, Alexander. "The Original Understanding and the Segregation Decision," *Harvard Law Review* 69 (November 1955): 1-65.

Cox, LaWanda. "The Promise of Land for the Freedmen," *Mississippi Valley Historical Review* 65 (December 1958): 413-439.

Durden, Robert F. "A. Lincoln: Honkie or Equalitarian?" *South Atlantic Quarterly* 71 (Summer 1972): 280-291.

————. "Ambiguities in the Antislavery Crusade of the Republican Party," in Martin Duberman, ed., *The Antislavery Vanguard: New Essays on the Abolitionists.* Princeton, 1965.

Fehrenbacher, Don E. "Only His Stepchildren: Lincoln and the Negro," *Civil War History* 22 (December 1974): 293-310.

Flanigan, Daniel J. "Criminal Procedure in Slave Trials in the Antebellum South," *Journal of Southern History* 40 (November 1974): 537-564.

Frantz, Laurent B. "Congressional Power to Enforce the Fourteenth Amendment Against Private Acts," *Yale Law Journal* 73 (July 1964): 1352-1384.

Fredrickson, George M. "A Man But Not a Brother: Abraham Lincoln and Racial Equality," *Journal of Southern History* 41 (February 1975): 39-58.

Gerteis, Louis S. "Salmon P. Chase, Radicalism, and the Politics of Emancipation, 1861-1864," *Journal of American History* 60 (June 1973): 42-62.

Hamilton, Howard Devon. "The Legislative History of the Thirteenth Amendment," *National Bar Journal* 9 (March 1951): 26-134.

Johnson, Ludwell H. "Lincoln's Solution to the Problem of Peace Terms, 1864-1865," *Journal of Southern History* 34 (November 1968): 576-586.

Kaczorowski, Robert J. "The Nationalization of Civil Rights: Constitutional Theory and Practice in a Racist Society, 1866-1883," Ph.D. dissertation, University of Minnesota, 1971.

————. "Searching for the Intent of the Framers of the Fourteenth Amendment," *Connecticut Law Review* 5 (Winter 1973): 368-398.

Kelly, Alfred H. "The Fourteenth Amendment Reconsidered: The Segregation Question," *Michigan Law Review* 54 (June 1956): 1049-1086.

Kinoy, Arthur. "The Constitutional Right of Negro Freedom," *Rutgers Law Review* 21 (Spring 1967): 387-441.

————. "The Constitutional Right of Negro Freedom Revisited: Some First Thoughts on Jones v. Alfred H. Mayer Company," *Rutgers Law Review* 22 (Spring 1968): 537-552.

————. "Jones v. Alfred H. Mayer Co.: An Historic Step Forward," *Vanderbilt Law Review* 22 (April 1969): 475-483.

Kohl, Robert L. "The Civil Rights Act of 1866, Its Hour Come Round at Last: Jones v. Alfred H. Mayer Co.," *Virginia Law Review* 55 (March 1969): 272-300.

Krug, Mark. "The Republican Party and the Emancipation Proclamation," *Journal of Negro History* 48 (April 1963): 98-114.

McGovney, Dudley O. "American Citizenship," *Columbia Law Review* 11 (March 1911): 231-250.

May, J. Thomas. "Continuity and Change in the Labor Program of the Union Army and the Freedmen's Bureau," *Civil War History* 17 (September 1971): 245-254.

Paludan, Phillip S. "The American Civil War Considered as a Crisis in Law and Order," *American Historical Review* 77 (October 1972): 1013-1034.

———. "The American Civil War: Triumph Through Tragedy," *Civil War History* 20 (September 1974): 239-250.

———. "John Norton Pomeroy: State Rights Nationalist," *American Journal of Legal History* 12 (October 1968): 275-293.

Sherman, Gordon E. "Emancipation and Citizenship," *Yale Law Journal* 15 (April 1906): 263-283.

Syrett, John. "The Confiscation Acts: Efforts at Reconstruction During the Civil War," Ph.D. dissertation, University of Wisconsin, 1971.

Index

About the Author

Herman Belz is associate professor of history at the University of Maryland. He is a specialist in American constitutional history and the Civil War and Reconstruction period, and is the winner of the 1966 Albert J. Beveridge Award. His earlier publications include *Reconstructing the Union* and articles in such journals as *Review of Politics, Journal of American History, Journal of Southern History,* and *American Journal of Legal History.*